GREAT
WHISKIES

GREAT
WHISKIES

500 OF THE BEST FROM AROUND THE WORLD

EDITOR-IN-CHIEF **CHARLES MACLEAN**

LONDON, NEW YORK, MUNICH,
MELBOURNE, DELHI

DK INDIA
Editorial Manager Glenda Fernandes
Senior Art Editor (Lead) Navidita Thapa
DTP Manager Sunil Sharma
Designer Heema Sabharwal
DTP Designers Manish Chandra Upreti,
Mohammed Usman, Neeraj Bhatia

DK UK
Editor Shashwati Tia Sarkar
Designer Katherine Raj
Managing Editor Dawn Henderson
Managing Art Editor Marianne Markham
Senior Jacket Creative Nicola Powling
Production Editor Ben Marcus
Production Controller Dominika Szczepanska
Creative Technical Support Sonia Charbonnier

Material first published in *World Whisky,* 2009
This edition first published in 2011
by Dorling Kindersley Limited,
80 Strand, London WC2R 0RL
Penguin Group (UK)

4 6 8 10 9 7 5 3
004 – 179127 – April/2011

A CIP catalogue record for this book
is available from the British Library.
ISBN 978-1-4053-6018-0

Colour reproduction by Media Development & Printing Ltd
Printed and bound in Singapore by Star Standard

Discover more at **www.dk.com**

CONTENTS

INTRODUCTION

There's an old saying in Scotland: "There's no bad whisky. Just good whisky and better whisky". The whiskies featured in this book come from all over the world. As you will see, great whisky is now being made in South Asia, Australasia, and Europe, not just the "established" whisky countries of Scotland, Ireland, USA, Canada, and Japan.

Whisky is recognised as the most complex spirit on the planet. It is made from the simplest and most natural of ingredients – cereal grains, water, and yeast – yet the craft and tradition that goes into its making elevate it to the rank of "noble spirit", presenting a huge spectrum of aromas and tastes. Like people, every whisky is different – each has its own personality. Some are big, bold, and rowdy; others delicate, elegant, and shy. Some you may not take to immediately may later become good friends. My selection has been guided by six of the world's leading whisky writers – Dave Broom, Tom Bruce-Gardyne, Ian Buxton, Peter Mulryan, Hans Offringa and Gavin D. Smith – and I am deeply grateful to them for writing up the individual entries.

How you choose to enjoy whisky – with or without water or ice; with soda or lemonade; with ginger ale or cola – is a matter of personal preference. In China they like it with iced tea, in Brazil with coconut water. However "flavour" is not just about taste, it also embraces smell. Indeed, to truly appreciate the nuances of flavour in whisky, particularly malt whisky, you should add nothing but a dash of water, and present the drink in a glass that allows you to consider its aroma to the full.

Secreted within this listing of world whiskies are tours that will guide you to whisky regions of Scotland, Ireland, the USA, and Japan. No experience adds more to the enjoyment of whisky than visiting a working distillery, to savour the aromas, appreciate the skill, dedication, and time that goes into making this profound spirit, and of course, to sample a dram right at its source.

Maybe you are just setting out on this journey of discovery; perhaps you're well down the road to becoming a connoisseur. Either way, I hope this book will be a useful guide and will introduce you to some interesting flavours.

Explore and enjoy!

Charles MacLean

8PM

India
Owner: Radico Khaitan
www.radicokhaitan.com

Launched as recently as 1999, 8PM had the singular distinction of selling a million cases in its first year (it now sells 3 million). The brand owner is Radico Khaitan, based at Rampur Distillery, Uttar Pradesh. Established in 1943, it is now a gigantic unit with a capacity of over 90 million litres (20 million gallons) of alcohol a year.

The company owns other whisky brands, including Whytehall, and it has recently formed a partnership with Diageo, the world's largest drinks conglomerate, to produce Masterstroke *(see p248)*.

◄ 8PM CLASSIC
BLEND
Made from "a mix of quality grains", this has a core that promises "*thaath*" (boldness, opulence) and "the reach of a man to the dream world".

8PM ROYALE
BLEND
A blend of Indian spirits and mature Scotch malt whiskies.

100 PIPERS

Owner: Chivas Brothers

Created in 1965 by Seagram, and named after an old Scots song, 100 Pipers was originally a contender in the "value" sector of the Scotch whisky market, where it was an immediate success. The blend contains malts from Allt-a-Bhainne and Braeval (distilleries that mainly supply malts for blends), and probably some Glenlivet and Longmorn as well. Seagrams developed the brand very effectively and it has continued to prosper under the new owners, Chivas Brothers (themselves owned by Pernod Ricard). It is one of the bestselling whiskies in Thailand, a dynamic market for Scotch, and is growing rapidly in many countries, especially Spain, Venezuela, Australia, and India.

100 PIPERS ▶
BLEND 40% ABV
Pale in colour. A light and very mixable whisky, with a smooth yet subtly smoky taste.

A

GREAT WHISKIES

9

ABERFELDY

Scotland
Aberfeldy, Perthshire
www.dewarswow.com

Aberfeldy was built by John Dewar & Sons in 1898 to supply malts for the company's blends, but now also offers some single malt bottlings. Its life-long bond with Dewar's White Label is celebrated at its impressive, fully interactive visitor centre, Dewar's World of Whisky, opened in 2000. Visitors see the rudiments of malt whisky distilling, but the main emphasis is on the art of blending and the role of Tommy Dewar (1864–1930), arguably the greatest whisky baron of them all.

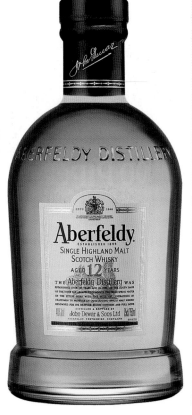

◀ ABERFELDY 12-YEAR-OLD
SINGLE MALT: HIGHLANDS
40% ABV
The standard expression has a clean, apple-scented nose with a medium-bodied fruity character in the mouth.

ABERFELDY 21-YEAR-OLD
SINGLE MALT: HIGHLANDS
40% ABV
Launched in 2005, this has greater depth and richness than the 12-year-old, with a sweet, heathery nose and a slightly spicy catch on the finish.

ABERLOUR

Scotland
Aberlour, Banffshire
www.aberlour.com

Aberlour's extreme popularity in France makes it one of the top ten bestselling malts in the world. As part of the old Campbell Distillers, it has been owned by the French group Pernod Ricard since 1975. Its malt is used in a great number of blends, particularly in Clan Campbell, but up to half the production is bottled as a single malt in a wide range of age statements and finishes.

ABERLOUR 12-YEAR-OLD SHERRY MATURED ▶
SINGLE MALT: SPEYSIDE
40% ABV
With its deep, reddish hue from new sherry wood, this expression has a nutty, Christmas-cake character and a creamy, buttery texture.

ABERLOUR A'BUNADH
SINGLE MALT: SPEYSIDE
60% ABV
A'bunadh (*a-boon-ahh*), "the origin" in Gaelic, is a cask strength, non chill-filtered malt matured in Oloroso casks. It has a sumptuous character of fruitcake and spice.

ALBERTA

Canada
1521 34th Avenue Southeast,
Calgary, Alberta
Owner: Jim Beam

Alberta Distillery was founded in
Calgary in 1946 to take advantage
of the immense Canadian prairies
and the fine Rocky Mountain
water. Rye is at the heart of
many Canadian whiskies, and is
predominant at Alberta. Maturing
takes place in first-fill bourbon
casks, or even in new white-oak
casks. Other brands from Alberta
include Tangle Ridge *(see p339)*
and Windsor Canadian *(see p374)*.

◀ ALBERTA SPRINGS 10-YEAR-OLD
CANADIAN RYE 40% ABV
A sweet aroma, with rye bread and
black pepper. The taste is very sweet,
even somewhat cloying, becoming
charred and caramelized.

ALBERTA PREMIUM
CANADIAN RYE 40% ABV
This is described as "Special Mild
Canadian Rye Whisky". The aroma
presents vanilla toffee, a hint of spice,
light citric notes, and fruitiness. The
taste is sweet above all, with stewed
apples, plums, and marzipan.

AMERICAN SPIRIT

USA

Wild Turkey Distillery,
US Highway 62 East,
Lawrenceburg, Kentucky
www.wildturkeybourbon.com

American Spirit is distilled at the Wild Turkey Distillery *(see p368)* by Austin Nicholls & Co, and was introduced in September 2007. According to Eddie Russell, who developed this expression with his father, Master Distiller Jimmy Russell, the name "American Spirit" seemed to suggest itself.

AMERICAN SPIRIT 15-YEAR-OLD ▶
BOURBON 50% ABV

Richly aromatic and characterful on the nose and silky-smooth in the mouth, with vanilla, brittle toffee, molasses, stewed fruits, spice, and a little mint. The finish is lengthy and spicy, with gentle oak and a final menthol note.

AMRUT

India

Amrut Distilleries, 36 Sampangi Tank
Road, Bangalore, Karnataka
www.amrutdistilleries.com

In Hindu mythology, the *amrut* was a golden pot containing the elixir of life. This family-owned Indian company focuses on innovation, quality, and transparency: they use barley grown in the Punjabi foothills of the Himalayas, malted in Jaipur, and distilled in small batches 900m (3,000ft) above sea level in Bangalore, where it is matured in ex-bourbon and new oak casks and bottled without chill-filtration.

◄ **AMRUT INDIAN SINGLE MALT CASK STRENGTH**
SINGLE MALT 61.9% ABV
Lightly fruity and cereal-like; bourbon casks introduce toffee. More woody, spicy, and malty with water. Similar in profile to a young Speyside malt.

AMRUT PEATED INDIAN SINGLE MALT
SINGLE MALT 62.78% ABV
Cereal and kippery smoke on the nose; oily, with salt and pepper. The taste is sweet and malty, with a whiff of smoke in the finish.

ANCIENT AGE

USA
Buffalo Trace Distillery,
1001 Wilkinson Boulevard,
Frankfort, Kentucky
www.buffalotrace.com

Ancient Age was, from 1969 to 1999, the name of what is now the Buffalo Trace Distillery *(see p66)*. The brand was introduced in the 1930s shortly after the end of Prohibition, initially being distilled in Canada. After World War II it was reformulated as a straight Kentucky-made bourbon, and went on to become one of the best-known brands produced by its proprietors.

ANCIENT AGE 10-YEAR-OLD ▶
BOURBON 40% ABV
This 10-year-old bourbon is complex and fragrant on the nose, with spices, fudge, oranges, and honey. It is medium-bodied and, after a slightly dry opening, the oily palate sweetens, developing vanilla and cocoa flavours and a lightly charred note.

WHISKIES

A

GREAT

ANCNOC

Scotland
*Knockdhu Distillery,
Knock, Huntly, Aberdeenshire
www.ancnoc.com*

Named after the nearby "Black Hill", the springs of which supply its water, anCnoc is the core expression of Knockdhu Distillery.

Historically significant for being the first distillery built by the Distillers Company Limited (DCL), Knockdhu's new owner Inver House has kept the character of the distillery. The traditional worm tubs for condensing the spirit add a slightly sulphury, meaty character to the new make.

◀ ANCNOC 1991
**SINGLE MALT: SPEYSIDE
46% ABV**
Vanilla, toffee, and wood on the nose. Fruity and full-bodied, with a hint of peatiness.

ANCNOC 12-YEAR-OLD
**SINGLE MALT: SPEYSIDE
40% ABV**
A relatively full-bodied Speyside malt, with notes of lemon peel and heather-honey on the nose, a fairly luscious mouthfeel, and some length on the finish.

ANGUS DUNDEE

Scotland
www.angusdundee.co.uk

With more than 50 years' experience in producing, blending, bottling, and distributing top-quality spirits, Angus Dundee is one of the few remaining truly independent family-owned companies in the Scotch whisky industry. It has two malt distilleries – Tomintoul and Glencadam – but is better known for its blending and broking activities. Other company-owned blends include Parkers and Scottish Royal.

THE DUNDEE ▶
BLEND 40% ABV
Hints of orange peel in a malty, medium-weight nose. There are some traces of smoke and some sweetness. Smooth on the palate.

OLD DUNDEE 12-YEAR-OLD
BLEND 43% ABV
Richer than its younger counterpart, with a longer finish. Orange notes develop into candied-peel. Soft in the mouth, and an elegant palate. There's a treacle tart flavour, but it's not cloying.

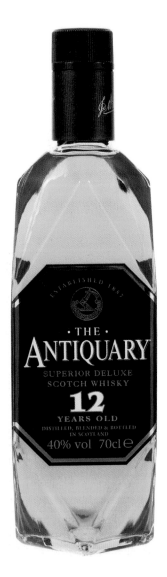

THE ANTIQUARY

Scotland
Owner: Tomatin Distillery
www.antiquary.co.uk

Introduced in 1857 and named after a novel by Sir Walter Scott, The Antiquary was a prized luxury blend in its heyday. Befitting its deluxe status, it has at its heart a very high malt-to-grain ratio, including some of the finest malts from Speyside and Highland distilleries and more than a splash of Tomatin. Islay seems to feature more strongly than previously.

◀ THE ANTIQUARY 12-YEAR-OLD
BLEND 40% ABV

Subtle fruitiness concealing a hint of apples. Outstanding smoothness, depth of flavour, and a long aftertaste. Other tasters have reported a striking peat influence, new to the blend.

THE ANTIQUARY 21-YEAR-OLD
BLEND 43% ABV

The subtle maltiness with muted peaty notes allows the heather, dandelion, and blackcurrant notes to flourish. A dash of Islay malt creates a truly exceptional dram: well-balanced, rich, and smooth. A stand-out blend that deserves to be more widely enjoyed.

ARDBEG

Scotland
Port Ellen, Islay
www.ardbeg.com

If Islay is the spiritual home
of Scotland's pungent, peat-
smoked whiskies, then Ardbeg
is undoubtedly one of the island's
leading disciples. The distillery
was first licensed in 1815 in the
parish of Kildalton, on Islay's
south coast just beyond Lagavulin
and Laphroaig. Reliance on the
blending market left Ardbeg in a
vulnerable position, however, and
when "the whisky loch" became
full to the brim in the early 1980s,
the distillery was mothballed. ☞

ARDBEG 10-YEAR-OLD ▶
SINGLE MALT: ISLAY 46% ABV
This non chill-filtered malt has notes
of creosote, tar, and smoked fish on
the nose. Any sweetness on the tongue
quickly dries to a smoky finish.

ARDBEG AIRIGH NAM BEIST
SINGLE MALT: ISLAY 46% ABV
A rich, spicy malt sweetened with
vanilla notes from 16 years in bourbon
casks. The name, pronounced *arry-nam
-bayst*, means "shelter of the beast".

19

ARDBEG

In 1997, Ardbeg was rescued by Glenmorangie who paid a reported £7m and then spent a further £1.4m on upgrading the distillery. At first, the years of non-production caused problems but, as the gaps in the inventory receded, the distillery was finally able to release a standard 10-year-old bottling. Since then, there has been a raft of new bottlings, which have added to Ardbeg's growing cult status among fans of Islay's smoky malt whiskies.

◀ ARDBEG BLASDA
SINGLE MALT: ISLAY 40% ABV
The Gaelic name translates as "sweet and delicious", a reference to a much gentler style than usual, made from malt peated at only 8ppm, one-third Ardbeg's usual levels.

ARDBEG UIGEADAIL
SINGLE MALT: ISLAY 54.2% ABV
Named after Loch Uigeadail – Ardbeg's water source – this has a deep gold colour and a treacle-like sweetness on the nose, with savoury, smoky notes following through on the tongue.

ARDMORE

Scotland
Kennethmont, Aberdeenshire
www.ardmorewhisky.com

Ardmore owes its existence to Teacher's Highland Cream *(see p341)*. The Teacher's blend was well-established in Scotland, particularly in Glasgow, where it was sold through Teacher's Dram Shops, and sales were growing abroad. To keep up with demand, Adam Teacher decided to build a new distillery in 1898 and found the ideal spot near Kennethmont, beside the main Aberdeen-to-Inverness railway. Famed for producing the smokiest malt on Speyside, Ardmore released a 12-year-old in 1999 to celebrate its centenary. In 2005 the distillery became part of Fortune Brands.

ARDMORE
TRADITIONAL CASK ▶
SINGLE MALT: SPEYSIDE
46% ABV
A smooth, relatively full-bodied malt, where the sweet American oak flavours from the cask are balanced by the dry, earthy character from the peat.

ARMORIK

France

Distillerie Warenghem,
Route de Guingamp,
22300 Lannion, Bretagne
www.distillerie-warenghem.com

The Warenghem Distillery was
founded in 1900 to produce apple
cider and fruit spirits. It was not
until 99 years later that the
owners decided to start making
other types of spirits, including
malted beers and whisky. There
are now two types of whisky made
here: Armorik, a single malt, and
WB (Whisky Breton), a blend. The
type of casks used for maturation
is not specified.

◀ ARMORIK
WHISKY BRETON
SINGLE MALT 40% ABV

A young spirit, Armorik is fresh and
very spicy, with a salty tang and a dry,
oaky influence in the finish.

ARRAN

Scotland
Lochranza, Isle of Arran
www.arranwhisky.com

When the distillery opened in
1993, it marked the return of
distilling on the Isle of Arran after
a hiatus of some 156 years. Arran
takes its water from Loch na Davie
on the island's north coast, and
the island itself is positioned in
the Gulf Stream, where the warm
waters and climate system are
said to beneficially speed up the
maturation period. Arran creates
a range of blends named for Robert
Burns, who was born nearby on
the mainland *(see p301)*.

ARRAN 10-YEAR-OLD ▶
SINGLE MALT: ISLANDS
46% ABV
Bottled without chill-filtering, this
has fresh bread and vanilla aromas,
with citrus notes that carry through
onto the tongue.

ARRAN 12-YEAR-OLD
SINGLE MALT: ISLANDS
46% ABV
This expression has an orange peel
and chocolate sweetness and a rich,
creamy texture thanks to the influence
of sherry wood.

AUCHENTOSHAN

Scotland
Dalmuir, Clydebank, Glasgow
www.auchentoshan.co.uk

While Glenkinchie sits just south of Edinburgh, Scotland's other main Lowland distillery lies west of Glasgow by the Erskine Bridge and the River Clyde.

Auchentoshan, licensed in 1823, produced a modest 225,000 litres (50,000 gallons) a year with a single pair of stills until it acquired a third still. Ever since, Auchentoshan, with its triple-distilled malt, has been almost unique in Scotland. This being the

◀ **AUCHENTOSHAN CLASSIC**
SINGLE MALT: LOWLANDS
40% ABV
With no age statement, this is a young introduction to the Auchentoshan range, with lots of vanilla sweetness and citrus.

AUCHENTOSHAN 12-YEAR-OLD
SINGLE MALT: LOWLANDS
40% ABV
This expression replaced the old 10-year-old and has a dense, spicy character thanks to the use of sherry casks.

standard style of Irish whiskey, it soon caught on among the burgeoning Irish community in Glasgow.

The Clydebank area was a key target for the Luftwasse in World War II and, after some heavy bombing in 1941, Auchentoshan has since drawn its cooling water from a pond created in a giant bomb crater.

Auchentoshan joined forces with the Islay distillery Bowmore in 1984, becoming Morrison Bowmore, now part of Suntory. In the past decade, the range of single malts has been greatly expanded.

AUCHENTOSHAN THREE WOOD ▶
SINGLE MALT: LOWLANDS 43% ABV
This is matured in three different types of cask, and sherry clearly has a big influence on the colour and sweet, candied-fruit flavours.

AUCHENTOSHAN 18-YEAR-OLD
SINGLE MALT: LOWLANDS 43% ABV
This is a classic nutty, spicy malt with plenty of age and complexity on the palate and some fruity sherry notes on the nose.

AUCHROISK

Scotland
Mulben, Banffshire
www.malts.com

This modern distillery lies on the
main road between Craigellachie
and Keith. The site was bought
by International Distillers &
Vintners (IDV) – now merged
within Diageo – in 1970 for £5m,
and Auchroisk (which means "ford
of the red stream" in Gaelic) was
up and running four years later.
The principal role of the distillery
was to supply malt for the J&B
blend, but after a decade it was
decided to release a distillery
bottling as well. This was called
the Singleton of Auchroisk. The
name was soon abandoned,
however, and replaced by a
10-year-old in the Flora & Fauna
range and occasional Rare Malt
series bottlings.

◀ **AUCHROISK FLORA & FAUNA
10-YEAR-OLD**
**SINGLE MALT: SPEYSIDE
43% ABV**
An aromatic Speyside with a wisp of
smoke and citrus notes, combined with
malty flavours that dry on the finish.

AULTMORE

Scotland
Keith, Banffshire

Alexander Edward was a seasoned distiller at Benrinnes before establishing the Craigellachie Distillery with Peter Mackie, the whisky baron and founder of the White Horse blend. In 1895, at the peak of the late-Victorian whisky boom, Edward built Aultmore, his third distillery, on the flat farmland between Keith and the sea. After acquisition by John Dewar & Sons and DCL, the distillery was one of five sold to Bacardi in 1998.

AULTMORE FLORA & FAUNA 12-YEAR-OLD ▶
SINGLE MALT: SPEYSIDE
40% ABV
The main distillery bottling is a crisp, herbal, aperitif-style malt with a gentle, perfumed nose and a malty flavour that dries on the finish.

AULTMORE SINGLE MALTS OF SCOTLAND 15-YEAR-OLD
SINGLE MALT: SPEYSIDE
46% ABV
This older expression has a floral, nutty, spicy aroma coupled with a trace of chocolate. It is medium- to full-bodied and luscious in texture.

BAGPIPER

India
Owner: United Spirits
www.unitedspirits.in

"The World's No.1 Non-Scotch
Whisky" sells nearly 14 million
cases a year. An IMFL (Indian
Made Foreign Liquor), probably
made from molasses alcohol and
concentrates, it was launched
by the United Spirits subsidiary
Herbertson's in 1987 and, in its
first year, sold 100,000 cases.
The brand has always been closely
associated with Bollywood, India's
huge film-production industry,
and has successfully won
accreditation from many film
stars. The company also
broadcasts a weekly Bagpiper
show on TV, and is a sponsor
of talent-spotting programmes.

◀ **BAGPIPER GOLD**
BLEND 42.8% ABV
Gold is the premium expression of
Bagpiper, but it still has a somewhat
artificial taste and is best drunk with
a mixer like cola.

BAILIE NICOL JARVIE

Scotland
Owner: Glenmorangie

Produced by Glenmorangie, Bailie Nicol Jarvie – or BNJ as it is commonly called in Scotland – is reputed to contain a healthy measure of both Glenmorangie and Glen Moray single malts. In fact, it has one of the highest malt contents of any blended whisky. It is excellent value and has gained something of a cult following, its adherents savouring the idea of being one of the cognoscenti, perhaps, for it is not at all heavily promoted. The label has a satisfying period feel.

BAILIE NICOL JARVIE ▶
BLEND 40% ABV
Smooth, subtle, and full of character, with a delicate balance of sweet Speyside, aromatic Highland, and peaty Islay malt whiskies blended with only the finest grain whisky.

BAKER'S

USA

Jim Beam Distillery,
149 Happy Hollow Road,
Clermont, Kentucky
www.jimbeam.com

Baker's is one of three whiskeys that were introduced in 1992 as Beam's Small Batch Bourbon Collection. It is named for Baker Beam, the former Clermont Master Distiller and grand-nephew of the legendary Jim Beam himself. He is also a cousin of the late Booker Noe, the high-profile distiller who instigated small-batch bourbon distilling. Baker Beam's namesake whiskey is distilled using the standard Jim Beam formula, but is aged for longer and offered at a higher bottling strength.

◀ **BAKER'S 7-YEAR-OLD**
BOURBON 53.5% ABV
Baker's is a fruity, toasty expression of the Jim Beam formula: medium-bodied, mellow, and richly flavoured, with notes of vanilla and caramel.

30

BAKERY HILL

Australia
*28 Ventnor Street,
North Balwyn, Victoria
www.bakeryhilldistillery.com.au*

David Baker, chemist and founder
of Bakery Hill Distillery, was
determined to prove that top-
quality malt whisky could be made
in Australia. He has succeeded: his
single cask, non chill-filtered malts
are already winning awards. At the
moment, however, they are only
available from the distillery, near
Melbourne, Victoria. The barley
strains Australian Franklin and
Australian Schooner are sourced
locally and sometimes malted over
locally cut peat.

BAKERY HILL CASK STRENGTH PEATED MALT ▶
SINGLE MALT 59.88% ABV
Intense peatiness on the nose, with
dark cherry. The taste is sweet (toffee,
honeycomb), with some salt and
smoke. It has a good texture.

BAKERY HILL PEATED MALT
SINGLE MALT 46% ABV
A sweet and oaky balance of peat and
malt on the nose. These aromas carry
through in the taste.

BALBLAIR

Scotland
Edderton, Tain, Ross-shire
www.balblair.com

Founded in 1790 by John Ross, Balblair is one of only a handful of 18th-century distilleries that has survived to this day. It remained in family hands for over 100 years. Since 1996, the distillery has been owned by Inver House Distillers, who began with a core range called Elements. This was succeeded by a range of vintage malts in a similar style to The Glenrothes bottlings, right down to the bulbous bottle shape.

◄ BALBLAIR 75
SINGLE MALT: HIGHLANDS
46% ABV
The sherry-matured vintage expression has a distinct rum-and-raisin character, with notes of butterscotch and some underlying fruit flavours that taper to a long finish.

BALBLAIR 89
SINGLE MALT: HIGHLANDS
43% ABV
Matured mainly in ex-bourbon casks, this has a slightly sweeter nose than the 75, with notes of toffee-apple, tropical fruits, and vanilla ice cream.

BALLANTINE'S

Scotland
www.ballantines.com

Ballantine's was a pioneer in developing aged blends. Its range is arguably the most extensive in the world today, and includes Ballantine's Finest (the standard bottling), as well as Ballantine's 12-year-old, 17-year-old, 21-year-old, and 30-year-old. The range is the world's second biggest Scotch whisky by volume and the top-selling super-premium brand in Asia.

The blend is noted for its complexity, with over 40 different malts and grains being used. The two Speyside single malts ☞

BALLANTINE'S FINEST ▶
BLEND 40% ABV

A sweet, soft-textured blend, with the Speyside malts giving chocolate, vanilla, and apple notes.

BALLANTINE'S 12-YEAR-OLD
BLEND 40% ABV

Golden-hued, with a honey sweetness on the nose, and vanilla from the oak. Creamy texture and balanced palate, with floral, honey, and oaky vanilla notes. Some tasters detect a hint of salt.

BALLANTINE'S

Glenburgie and Miltonduff form the base for the blend, but malts from all parts of Scotland are also employed. For maturation, Ballantine's principally favours the use of ex-bourbon barrels, for the vanilla influences and sweet creamy notes they characteristically bring to the blend.

The Glenburgie Distillery has been completely remodelled and modernized and is today Ballantine's spiritual home.

◀ BALLANTINE'S 21-YEAR-OLD
BLEND 43% ABV

The sought-after older expressions of Ballantine's are deep in colour, with traces of heather, smoke, liquorice, and spice on the nose. The 21-year-old has a complex, balanced palate, with sherry, honey, and floral notes.

BALLANTINE'S 17-YEAR-OLD
BLEND 43% ABV

A deep, balanced, and elegant whisky with a hint of wood and vanilla. The body is full and creamy, with a vibrant, honeyed sweetness and hints of oak and peat smoke on the palate.

BALMENACH

Scotland
*Cromdale, Grantown-on-Spey,
Morayshire*
www.inverhouse.com

In 1824 James McGregor, like
many illicit distillers, decided to
come in from the cold and take
out a licence for his farm distillery
near Grantown-on-Spey. It was
owned by the family for 100
years until they sold out to DCL.
Apart from during World War II,
the distillery was in constant
production until 1993, when its
whisky was available as part of
the Flora & Fauna range. In 1997,
Balmenach was sold to Inver House,
who fired up the stills the following
year. A full distillery bottling has
had to wait, owing to a dearth of
inherited stocks.

BALMENACH GORDON & MACPHAIL 1990 ▶
**SINGLE MALT: SPEYSIDE
43% ABV**

Citrus, grass, and malt on the nose,
slight smoke on the palate. Opens up
with water.

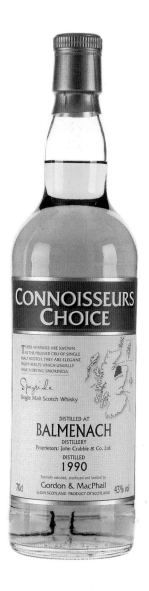

BALVENIE

Scotland

Dufftown, Keith, Banffshire
www.thebalvenie.com

Within six years of setting up
Glenfiddich in 1886, William
Grant was converting Balvenie
New House (a derelict Georgian
pile) next door into another
distillery using second-hand stills.
This expansion was partly a result
of a request from an Aberdeen
blender who desperately needed
1,800 litres (400 gallons) of
Glenlivet-style whisky a week.

◀ THE BALVENIE
DOUBLEWOOD 12-YEAR-OLD
SINGLE MALT: SPEYSIDE
40% ABV

After a decade in American oak,
Doublewood spends two years in
ex-sherry casks to give it a smooth,
confected, slightly nutty character.

THE BALVENIE SIGNATURE
12-YEAR-OLD
SINGLE MALT: SPEYSIDE
40% ABV

A vatting of three types of cask – sherry,
first-fill bourbon, and refill bourbon –
which give a mix of confected fruit and
vanilla with a syrupy texture.

Although physically dwarfed by Glenfiddich, Balvenie is no boutique distillery: it can produce 6.4 million litres (1.4 million gallons) a year and has built up an impressive range of single malts. As an artisan distillery, it grows some of its own barley, in contrast to Glenfiddich. It has also retained its floor maltings to satisfy part of its requirements, and employs a coppersmith and a team of coopers. Indeed, Balvenie's attention to maturation and different wood finishes rivals even that of Glenmorangie.

THE BALVENIE SINGLE BARREL 15-YEAR-OLD ▶
SINGLE MALT: SPEYSIDE 47.8% ABV

This 15-year-old is bottled one cask at a time, so each is subtly different from the last, although sharing a sweet woody character and nutty flavour.

THE BALVENIE VINTAGE CASK 1976
SINGLE MALT: SPEYSIDE 53.8% ABV

Autumnal wet leaves and damp, woody aromas. Heavy tannins on the palate, balanced by fruitiness; slightly sweet in the finish.

BARTON

USA

Tom Moore Distillery, 1 Barton Road, Bardstown, Kentucky

The Tom Moore Distillery in Bardstown, Nelson County makes what were formerly known as the Barton brand whiskeys. Bardstown is in the true heartland of bourbon, and once boasted more than 20 distilleries. The whiskeys made at Tom Moore are typically youthful, dry, and aromatic.

In 2009, the Sazerac Company Inc, which also owns Buffalo Trace, acquired the Tom Moore Distillery from Constellation Brands, as well as all the Barton whiskeys produced there, including Very Old Barton, Kentucky Gentleman *(see p211)*, Ridgemont *(p299)*, Kentucky Tavern, Ten High, and Tom Moore.

◄ VERY OLD BARTON
BOURBON 43% ABV
Six years is comparatively old for a Barton whiskey, hence its name. The nose is rich, syrupy, and spicy, with a prickle of salt. Big-bodied in the mouth, it is fruity and spicy, with spices and ginger in the drying finish.

BASIL HAYDEN'S

USA

Jim Beam Distillery,
149 Happy Hollow Road,
Clermont, Kentucky
www.jimbeam.com

Basil Hayden's was one of the
three whiskeys that made up
Beam's pioneering Small Batch
Bourbon Collection, introduced
in 1992. Basil Hayden was an early
Kentucky settler from Maryland
who began making whiskey in the
late-18th century near Bardstown,
and it is claimed that the recipe
for this particular expression dates
from that period.

BASIL HAYDEN'S
8-YEAR-OLD ▶
BOURBON 40% ABV

The nose is light, aromatic, and spicy,
with flavours of soft rye, wood-polish,
spices, pepper, vanilla, and a hint of
honey on the comparatively dry palate.
The finish is long, with notes of
peppery rye.

THE BELGIAN OWL

Belgium
The Owl Distillery,
Rue Sainte Anne 94,
B4460 Grâce-Hollogne
www.belgianwhisky.com

Master Distiller Etienne Bouillon founded this distillery in the French-speaking part of Belgium in 2004. He uses home-grown barley and first-fill bourbon casks to produce a 3-year-old single malt whisky. The first batch was bottled in the autumn of 2007.

The Belgian Owl Distillery was formerly known under the names Lambicool and PUR.E.

◀ **BELGIAN SINGLE MALT**
SINGLE MALT 46% ABV
This non chill-filtered malt offers vanilla, coconut, banana, and ice cream, topped with fig, followed by a crescendo of other flavours such as lemon, apples, and ginger. A long finish, with ripe fruits and vanilla.

BELL'S

Scotland
www.bellswhisky.co.za

"Several fine whiskies blended together please the palates of a greater number of people than one whisky unmixed", wrote the first Arthur Bell. In keeping with this spirit, the current owners of Bell's, Diageo, lay great emphasis on the skill of the blenders. Bell's acquired Blair Athol (the source of the single malt at the heart of the blend) and Dufftown distilleries in 1933, adding Inchgower in 1936. The blend itself has undergone constant evolution; the company insists that, in blind taste tests, drinkers prefer the new version.

BELL'S ORIGINAL ▶
BLEND 40% ABV
As well as Blair Athol, Dufftown and Inchgower are important components here, along with Glenkinchie and Caol Ila. Medium-bodied blend, with a nutty aroma and a lightly spiced flavour.

BELL'S SPECIAL RESERVE
BLEND 40% ABV
Special Reserve has smoky hints from the Islay malts, tempered with warm pepper and a rich honey complexity.

WHISKIES

B

GREAT

41

BEN NEVIS

Scotland
Lochy Bridge, Fort William
www.bennevisdistillery.com

Scotland's most northerly west
coast distillery was founded in
1825 by "Long John" Macdonald,
who was the inspiration for the
once-popular blend of that name
(see p238). Sitting by Loch
Linnhe, Fort William, the 19th
century distillery even had its
own small fleet of steamers to
ferry the whisky down the loch.

Periodic closures during the
1970s and 80s have caused gaps
in its inventory, but despite this
a number of older single malts
have been released alongside the
various Dew of Ben Nevis blends.
The 10-year-old is the only regular
distillery bottling, although single-
cask and wood-finished releases
appear occasionally. Various
independent bottlings have also
been released.

◄ BEN NEVIS 10-YEAR-OLD
SINGLE MALT: HIGHLANDS
46% ABV
A big, mouth-filling West Highlands
malt with a sweet smack of oak and
an oily texture that finishes dry.

BENRIACH

Scotland
Longmorn, Elgin, Morayshire
www.benriachdistillery.co.uk

Of all the Speyside distilleries
built on the crest of the great
speculative wave of whisky-making
at the end of the 19th century, few
crashed so badly as BenRiach. It
opened in 1897 but only operated
until 1903, when it was closed for
the first half of the 20th century.
Then, in 1965, after a major
refurbishment, its pair of stills
was fired up again. Its subsequent
owners, Seagram, having no
distillery on Islay, decided to ☞

BENRIACH 12-YEAR-OLD ▶
SINGLE MALT: SPEYSIDE
40% ABV
More classically Speyside in character
than the 10-year-old, with a heathery
nose, creamy vanilla ice cream flavour,
and a hint of honey.

BENRIACH CURIOSITAS
10-YEAR-OLD
SINGLE MALT: SPEYSIDE
40% ABV
A bitter-sweet whisky with a dense
peaty flavour. Beneath the smoke,
there are flavours of digestive biscuits,
cereal, and some citrus notes.

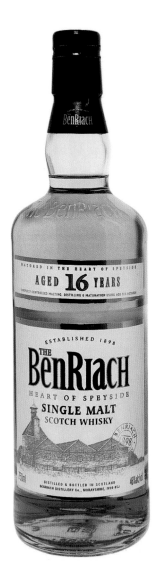

BENRIACH

produce a powerful peat-smoked malt at BenRiach in 1983. There were still some stocks of this peated BenRiach left when a South African consortium led by Billy Walker took over in 2004 from Chivas Brothers. This led to the Curiositas and Authenticus bottlings – the only commercially available Speyside single malts distilled from peated malted barley.

With 5,000 different casks dating back to 1970 and different levels of peating to play with, Billy Walker has dramatically expanded the range of BenRiach malts available, although he has quite some way to go if he wants to rival Bruichladdich's 200-plus releases.

◀ BENRIACH 16-YEAR-OLD
**SINGLE MALT: SPEYSIDE
40% ABV**
A nutty, spicy Speysider, with a honeyed texture in the mouth and perhaps the faintest wisp of smoke.

BENRIACH 20-YEAR-OLD
**SINGLE MALT: SPEYSIDE
40% ABV**
The long years in oak have given this expression a dry, woody flavour, with sharp citrus notes and a clean finish.

BENRINNES

Scotland
Aberlour, Banffshire
www.malts.com

The original Benrinnes Distillery was founded in 1826 at Whitehouse Farm on lower Speyside by Peter McKenzie, but was swept away in a flood three years later. In 1834 a new distillery called the Lyne of Ruthrie was built a few miles away and, despite bankruptcies and a bad fire in 1896, it has survived as Benrinnes. What you see today is a modern post-war distillery, which was completely rebuilt in the mid-1950s. It has six stills that operate a partial form of triple distillation, with one wash still paired with two spirit stills.

BENRINNES FLORA & FAUNA 15-YEAR-OLD ▶

SINGLE MALT: SPEYSIDE
43% ABV

The only official distillery bottling is fairly sumptuous, with some smoke and spicy flavours and a creamy mouthfeel.

BENROMACH

Scotland
Forres, Morayshire
www.benromach.com

With just a single pair of stills and a maximum production of 500,000 litres (110,000 gallons) of pure alcohol a year, Benromach was always something of a pint-sized distillery. It was founded in 1898 and changed hands no fewer than six times in its first 100 years. At one point, it found itself part of National Distillers of America, sharing a stable with bourbon brands such as Old Crow and Old Grand-Dad. Then, like so

◄ BENROMACH TRADITIONAL
SINGLE MALT: SPEYSIDE
40% ABV
This expression has a clean, light, floral character with a gentle phenolic edge and a trace of caramel.

BENROMACH CASK STRENGTH 1981
SINGLE MALT: SPEYSIDE
54.2% ABV
The nose is quite closed at first, but with water it opens up to reveal ripe orchard fruits and notes of cinnamon and sherry trifle.

many dispossessed distilleries, Benromach became part of the giant DCL who, as UDV, mothballed the distillery in 1983, along with many others. This time the stills were ripped out and the warehouses knocked down, and it seemed Benromach would never produce whisky again.

Benromach's saviour was the famous firm of independent bottlers Gordon & MacPhail of Elgin, who bought the distillery in 1993. A new pair of stills was installed, and the first spirit flowed from it in 1999, when Prince Charles officially opened the new Benromach.

BENROMACH ORIGINS ▶
SINGLE MALT: SPEYSIDE
50% ABV
Origins is a new series. Batch 1 Golden Promise is named for the strain of barley used. Maturation is in first- and second-fill sherry casks.

BENROMACH 25-YEAR-OLD
SINGLE MALT: SPEYSIDE
43% ABV
The bourbon-cask brother to the sherried Vintage. Mellow, soft in the mouth, with a fruity citrus character.

BERNHEIM

USA

Heaven Hill Distillery,
1701 West Breckinridge Street,
Louisville, Kentucky
www.bernheimwheatwhiskey.com

The Bernheim brand takes its name from Heaven Hill's Bernheim Distillery in Louisville, Kentucky, where Heaven Hill whiskeys have been produced since the plant was acquired in 1999. Launched in 2005, Bernheim is the only straight wheat whiskey on the US market.

Heaven Hill father and son Master Distillers Parker and Craig Beam developed the wheat formula with a minimum of 51 per cent winter wheat, and the recipe also includes corn and malted barley.

◀ BERNHEIM ORIGINAL
WHEAT WHISKEY 45% ABV
Bernheim exhibits light fruit notes on the spicy nose, with freshly sawn wood, toffee, vanilla, sweetish grain, and a hint of mint on the palate. A long, elegant, honeyed, and spicy finish.

BLACK & WHITE

Scotland
Owner: Diageo

A fondly regarded brand from the
Buchanan's stable, Black & White
originally went by the name
Buchanan's Special. The story
goes that, in the 1890s, James
Buchanan supplied his whisky
to the House of Commons in a
very dark bottle with a white
label. Apparently incapable of
memorizing the name, British
parliamentarians simply called
for "Black and White". Buchanan
adopted the name and
subsequently adorned the label
with two dogs – a black Scottish
terrier and a white West Highland
terrier. Today it is marketed by
Diageo in France, Brazil, and
Venezuela, where it continues
to enjoy a popularity long since
lost in its homeland.

BLACK & WHITE ▶
BLEND 40% ABV
A high-class, traditional-style blend.
Layered hints of peat, smoke, and oak.

BLACK BOTTLE

Scotland
Owner: Burn Stewart Distillers

Burn Stewart Distillers have made great efforts to invest in the blend quality of Black Bottle, and many commentators agree that the blend profile now resembles that of the original, created in 1879. At the time of writing, the excellent 10-year-old expression is due to be discontinued. This is a quality blend to taste before supplies dry up.

◄ BLACK BOTTLE
BLEND 40% ABV
Black Bottle contains malt from seven Islay distilleries, along with hefty helpings of the company's Deanston malt. The nose is fresh and fruity, with hints of peat, while the palate is full, with a slightly honeyed sweetness followed by a distinctive smoky flavour. The finish is long and warming, with a smoky Islay character.

BLACK BOTTLE 10-YEAR-OLD
BLEND 40% ABV
Like the original blend, the 10-year-old contains malt from seven Islay distilleries, but this expression is richer and more rounded.

BLACK DOG

Owner: Whyte & Mackay

Walter Millard, a Scot trading from
Calcutta, was looking for a blended
Scotch to sell in India. In 1883,
after some research, he appointed
Charles Mackinlay & Co. (now
part of Whyte & Mackay) to make
up the blend. As a keen fisherman,
he named it Black Dog after a
favourite salmon fly. Black Dog
was re-introduced to India in
2006. The following year, United
Spirits, the largest distiller in
India, bought Whyte & Mackay.

BLACK DOG CENTENARY ▶
BLEND 40% ABV
Sweet malt, light butterscotch, and
cream, with light herbal notes on the
nose. A firm body, with malt, oak, dark
chocolate, and caramel in the mouth.

51

BLACK VELVET

Canada
*2925 9th Avenue North,
Lethbridge, Alberta
www.blackvelvetwhisky.com*

Black Velvet is the third bestselling
Canadian whisky in the US. It was
created by Gilbey Canada in the
1950s as Black Label, and made
at the Old Palliser Distillery in
Toronto. It was so successful that,
in 1973, the Black Velvet Distillery
was established at Lethbridge, in
the shadow of the Rockies, only a
couple of hours drive from the US
border. In 1999, both Black Velvet
and Palliser were sold to Barton
Brands, then later became part
of Constellation Brands.

◀ BLACK VELVET RESERVE
BLEND 40% ABV
A light and mellow nose with vanilla
notes. The palate is mild and sweet,
with butterscotch, a faint citrus note,
and light spiciness. Velvet-smooth
texture, but the flavour lacks depth.

BLADNOCH

Scotland
Bladnoch, Wigtown, Wigtonshire
www.bladnoch.co.uk

Scotland's most southerly
distillery was bought and sold
several times over the 20th
century, spending long periods
lying idle in between. Finally,
Guinness UDV (now Diageo) sold
it to Raymond Armstrong from
Northern Ireland in 1994. The
deal brokered was that Bladnoch
would never produce whisky again
but Diageo relented in 2000 and
the distillery is now allowed to
produce 250,000 bottles a year.
Occasional older bottlings and
a Flora & Fauna release can be
found. Bladnoch will also sell
you whisky by the cask.

BLADNOCH 15-YEAR-OLD ▶
SINGLE MALT: LOWLANDS
55% ABV
A light, crisp, apertif-style whisky
with a trace of green apples.

BLADNOCH 18-YEAR-OLD
SINGLE MALT: LOWLANDS
55% ABV
This smooth Lowland malt is bottled
at full cask strength without chill-
filtration, but is in short supply.

BLAIR ATHOL

Scotland
Pitlochry, Perthshire
www.malts.com

In 1798 John Stewart and Robert Robertson took out a licence for their Aldour Distillery on the edge of Pitlochry. In an area crawling with illicit stills, life was tough for legitimate, tax-paying distilleries, and Aldour soon closed. It was resurrected in 1826 by Alexander Connacher, who renamed it Blair Athol. Within 30 years, some of the malt was being sold to the Perth blender Arthur Bell & Sons, who finally bought the distillery in 1933 *(see p41)*. Except for the 12-year-old and the occasional rare malt, nearly every drop goes into blends, particularly Bell's.

◀ **BLAIR ATHOL FLORA &
FAUNA 12-YEAR-OLD**
SINGLE MALT: HIGHLANDS
43% ABV
Smooth, well-rounded flavours, with spice and candied fruit, and a trace of smoke on the finish.

BLANTON'S

USA

Buffalo Trace Distillery,
1001 Wilkinson Boulevard,
Frankfort, Kentucky
www.buffalotrace.com

Colonel Albert Bacon Blanton
worked for no fewer than 55 years
at what is now the Buffalo Trace
Distillery, starting as office boy in
1897 and graduating to distillery
manager in 1912. When he retired
in 1955 the distillery was renamed
Blanton's in his honour. This single
barrel expression was created in
1984 by Master Distiller Elmer
T. Lee, who worked with Blanton
during the 1950s.

BLANTON'S SINGLE BARREL ▶
BOURBON 46.5% ABV
The nose of Blanton's is soft, with
toffee, leather, and a hint of mint.
Full-bodied and rounded on the
palate, this is a notably sweet bourbon,
embracing vanilla, caramel, honey, and
spices. The finish is long and creamy,
with a hint of late spice.

BLENDERS PRIDE

India
Owner: Pernod Ricard
www.pernod-ricard.com

Since it fell under the ownership of Pernod Ricard, this brand has been neck and neck with Royal Challenge *(see p305)* as the bestseller in its sector. It is a premium IMFL (Indian Made Foreign Liquor, made from Scotch malts and Indian grains), whose name comes from a story about the master blenders who exposed a cask of whisky to the warmth of the sun at regular intervals. The delicate sweetness and aromatic flavour of the blend are testimony to the success of their experiment.

◄ **BLENDERS PRIDE**
BLEND 42.8% ABV
A smooth and rich mouthfeel, with a sweet taste that gives way to a disappointingly dull finish.

BOOKER'S

USA

Jim Beam Distillery,
149 Happy Hollow Road,
Clermont, Kentucky
www.jimbeam.com

A brand created by the global Jim
Beam company, Booker's is named
after Jim Beam's grandson, Booker
Noe. It is made to the same Jim
Beam formula as Baker's *(see p30)*,
and is still bottled unfiltered and
undiluted to maintain its natural
barrel flavours.

**BOOKER'S KENTUCKY
STRAIGHT** ▶
BOURBON 60.5–63.5% ABV
Big, fruity, and spicy on the nose,
Booker's is sweet and slightly nutty
on the palate, with heat and spiciness
in the oaky finish. A big, traditional,
classy bourbon.

57

BOWMORE

Scotland
Bowmore, Isle of Islay
www.bowmore.co.uk

The oldest surviving distillery
on Islay was founded in 1779. The
distillery remained small for years
until the Glasgow firm of W. & J.
Mutter in bought it in 1837,
increasing its annual production
to 900,000 litres (200,000 gallons)
and storing the casks in their
warehouse beneath Glasgow
Central Station. In 1963 it was
bought by Glasgow broker Stanley
P. Morrison, and today is the
flagship distillery of Morrison
Bowmore, itself part of the
Japanese drinks giant Suntory.

◀ **BOWMORE 12-YEAR-OLD**
SINGLE MALT: ISLAY 40% ABV
Gently aromatic, with a mix of citrus
fruits and smoke on the nose, which
carries through to the tongue, together
with some dark chocolate.

BOWMORE LEGEND
SINGLE MALT: ISLAY 40% ABV
Dry and bracing, with a faint
citrus flavour that develops into
a smoky finish.

Bowmore stands on the shores of Loch Indaal. With the salty sea breeze blowing right into the warehouses, some of it is bound to seep into the casks. The distillery has two pairs of stills, six Oregon-pine washbacks, and its own floor maltings, which can supply up to 40 per cent of Bowmore's needs. Whether using its own malt, which is peated to around 25 ppm, improves the flavour of Bowmore would be hard to prove, but to see the whole process, from the freshly steeped barley to the peat-fired kiln and its dense blue smoke, certainly makes a visit to the Bowmore Distillery that much more special.

BOWMORE 15-YEAR-OLD ▶
SINGLE MALT: ISLAY 43% ABV
The deep mahogany colour comes from two years in Oloroso casks, which also give a raisin-like sweetness to Bowmore's signature note of smoke.

BOWMORE 17-YEAR-OLD
SINGLE MALT: ISLAY 43% ABV
Rich caramel on the nose with a background of peat. Creamy texture, with malt, peat, and fruit interplay on the palate, and a long, warming finish.

Whisky Tour: Islay

The Hebridean island of Islay is the destination for "peat freaks", particularly during the annual malt and music festival, Fèis Ìle, in May. You can either fly to Islay from Glasgow then hire a car to get around, or use the Caledonian MacBrayne ferry from Kennacraig to bring your own vehicle. A four-day itinerary should take in all eight distilleries.

DAY 1: CAOL ILA, BUNNAHABHAIN

1 If arriving in Port Askaig by ferry, the logical place to stay is the charming, family-run Port Askaig Hotel on the coast. From there you can walk to **Caol Ila**, a large Diageo distillery that is the most highly productive on the island.

2 It's a car trip or hike along the coastal path from Port Askaig to **Bunnahabhain**, which makes the most lightly peated of the Islay whiskies. It is possible to rent one of the distillery cottages to stay in.

WASHBACKS AT CAOL ILA

DAY 2: KILCHOMAN, BRUICHLADDICH

3 Tiny **Kilchoman** is Islay's newest and smallest distillery. It's also a farm with a friendly café. Like other Islay distilleries, it sells special bottlings that may not be available elsewhere. This is a great spot for lunch and the dishes use locally sourced ingredients.

4 Drive back over the hill to **Bruichladdich**, which produces a huge array of whiskies. It is near Port Charlotte, where you can learn about illicit whisky production in the Museum of Islay Life, then enjoy dinner at the Port Charlotte Hotel.

BRUICHLADDICH

SCOTLAND

B8018

KILCHOMAN 3

BRUICHLADDICH 4

PORT CHARLOTTE

miles
0   2

0   2
kilometres

N
W   E
S

TOUR STATISTICS

DAYS: 4
LENGTH: 60 miles (96km)
TRAVEL: Car, walking
DISTILLERIES: 8

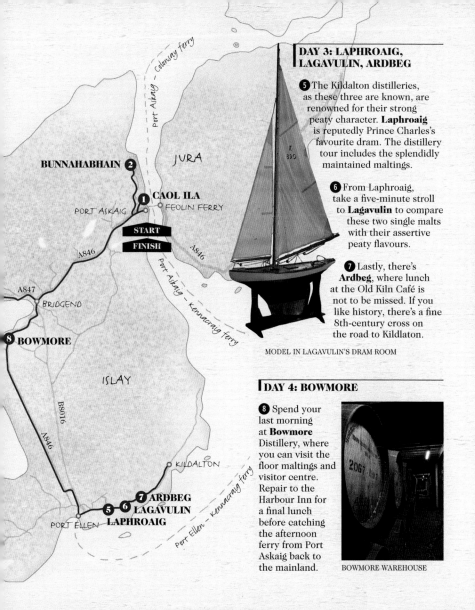

BUNNAHABHAIN **2**

JURA

1 CAOL ILA
PORT ASKAIG ◦ FEOLIN FERRY

Port Askaig – Colonsay ferry

START
FINISH

A846

A846

Port Askaig – Kennacraig ferry

A847

BRIDGEND

8 BOWMORE

ISLAY

B8016

A846

KILDALTON

7 ARDBEG
6 LAGAVULIN
5 LAPHROAIG
PORT ELLEN

Port Ellen – Kennacraig ferry

DAY 3: LAPHROAIG, LAGAVULIN, ARDBEG

5 The Kildalton distilleries, as these three are known, are renowned for their strong peaty character. **Laphroaig** is reputedly Prince Charles's favourite dram. The distillery tour includes the splendidly maintained maltings.

6 From Laphroaig, take a five-minute stroll to **Lagavulin** to compare these two single malts with their assertive peaty flavours.

7 Lastly, there's **Ardbeg**, where lunch at the Old Kiln Café is not to be missed. If you like history, there's a fine 8th-century cross on the road to Kildalton.

MODEL IN LAGAVULIN'S DRAM ROOM

DAY 4: BOWMORE

8 Spend your last morning at **Bowmore** Distillery, where you can visit the floor maltings and visitor centre. Repair to the Harbour Inn for a final lunch before catching the afternoon ferry from Port Askaig back to the mainland.

BOWMORE WAREHOUSE

BRAUNSTEIN

Denmark
Braunstein, Carlsensvej 5, 4600 Koge
www.braunstein.dk

A microbrewery located in an old warehouse in Koge harbour, Braunstein uses a small still to make spirit from malted barley. The resulting spirit is clean, fresh, and fruity. Maturation takes place in ex-Oloroso sherry casks. A new edition of the whisky is added each year. The distillery also manufactures aquavit, herbal spirits, schnapps, and a beer called BB Amber Lager. Tastings are held each month.

Dansk Single Malt

BRAUNSTEIN
WHISKY

◀ **BRAUNSTEIN**
SINGLE MALT (VARIABLE ABV)
Fruits, raisins, and chocolate come to the fore in this single malt that varies in strength from batch to batch.

BRUICHLADDICH

Scotland
Bruichladdich, Isle of Islay
www.bruichladdich.com

Islay's most westerly distillery stands on the shores of Loch Indaal, across the water from Bowmore. Unlike older Islay distilleries, it was purpose-built in 1881 with state-of-the-art cavity walls and its own steam generator.

After repeated sales, it was closed down in 1994, seemingly for good. Then, days before Christmas 2000, it was rescued by a private consortium led by the independent bottler Murray McDavid. From the start, the ☞

BRUICHLADDICH 18-YEAR-OLD ▶
SINGLE MALT: ISLAY 46% ABV
There have been two versions of this limited-release bottling: the first finished in German sweet-wine casks, the second in sweet Jurançon casks from France.

BRUICHLADDICH 21-YEAR-OLD
SINGLE MALT: ISLAY 46% ABV
Aged in Oloroso casks and suitably deep in colour, this is a pungent, sulphury malt for those who like their whiskies well-sherried.

63

B

BRUICHLADDICH

🥃 distiller has been Jim McEwan, who left a long career at Bowmore to join the new venture in 2001.

In 2003 Bruichladdich became the first distillery on Islay to bottle its whiskies on the island. From the heavily sherried Blacker Still and the pink-hued Flirtation, to 3D, Infinity, and The Yellow Submarine, the range of bottlings has been staggering. To date, over 200, many of them in very limited quantities, have been released. While this may cause some frustration among Bruichladdich's devoted fans, it does allow this privately-owned distillery to punch way above its weight.

◀ **BRUICHLADDICH WAVES**
SINGLE MALT: ISLAY 46% ABV
A multi-vintage vatting that offers a moderately peated style of Bruichladdich.

BRUICHLADDICH PEAT
SINGLE MALT: ISLAY 46% ABV
A powerful phenolic whisky with the scent of bonfires, seaweed, and sweet smoked bacon.

BUCHANAN'S

Scotland
Owner: Diageo

James Buchanan was one of the
most notable whisky barons – the
Victorian entrepreneurs who
brought Scotch to world attention,
amassing personal fortunes along
the way. Starting as an agent in
1879, he soon began trading on his
own and rapidly saw his whisky
adopted in the House of Commons.
Today the Buchanan's brand is
showing signs of prospering once
again under its owners, Diageo.
Mainly seen in Venezuela, Mexico,
Colombia, and the US, Buchanan's
is positioned as a premium-style
blend. There are two expressions:
a 12-year-old and the Special
Reserve at 18 years old.

BUCHANAN'S 12-YEAR-OLD ▶
BLEND 40% ABV
Rich on the nose, with sherry and
spice. Thinner on the palate, with
bitter, dried-lemon notes. Winey,
with a touch of dry wood.

BUFFALO TRACE

USA
Buffalo Trace Distillery,
1001 Wilkinson Boulevard,
Frankfort, Kentucky
www.buffalotrace.com

Formerly known as Ancient Age
(see p15), Buffalo Trace is located
at a crossing point where, in the
past, herds of migrating buffalo
forded the Kentucky River. The
trail they followed was known
as the Great Buffalo Trace.

Buffalo Trace boasts the
broadest age-range of whiskey
in the USA (from 4 to 23 years)
and is the only US distillery using
five recipes – a wheat whiskey,
a rye whiskey, two rye bourbons,
and a barley. The Buffalo Trace
Experimental Collection of
cask strength, wine-barrel-aged
whiskies was launched in 2006.

◄ BUFFALO TRACE KENTUCKY STRAIGHT BOURBON
BOURBON 45% ABV
Aged a minimum of nine years, this
has aromas of vanilla, gum, mint, and
molasses. Sweet, fruity, and spicy on
the palate, with emerging brown sugar
and oak. The finish is long, spicy, and
fairly dry, with developing vanilla.

BULLEIT

USA

Four Roses Distillery,
1224 Bonds Mill Road,
Lawrenceburg, Kentucky
www.bulleitbourbon.com

Bulleit Bourbon originated in the 1830s with tavern-keeper and small-time distiller Augustus Bulleit, but production ceased after his death in 1860. However, the brand was revived, using the original recipe, in 1987 by his great-great-grandson Tom Bulleit. Seagram subsequently took over the label and from there it passed to Diageo. Bulleit Bourbon is now distilled for Diageo by Four Roses Distillery *(see p124)*, and has a high rye content of 29 per cent.

BULLEIT BOURBON ▶
BOURBON 40% ABV
Rich, oaky aromas lead into a mellow flavour, focused around vanilla and honey. The medium-length finish features vanilla and a hint of smoke.

BUNNAHABHAIN

Scotland
Port Askaig, Islay
www.bunnahabhain.com

Before the Islay distilleries found
fame for their heavily peat-smoked
single malts, their market was not
the whisky drinker, but the big
blending houses. The blenders
only required limited quantities
of smoky malt, however, as too
much would leave their whiskies
unbalanced. With this is mind,
Bunnahabhain used unpeated
or lightly peated malt.

Bunnahabhain also produces
limited-edition bottlings for the
Fèis Ìle, Islay's annual festival.

◀ BUNNAHABHAIN 12-YEAR-OLD
SINGLE MALT: ISLAY 40% ABV
A clean, refreshing whisky with a scent
of ozone and sea spray, which gives
way to a nutty malty sweetness in
the mouth.

BUNNAHABHAIN 18-YEAR-OLD
SINGLE MALT: ISLAY 43% ABV
With its richer sherry influence, this
has less of the malty distillery character
than the 12-year-old. Instead it has
a broader texture and woody flavour.

BUSHMILLS

Ireland

*2 Distillery Road, Bushmills,
County Antrim*
www.bushmills.com

Old Bushmills has the amazing
ability to be all things to all
people: a thoroughly modern
distillery housed in a beautiful
Victorian building; a boutique
distillery that nevertheless
produces global brands; and
a working distillery that
welcomes the public.

Bushmills produces only malt
whiskey, so the grain used in its
blends is made to order in the
Midleton Distillery. This is ☞

BUSHMILLS ORIGINAL ▶
BLEND 40% ABV

A fruity, easy-to-drink, vanilla-infused
mouthful. Its clean, clear character
makes it very approachable. A lovely
entry to the world of Irish whiskey.

BUSHMILLS BLACK BUSH
BLEND 40% ABV

A living legend, Black Bush is the
lovable rogue of the family. It is
a very classy glassful of honey-nut
scrumptiousness with an extremely
silky mouthfeel. The benchmark for
Irish blends.

BUSHMILLS

 matured on site in one of the ten working warehouses.

Unusually, Old Bushmills doesn't have a problem selling single malts and blends under the same brand name: it is a distillery that isn't afraid to push the boundaries.

◄ BUSHMILLS MALT 10-YEAR-OLD
SINGLE MALT 40% ABV

As you'd expect from a triple-distilled, peat-free whiskey, this charmer appeals to just about everyone. There's a hint of sherry wood, but it is the malt that's showcased here – sweet with hints of fudgy chocolate. A classic and very approachable Irish malt.

BUSHMILLS MALT 16-YEAR-OLD
SINGLE MALT 40% ABV

This malt isn't just a straight ageing of the classic 10-year-old. It's a half-and-half mix of bourbon- and sherry-cask-matured malt, married for a further nine months in port pipes. The three woods bring their own magic to bear, and produce a riot of dried-fruit flavours cut with almonds and the ever-present honey.

CAMERON BRIG

Scotland

Cameronbridge Distillery, Winygates, Leven, Fife

Greatly misunderstood, little drunk in their own right, and sadly misrepresented, grain whiskies are Scotch's poor relation. Yet, they are the essential component and base of all blends and, when found as a single grain bottling, the source of much pleasure.

Cameron Brig is made at Diageo's Cameronbridge distillery in Fife, a massive complex of giant continuous stills. The sheer scale of grain whisky production offends some purists but, at its best, good grain whisky is very good indeed. You would not expect anything less from Diageo in its only offering in this category, and Cameron Brig won't disappoint.

CAMERON BRIG 12-YEAR-OLD ▶

SINGLE GRAIN 40% ABV
The nose is clean and grassy, with some honey. Smooth palate; nutty and firm, with a hint of bitter coffee in the finish.

CANADIAN CLUB

Canada

Hiram Walker Distillery,
Riverside Drive East,
Walkerville, Ontario
www.canadianclubwhisky.com

Canadian Club is the oldest and most influential whisky brand in Canada. Created by businessman Hiram Walker in 1884, it was named simply "Club" and aimed at discerning members of gentlemen's clubs. Unusually, in an era when most whiskies were sold in bulk, it was supplied in bottles (and thus could not be adulterated by the retailer), a practice soon adopted by other Canadian and American distillers.

◀ CANADIAN CLUB RESERVE
BLEND 40% ABV
Blended at birth, then aged in small oak barrels to give a richer flavour.

CANADIAN CLUB 6-YEAR-OLD 100 PROOF
BLEND 50% ABV
The higher strength allows the signature flavours to come through better with a mixer.

The company has had numerous Royal Warrants, from Queen Victoria to Elizabeth II. A less lofty customer, Al Capone, smuggled thousands of cases across the border during Prohibition.

The Canadian Club brands were sold to Fortune Brands, the owner of Jim Beam *(see p204)*, in 2005. Canadian Club is always "blended at birth" – that is, the component whiskies are mixed prior to a maturation of at least five years. The standard is a 6-year-old; older versions, such as the 20-year-old, are sometimes released onto the domestic and export markets.

CANADIAN CLUB PREMIUM ▶
BLEND 40% ABV
Creamy and cereal-like; rather spirity. Drier than most Canadian whiskies, with light smokiness and nuttiness.

CANADIAN CLUB CLASSIC
BLEND 40% ABV
Nose of tropical fruits, oak, and honey, with some toffee. The palate is very smooth and very sweet, with a banana aftertaste.

CANADIAN MIST

Canada
*202 MacDonald Road,
Collingwood, Ontario
www.canadianmist.com*

Launched in 1965, this whisky
now sells 3 million cases a year
in the US. Its distillery is odd in
several ways: the equipment is
all stainless steel; it is the only
Canadian distillery to use a
mashbill of corn and malted
barley; and it imports its rye
spirit from sister distillery Early
Times (*see p111*) in Kentucky.
Almost all the spirit is tankered
to Kentucky for blending. In
addition to the popular Canadian
Mist brand, the 1185 Special
Reserve is also available.

◀ **CANADIAN MIST**
BLEND 40% ABV
Lightly fruity on the nose, with vanilla
and caramel notes. Mild, sweet flavour
with traces of vanilla toffee.

CAOL ILA

Scotland
Port Askaig, Islay
www.malts.com

For years, Caol Ila played second fiddle to Lagavulin within the Diageo stable. This is beginning to change, as its owners are now promoting Caol Ila as a top-quality single malt.

The distillery was built in 1846, and by 1857 was in the hands of Glasgow blender Bulloch Lade, who reconstructed Caol Ila on a larger scale in 1879. The distillery was effectively demolished in 1972, re-opening two years later with the warehouse the only original part remaining.

CAOL ILA 12-YEAR-OLD ▶
SINGLE MALT: ISLAY 43% ABV
Malty sweetness and citrus aromas balance the scent of tar and peat. Oily textured, with treacly, smoky flavours.

CAOL ILA DISTILLERS EDITION 1995
SINGLE MALT: ISLAY 43% ABV
Sweet, smoky, and malty, with aromatic spices (cinnamon), especially in the lingering finish. The most rounded expression of the core range.

CARDHU

Scotland

Knockando, Aberlour, Morayshire
www.malts.com

Cardhu Distillery was a small farm
distillery until Elizabeth Cumming
rebuilt it in the 1880s. Soon after,
it was sold to Johnnie Walker and
became the spiritual home of the
blend. In the 1990s, increased
demand in Spain for Cardhu
12-year-old led owners Diageo to
re-christen the whisky as Cardhu
Pure Malt, so they could add other
malts and thereby increase
production. But outrage within the
industry forced Diageo to withdraw
the brand and revert to selling
Cardhu as a genuine single malt.

◀ CARDHU 12-YEAR-OLD
SINGLE MALT: SPEYSIDE
40% ABV
A heathery, pear-drop-scented malt.
Light to medium body; malty, slightly
nutty flavour that finishes fairly short.

CARDHU SPECIAL CASK RESERVE
SINGLE MALT: SPEYSIDE
40% ABV
More depth and body than the
12-year-old, with an aroma of peaches
and a sweeter, more creamy texture.

CATDADDY

USA
Piedmont Distillers,
203 East Murphy Street,
Madison, North Carolina
www.catdaddymoonshine.com

Piedmont is the only licensed distillery in North Carolina, and its Catdaddy Moonshine celebrates the state's great heritage of illicit distilling. In 2005, ex-New Yorker Joe Michalek established Piedmont in Madison. It is the first legal distillery in the Carolinas since before Prohibition. "According to the lore of moonshine, only the best moonshine earns the right to be called the Catdaddy," says Joe Michalek. "True to the history of moonshine, every batch of Catdaddy is born in an authentic copper pot still."

CATDADDY
CAROLINA MOONSHINE ▶
CORN WHISKEY 40% ABV
Triple-distilled from corn in small batches, Catdaddy is sweet and spicy, with notes of vanilla and cinnamon.

CATTO'S

Scotland
Owner: Inver House Distillers

James Catto, an Aberdeen-based
whisky blender, set up in business
in 1861. His whiskies achieved
international distribution on the
White Star and P&O shipping
lines. After the death of his son
Robert in World War I, the
company passed to the distillers
Gilbey's. More recently, it was
acquired by Inver House Distillers.
Catto's is a deluxe, fully matured,
and complex blend. Two versions
are available: a non-age standard
bottling and a 12-year-old
expression with a yellow-gold,
straw-like appearance that belies
its complexity and warm finish.

◄ **CATTO'S**
BLEND 40% ABV
The standard Catto blend is aromatic
and well-rounded in character, with
a smooth, mellow finish.

CHARBAY

USA
Domaine Charbay,
4001 Spring Mountain Road,
St Helena, California
www.charbay.com

The father-and-son partnership of
Miles and Marko Karakasevic are
12th and 13th generation wine-
makers and distillers. Charbay
Double Barrel Hop-Flavored
Whiskey is double-distilled in
a 1,000-US-gallon (3,750-litre)
copper alambic Charentais pot
still. It is made using two-row
European malted barley, with the
addition of hops to the mash for
greater aromatic effect. The spirit
is put into new American white-
oak barrels for maturation.

CHARBAY DOUBLE BARREL ▶
DOUBLE BARREL WHISKEY
64% ABV
The floral nose also features honey,
vanilla, oranges, oak, and smoky spice.
This big-bodied whiskey offers citrus,
spice, and honey on the palate, moving
into a long, hoppy, vanilla, and dried-
fruit finish.

CHICHIBU

Japan

*Distribution: Number One Drinks,
Netherconesford, King Street,
Norwich, UK
www.one-drinks.com*

The newest Japanese distillery was
founded in 2007 by Ichiro Akuto,
previously of Hanyu *(see p175).*
A small plant, it features what
might be the only Japanese oak
washbacks in the world. Ageing
takes place in a mix of Japanese
oak, ex-bourbon, ex-sherry, and
a few ex-cognac casks. Two styles
are being tested: one for early
maturation; the other for long-
term ageing. There are plans
to malt (or at least kiln) with
Japanese peat.

◀ **CHICHIBU NEWBORN**
NEW MAKE 62.5% ABV
This cannot legally be called whisky,
but gives an idea of the quality to
come. Warming, with the typical
unripe fruit character of new makes,
along with some green pear and
jasmine. The palate is clean with
well-balanced sweetness.

CHIVAS REGAL

Scotland
Owner: Chivas Brothers

Chivas Brothers was founded in the early 19th century and prospered, due in part to some favourable royal connections. The business is owned today by French multi-national Pernod Ricard.

At the heart of Chivas Regal blends are Speyside single malt whiskies, in particular Strathisla Distillery's rich and full single malt. To safeguard the supply of this critically important ingredient, Chivas Brothers bought the distillery in 1950.

CHIVAS REGAL 25-YEAR-OLD ▶
BLEND 40% ABV
The flagship blend, Chivas Regal 25-year-old is classy and rich. A luxury blend for indulgent sipping. Well-mannered, balanced, and stylish.

CHIVAS REGAL 12-YEAR-OLD
BLEND 40% ABV
An aromatic infusion of wild herbs, heather, honey, and orchard fruits. Round and creamy on the palate, with a full, rich taste of honey and ripe apples and notes of vanilla, hazelnut, and butterscotch. Rich and lingering.

CLAN CAMPBELL

Scotland
Owner: Chivas Brothers

Launched as recently as 1984,
Clan Campbell is a million-case-
selling brand from Chivas Brothers,
the whisky arm of drinks giant
Pernod Ricard. It is not available
in the UK, but is a leader in the
important French market, and
may also be found in Italy, Spain,
and some Asian countries. Despite
its relative youth, its origins are
now inextricably entwined with
Scottish heritage, thanks to clever
marketing and a link to the Duke
of Argyll, head of the clan. Indeed,
what is claimed to be the oldest
whisky-distilling relic in Scotland
– a distiller's worm – was by good
fortune found on Campbell lands.

◀ CLAN CAMPBELL
BLEND 40% ABV
The malt component of Clan Campbell
comes largely from Speyside (Aberlour
and Glenallachie especially). A smooth,
light whisky with a fruity finish.

CLAN MACGREGOR

Scotland
Owner: William Grant & Sons

This secondary (ie budget-priced) blend is sold largely in North America and from Venezuela to the Middle East to Thailand, but not by and large in its Scottish homeland. Sales approach an impressive 1.5 million cases a year and it is one of the world's fastest-growing Scotch whisky brands. Owned by William Grant & Sons, it is primarily a mix of Grant's own malts (Glenfiddich, Balvenie, and Kininvie) and grain whisky from its substantial Girvan operation. The label proudly carries the badge, motto, and personal crest of the 24th clan chief, Sir Malcolm MacGregor of MacGregor.

CLAN MACGREGOR ▶
BLEND 40% ABV
A blend of grain whiskies and some Speyside malt. Light in style, fragrant, with just a little fruitiness.

THE CLAYMORE

Scotland
Owner: Whyte & Mackay

A claymore is a Highland broadsword. The name was deemed appropriate by DCL (forerunner of drinks giant Diageo) when, in 1977, it attempted to recover some of the market share it had lost when it withdrew Johnnie Walker Red Label from the UK market. Competitively priced, The Claymore was an immediate success. In 1985, the brand was sold to Whyte & Mackay. It continued to sell well for some time, but in recent years has declined and is now principally seen as a low-priced secondary brand. Dalmore is believed to be the main malt whisky in the blend.

◀ **THE CLAYMORE**
BLEND 40% ABV
The nose is heavy and full, with silky mellow tones. Well-balanced and full-bodied on the palate. Polished finish.

CLONTARF

Ireland
www.clontarfwhiskey.com

Clontarf has been in the doldrums
for a number of years now, and in
that time the taste and style have
fluctuated wildly. There isn't a
distillery in Clontarf; this is simply
a brand, so the whiskeys can come
from anywhere. This is a problem,
as the consumer loves consistency
– especially from blended whiskeys.
And with Clontarf you never quite
know what you are buying.

CLONTARF SINGLE MALT ▶
SINGLE MALT 40% ABV
Sweet and thin with some nice
mouthfeel. Cereal notes with hints
of honey, but a bit one-dimensional.

CLONTARF CLASSIC BLEND
BLEND 40% ABV
Toffee popcorn comes to mind when
tasting this blend, but not in a good
way, unfortunately.

CLUNY

Scotland
Owner: Whyte & Mackay

Although it is produced by Whyte & Mackay, Cluny is supplied in bulk to Heaven Hill Distilleries, who have bottled the whisky in the US since 1988. Today it is one of America's top-selling domestically bottled blended Scotch whiskies. It contains over 30 malts from all regions of Scotland (Isle of Jura, Dalmore, and Fettercairn single malts among them), along with grain whisky that is almost certainly largely sourced from Whyte & Mackay's Invergordon plant. Cluny is sold primarily on its competitive price. Under Whyte & Mackay's new Indian ownership, it may be a candidate for further international development.

◄ **CLUNY**
BLEND 40% ABV
Subtle sweet-and-sour nose, with a slight metallic, bitter tang on the palate.

CLYNELISH

Scotland
Brora, Sutherland
www.malts.com

A large box-shaped distillery
dating from 1967, Clynelish has
six stills and a capacity of 3.4
million litres (750,000 gallons).
Within its grounds is a much older
distillery that ran alongside it until
1983. This was Brora, founded in
1819 by the Marquis of Stafford.
Known briefly as Old Clynelish,
Brora made a heavily peated malt
during the 1970s to ensure a
supply of Islay-style malts for
blends like Johnnie Walker Black
Label. In 1983 Brora closed for
good, leaving just Clynelish.
There have been various rare
malts and independent
bottlings from Douglas Laing
and Cadenhead, among others.

CLYNELISH 14-YEAR-OLD ▶
SINGLE MALT: HIGHLANDS
46% ABV
A mouthfilling malt, quite fruity with
a creamy texture, a wisp of smoke,
and a firm, dry finish.

COLERAINE

Ireland

*Coleraine Distillery Ltd,
Hawthorn Office Park,
Stockman's Way, Belfast*

Never underestimate the selling power of nostalgia: the sole reason this blend is still produced is because whiskey drinkers are very brand loyal, and the name Coleraine still has resonance some three decades after the distillery fell silent. It once produced a single malt of some repute, then in 1954 it started to make grain whiskey for Bushmills, before it was eventually wound down in the 1970s. The reputation of the distillery was such, however, that customers still look out for the name, and so a brand and blend were created to fill a niche. Although the company is called Coleraine Distillery, the whiskey is produced elsewhere.

◄ **COLERAINE**
BLEND 40% ABV
Light, sweet, and grainy. Probably best suited to drinking with a mixer.

COMPASS BOX

Scotland
www.compassboxwhisky.com

Compass Box was formed in
2000 and describes itself as an
"artisanal whisky maker", which
may seem disingenuous since it
isn't a distiller but a blender, albeit
a highly innovative one. Its
technique of inserting additional
oak staves into a barrel to produce
Spice Tree led to pressure from
the Scotch Whisky Association
and the eventual withdrawal of the
product. For all this, the company
has been highly influential and in
its short life has won more than
60 medals and awards.

COMPASS BOX
THE PEAT MONSTER ▶
BLENDED MALT
ISLAY / SPEYSIDE 46% ABV
Rich and loaded with flavour: a
bacon-fat smokiness, full-blown peat,
hints of fruit and spice. A long finish,
echoing peat and smoke.

COMPASS BOX ASYLA
BLEND 40% ABV
A frequent award-winner. Sweet,
delicate, and very smooth on the
palate. Flavours of vanilla cream,
cereals, and a subtle apple character.

CONNEMARA

Ireland

*Cooley Distillery, Riverstown,
Cooley, County Louth
www.connemarawhiskey.com*

In the eyes of the Irish whiskey industry – and many a traditionalist beside – Irish whiskey was a triple-distilled and unpeated drink. Then along came Cooley's John Teeling, who started making Irish whiskey that was double-distilled and peated. It caused quite a stir. Yet, over the last 15 years, Connemara has gone from being a curiosity to winning gold medals.

◀ CONNEMARA
SINGLE MALT 40% ABV
Definitely its own whiskey rather than "Scotch Light". It is rural, not coastal, so has no iodine or sea spray, just bog heather, barley, and far off peat reek.

CONNEMARA CASK STRENGTH
SINGLE MALT 60.7% ABV
A good splash of water unleashes the nose, which is huge and slightly minty. In the mouth, the beast that had been held in check by the alcohol gets loose and explodes into sparks of dry peat and aromatic timber. The finish is as dry as they come.

CRAGGANMORE

Scotland
Ballindalloch, Morayshire
www.malts.com

This was a well-conceived distillery from the start. Built in 1869, it had a reliable source of pure water from the Craggan burn, nearby access to peat and barley, and its proximity to Ballindalloch station enabled it to become the first distillery in Scotland to have its own railway siding, to bring in supplies and carry off the freshly filled casks.

Unusual flat-topped stills, and worm tubs, may contribute to Cragganmore's famed complexity.

CRAGGANMORE 12-YEAR-OLD ▶
SINGLE MALT: SPEYSIDE
40% ABV
Floral, heathery aromas, then a robust woody complexity with a trace of smoke on the palate.

CRAGGANMORE DISTILLERS EDITION 1992
SINGLE MALT: SPEYSIDE
43% ABV
Double-matured, including a spell in a port cask, there is a cherry and orange sweetness that dies away into a lightly smoky finish.

GREAT WHISKIES

C

CRAIGELLACHIE

Scotland
Craigellachie, Banffshire

Although the name of John Dewar
& Sons is writ large above the
modern, plate-glass still house that
sits on the main road out of
Craigellachie, the distillery was
originally tied to White Horse.
Peter Mackie, the man behind the
famous blend, built Craigellachie
in 1891 in partnership with
Alexander Edward. Of all the
Victorian whisky barons, Mackie
was the most connected to malt
distilling, having served as an
apprentice at Lagavulin, whose
whisky was also part of White
Horse. Since 1998, Craigellachie
has been owned by Bacardi.

◄ CRAIGELLACHIE
14-YEAR-OLD
**SINGLE MALT: SPEYSIDE
40% ABV**
Rich and aromatic, with a scent of
fruit pie and a touch of smoke. More
delicate on the tongue, and some
woody notes on the finish.

CRAOI NA MONA

Ireland
*Cooley Distillery, Riverstown, Cooley,
County Louth*

Craoi na Móna is Gaelic for "heart
of peat". Produced by Cooley,
though not one of its own brands,
this whiskey can be found in
places as diverse as Moscow and
London, but so far it hasn't been
spotted in Dublin. Given the huge
rise in the popularity of Irish
whiskey recently, it's not
surprising that so many drinks
companies are trying to cut
themselves a slice of the action.
But the market place is very
crowded and the amount of
whiskey being produced in Ireland
is limited. What's left then are
too many small companies selling
whiskey that's very young indeed.

CRAOI NA MONA ▶
SINGLE MALT 40% ABV
Sweet and young, this is a decidedly
immature peated malt.

CRAWFORD'S

Scotland
Owner: Whyte & Mackay / Diageo

Crawford's 3 Star was established by Leith firm A. & A. Crawford, and by the time the company joined the Distillers Company (DCL) in 1944 the blend was a Scottish favourite. Although its popularity continued, it was not of strategic significance to its owners, hence the decision to license the brand to Whyte & Mackay in 1986. Whyte & Mackay are today owned by the Indian UB Group, so the future of this venerable label may lie on the subcontinent. Diageo, successors to DCL, retain the rights to the name Crawford's 3 Star Special Reserve outside the UK. Benrinnes single malt *(see p45)* has been a long-time component in the Crawford's blend.

◄ CRAWFORD'S 3 STAR SPECIAL RESERVE
BLEND 40% ABV
A spirity, fruity, fresh-tasting blend, with a smack of citrus, a sweet centre, and a dry, slightly sooty finish.

CRESTED TEN

Ireland
*Midleton Distillery, Midleton,
County Cork*

Launched in 1963, Crested Ten
was Jameson's first venture into
distillery bottling. The fact that
it came at least a century after
the Scots started branding and
distillery bottling shows how
far behind the times the Irish
industry was and how close
it came to vanishing entirely.
Crested Ten is a whiskey you'll
see lurking on a top shelf in many
Irish pubs. It's never on an optic,
probably because it's no good with
mixers. Instead, you'll have to ask
for it by name.

CRESTED TEN ▶
BLEND 40% ABV
An old-fashioned Irish whiskey with
plenty of pot-still character and its
Oloroso maturation in evidence. This
is a great big hug of a drink that will
reward those brave enough to take it
from the top shelf. Have it neat, cut
with just a splash of water.

95

CROWN ROYAL

Canada
Distillery Road, Gimli, Manitoba
www.crownroyal.ca

Crown Royal was created by Sam Bronfman, President of Seagram (*see p313*), to mark the state visit to Canada of King George VI and Queen Elizabeth in 1939, with its "crown-shaped" bottle and purple velvet bag. Although it was only available in Canada until 1964, it is now one of the best-selling Canadian whiskies in the US.

Since 1992, it has been produced at the Gimli Distillery on Lake Winnipeg. In 2001 Seagram's shed its alcohol interests and both Gimli Distillery and the Crown Royal brand went to Diageo.

◀ CROWN ROYAL
BLEND 40% ABV

Rich, robust, and balanced. Vanilla, oak, and fruit in the mouthfeel and taste.

CROWN ROYAL SPECIAL RESERVE
BLEND 40% ABV

A big, rich, rounded nose, with fruity (apple, guava, coconut) and floral notes.

CUTTY SARK

Scotland
Owner: Berry Brothers & Rudd

Blended and bottled in Glasgow by
The Edrington Group, Cutty Sark
was created in 1923 for Berry Bros
& Rudd Ltd, a well-established
London wine and spirit merchants
who are still the brand owner.

The first very pale-coloured
whisky in the world, Cutty Sark
uses some 20 single malt whiskies,
many from Speyside distilleries
such as Glenrothes and Macallan.
The wood for the oak casks is
carefully chosen to bring out the
characteristic flavour and aroma
of each whisky in the Cutty Sark
blend and to impart colour gently
during the long maturation.

CUTTY SARK ORIGINAL ▶
BLEND 40% ABV
Light and fragrant aroma, with hints
of vanilla and oak. Sweet and creamy,
with a vanilla note, and a crisp finish.

CUTTY SARK 12-YEAR-OLD
BLEND 43% ABV
Elegant and fruity, with a subtle vanilla
sweetness. Here the malts used are
between 12 and 15 years old.

DAILUAINE

Scotland

Carron, Banffshire
www.malts.com

Under the shadow of Benrinnes, a local farmer called William Mackenzie built Dailuaine in 1854. His son Thomas later went into partnership with James Fleming to form Dailuaine-Talisker Distilleries Ltd. In 1889 Dailuaine was rebuilt and became one of the biggest distilleries in Scotland. The architect Charles Doig erected his first pagoda roof here, to draw smoke from the kiln through the malt. The idea caught on at other distilleries. With all but 2 per cent of Dailuaine used as fillings, single malt bottlings are relatively rare.

◀ DAILUAINE GORDON & MACPHAIL 1993
SINGLE MALT: SPEYSIDE 43% ABV
Sweet and malty, with spicy notes of liquorice and aniseed. Oaky, toasty notes too. Creamier with a little water.

D

DALLAS DHU

Scotland
Forres, Morayshire

This late-Victorian distillery, founded in 1898 by the Master Distiller Alexander Edward, was one of many owned by the Distillers Company Limited (DCL) to be shut down in 1983 to await its fate. With just two stills and a waterwheel that had provided power for the distillery right up until 1971, Dallas Dhu never fully embraced the 20th century. But, while its stills have never been fired up again, it has lived on as a museum run by Historic Scotland. Thousands of visitors have taken the tour and tried a drop of the malt in a blend called Roderick Dhu.

DALLAS DHU RARE MALTS 21-YEAR-OLD ▶
SINGLE MALT: SPEYSIDE 61.9% ABV
Full-bodied, almost Highland character on the nose, with a trace of smoke and a robust, malty flavour.

DALMORE

Scotland
Alness, Ross-shire
www.thedalmore.com

While the Whyte & Mackay blend has a long association with Glasgow, its heart lies in the Highlands, in Dalmore on the banks of the Cromarty Firth. The distillery became part of Whyte & Mackay in 1960, and The Dalmore is now the company's flagship single malt.

The name Dalmore is a fusion of Norse and Gaelic and means "the big meadowland". The distillery stands facing the Black Isle, where some of Scotland's best barley is grown. With ample

◀ THE DALMORE 12-YEAR-OLD
SINGLE MALT: HIGHLANDS
40% ABV
The well-established 12-year-old has a gentle flavour of candied peel and vanilla fudge.

THE DALMORE 1974
SINGLE MALT: HIGHLANDS
45% ABV
Smooth and full-bodied, with sherry notes, bananas, dark chocolate orange, coffee, walnuts, and a long finish.

supplies of grain, plenty of local peat, and water from the River Alness, the site was well-chosen.

For years, the only distillery bottling of Dalmore was a 12-year-old single malt, but in time a 21- and 30-year-old were added, together with Gran Reserva (formerly known as the Cigar Malt) in 2002. That year also saw the sale at auction of a 62-year-old expression for a record-beating £25,877. Since then, the core range has swelled alongside limited-release bottlings. Many of these have played on different cask maturation, a subject that clearly fascinates Whyte & Mackay's Master Blender, Richard Paterson.

THE DALMORE 15-YEAR-OLD ▶
SINGLE MALT: HIGHLANDS
40% ABV
This has the characteristic rich, fruity sherry influence, but with rather more spice – cloves, cinnamon, and ginger.

THE DALMORE 40-YEAR-OLD
SINGLE MALT: HIGHLANDS
40% ABV
After years in American oak casks, this Dalmore was poured into second-fill Matusalem Oloroso sherry butts and then Amoroso sherry wood.

D

DALWHINNIE

Scotland
Dalwhinnie, Inverness-shire
www.malts.com

Founded in 1897, Dalwhinnie used to claim to be the highest distillery in Scotland, at 327m (1,073ft) above sea level, but it has since been eclipsed by Braeval. Its other claim to fame holds good, however: with a mean annual temperature of just 6°C (43°F), Dalwhinnie remains the coldest distillery in the country. In 1905 it became Scotland's first American-owned distillery, bought by the New York company Cook & Bernheimer, and the Stars and Stripes were raised above the owners' warehouse in Leith. Since 1926 it has been part of DCL (now Diageo), supplying blends such as Black & White.

◀ **DALWHINNIE 15-YEAR-OLD**
SINGLE MALT: HIGHLANDS
43% ABV
Sweet, aromatic, and subtly infused with smoke, this complex malt is thick on the tongue.

DEANSTON

Scotland
Deanston, Perthshire
www.burnstewartdistillers.com

Many distilleries evolved from illicit stills on the farm, others from breweries or malt mills, but only Deanston is a former cotton mill. It was founded in 1785 by Richard Arkwright, one of the great pioneers of the Industrial Revolution. The conversion to whisky-making took place in 1965, in a joint venture with Brodie Hepburn, who also owned Tullibardine. Deanston was soon producing a single malt – Old Bannockburn was released in 1971. Having spent most of the 1980s in mothballs, the distillery was bought by Burn Stewart, now part of Trinidad-based CL Financial, in 1990.

DEANSTON 12-YEAR-OLD ▶
SINGLE MALT: HIGHLANDS
40% ABV
A relatively light-bodied Highland malt, with a nutty flavour and hints of sherry.

DEWAR'S

Scotland
www.dewars.com

When it was bought by Bacardi in 1988, the whole Dewar's enterprise was reinvigorated. The brand was repackaged, with considerable investment made throughout the business, from distilling to bottling. New products were developed to augment the standard White Label – one of the biggest selling Scotch blends in the US. First of these was a 12-year-old expression, Special Reserve, followed by the 18-year-old Founder's Reserve bottling, and finally an ultra-premium non-age style known as Signature.

◀ **DEWAR'S 12-YEAR-OLD**
BLEND 40% ABV
Sweetish and floral. A full and rich blend, with honey and caramel, and liquorice notes in the long finish.

DEWAR'S WHITE LABEL
BLEND 40% ABV
Sweet and heathery on the nose. Medium-bodied, fresh, malty, and vaguely spicy, with a clean, slightly dry finish.

The main single malt in the Dewar's blends is Aberfeldy, although the group's other single malts – Aultmore, Craigellachie, Royal Brackla and MacDuff – are also used.

Dewar's is not widely available in the UK, but is dominant in the US. It is also important in parts of Europe and is gaining a following in Asia. Bacardi has expanded global distribution for Dewar's and greatly expanded its profile through increased advertising and marketing. Standards of production have been kept high, and some would say that the blend quality has improved, especially in the new products.

DEWAR'S 18-YEAR-OLD ▶
BLEND 43% ABV
Here the Dewar's nose is more delicately perfumed, with notes of pear and lemon zest. Soft on the palate, but drying, with a slightly spicy finish.

DEWAR'S SIGNATURE
BLEND 43% ABV
A limited-edition blend, with a heavy share of old Aberfeldy. Silky textured and mellow, with rich fruit and dark honey to the fore.

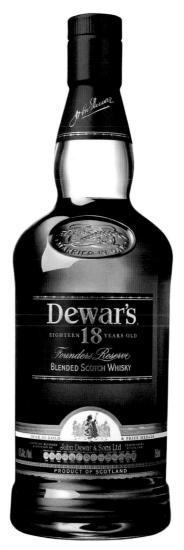

DIMPLE

Scotland
Owner: Diageo

Launched to marked success in 1890, Haig's Dimple brand is today part of the Diageo stable. It has always been a deluxe blend, noted for its distinctive packaging introduced by G. O. Haig in the 1890s. It stood out in particular for the wire net over the bottle, originally applied by hand and intended to prevent the cork popping out in warm climates or during sea transport. It was the first bottle of its type to be registered as a trademark in the United States, although this was done as late as 1958.

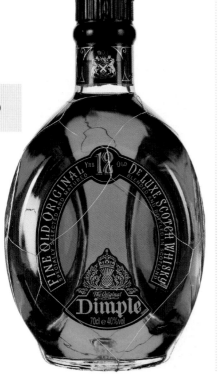

◀ DIMPLE 12-YEAR-OLD
BLEND 40% ABV
Aromas of fudge, with woody notes. Hints of mint, and an initial richness on the palate, with toffee apples and caramel; spiciness and dried fruits too.

DIMPLE 15-YEAR-OLD
BLEND 43% ABV
In this blend, there are hints of smoke, chocolate, and cocoa, completed by a long, rich finish.

DUFFTOWN

Scotland
Dufftown, Keith, Banffshire
www.malts.com

This epicentre of Speyside whisky-making was bound to have a distillery named after it, although it took until 1896, by which point there were already five distilleries in town. Within a year, Dufftown was owned outright by Peter Mackenzie, who also owned Blair Athol. He was soon selling whisky to the blender Arthur Bell & Sons, who eventually bought Dufftown in 1933. Now part of Diageo, Dufftown continues to supply malt for the Bell's blend and, until recently, had produced little in the way of its own single malt.

SINGLETON OF DUFFTOWN ▶
SINGLE MALT: SPEYSIDE
40% ABV
A sweet and eminently drinkable introductory malt. If this recently launched 12-year-old takes off, there should be plenty available – it comes from one of Diageo's biggest distilleries.

D

DUNGOURNEY 1964

Ireland
Midleton Distillery, Midleton, County Cork

No one is quite sure how, but for 30 years some of the last pot still to be produced at the old Midleton Distillery lay undiscovered in the corner of a warehouse at Dungourney. In 1994 the remarkable survivor was bottled and named after the river it had come from some three decades before. Dungourney 1964 is a time machine: one sniff and you are transported back to the days when Jameson, Powers, and Paddy came from competing distilleries.

◄ **DUNGOURNEY 1964**
IRISH POT STILL WHISKEY 40% ABV
The mushroom edge to the nose gives a hint of age, but the body is still firm. They made whiskey differently back then, which is why this tastes slightly oily, but the tell-tale, almost minty, kick of pure pot still whiskey is still evident.

DYC

Spain

Beam Global España SA,
Pasaje Molino del Arco,
40194 Palazuelos de Eresma, Segovia
www.dyc.es

The first whisky distillery in Spain was founded in 1959 close to Segovia. It stands next to the River Eresma, famous for the excellent quality of its water.

DYC (which stands for Destilerías y Crianza del Whisky) comes in three versions. The Fine Blend and the 8-year-old are both blends of various grains. The Pure Malt is a blended malt. American oak is used for maturation.

DYC 8-YEAR-OLD ▶
BLEND 40% ABV
Floral, spicy, smoky, grassy, with a hint of honey and heather. Smooth, creamy mouthfeel; malty with hints of vanilla, marzipan, apple, and citrus. A bittersweet, long, smooth finish.

DYC PURE MALT
BLENDED MALT 40% ABV
Fragrant bouquet with hints of citrus, sweetness, honey, and vanilla. Full-bodied, rich malt flavour. The finish is long, sophisticated, and subtle, with hints of heather, honey, and fruit.

EAGLE RARE

USA

Buffalo Trace Distillery,
1001 Wilkinson Boulevard,
Frankfort, Kentucky
www.buffalotrace.com

The Eagle Rare brand was
introduced in 1975 by Canadian
distilling giant Joseph E. Seagram
& Sons Inc. In 1989 it was
acquired by the Sazerac Company
of New Orleans. In its present
incarnation, Eagle Rare is part
of Sazerac's Buffalo Trace
Antique Collection, which
is updated annually.

◄ **EAGLE RARE 2008 EDITION**
BOURBON 45% ABV
This variant of Eagle Rare is from
barrels that were distilled in the spring
of 1991, and the nose offers caramel,
maple syrup, almonds, and vanilla,
while the palate boasts more vanilla,
worn leather, summer fruits, dark
chocolate, and a hint of mint. There is
a delicious, spicy, crème brûlée finish.

EARLY TIMES

USA

Brown-Forman Distillery,
850 Dixie Highway,
Louisville, Kentucky
www.brown-forman.com

Early Times takes its name from a settlement near Bardstown where it was created in 1860. It cannot be classified as a bourbon because some spirit is put into used barrels, and bourbon legislation dictates that all spirit of that name must be matured in new barrels.

This version of Early Times was introduced in 1981 to compete with the increasingly popular, lighter-bodied Canadian whiskies. The Early Times mashbill is made up of 79 per cent corn, 11 per cent rye, and 10 per cent malted barley.

EARLY TIMES ▶
KENTUCKY WHISKEY 40% ABV
Quite light on the nose, with nuts and spices. The palate offers more of the same, together with honey and butterscotch notes, leading into a medium-length finish.

EDDU

France
*Des Menhirs, Pont Menhir, 29700
Plomelin, Bretagne
www.distillerie.fr*

The Des Menhirs Distillery started life as a manufacturer of apple cider in 1986, but in 1998 branched out into whisky. Most fruit distillers that venture into whisky-making use their existing equipment to distil whisky on the side. Not so this company: Des Menhirs built a separate still for the exclusive production of whisky, which it distils not from barley but from buckwheat (*eddu* in Breton).

◀ EDDU SILVER
BUCKWHEAT WHISKY 40% ABV
Aromatic rose and heather on the nose. Fruity, with a touch of honey, marmalade, and some nutmeg. Velvety body, with vanilla and oak in the finish.

EDDU GREY ROCK
BLEND 40% ABV
A blended variety containing 30 per cent buckwheat. Orange and apricot flavours combine with broom flower. A faint sea breeze is framed by a hint of cinnamon. Balanced flavours and a long, long finish.

EDGEFIELD

USA

2126 Southwest Halsey Street,
Troutdale, Oregon
www.mcmenamins.com

Operated by the McMenamin's
hotel and pub group, Edgefield
Distillery is located in a former
dry store for root vegetables on
the beautiful Edgefield Manor
Estate at Troutdale. The distillery
has been in production since
February 1998 and features a
4-m (12-ft) tall copper and
stainless-steel still. According
to McMenamin's, it resembles a
hybrid of a 19th-century diving
suit and oversized coffee urn, a
design made famous by Holstein
of Germany, the world's oldest
surviving still manufacturer.

EDGEFIELD HOGSHEAD ▶
OREGON WHISKEY 46% ABV
Hogshead whiskey has banana and
malt on the sweet, floral nose, with
vanilla and caramel notes on the
palate, plus barley, honey, and oak
in the medium-length finish.

E

EDRADOUR

Scotland
Pitlochry, Perthshire
www.edradour.co.uk

With an output of just 90,000 litres (6,600 gallons) of pure alcohol a year, this picturesque distillery would have been one of many farm distilleries in the Perthshire hills when it was founded in 1825. Today it feels much more special, and a world apart from the large-scale malt distilleries of Speyside. It became part of Pernod Ricard in 1975 but, as the French group expanded to become a huge global player in the whisky industry, tiny Edradour began to look increasingly out of place. In 2002 it was finally sold to Andrew Symington, owner of independent bottler Signatory.

◀ **EDRADOUR 10-YEAR-OLD**
SINGLE MALT: HIGHLANDS
40% ABV
Clean peppermint nose, with a trace of smoke. Richer, nutty flavours and a silky texture on the tongue.

ELIJAH CRAIG

USA
Heaven Hill Distillery,
1701 West Breckinridge Street,
Louisville, Kentucky
www.heaven-hill.com

The Reverend Elijah Craig
(1743–1808) was a Baptist
minister who is widely viewed as
the "father of bourbon", having
reputedly invented the concept of
using charred barrels to store and
mature the spirit he made. There
seems to be no hard evidence that
he was the first person to make
bourbon, but the association
between a "man of God" and
whiskey was seen as a useful
tool in the struggle against
the temperance movement.

ELIJAH CRAIG 12-YEAR-OLD ▶
BOURBON 47% ABV
A classic bourbon, with sweet,
mature aromas of caramel, vanilla,
spice, and honey, plus a sprig of mint.
Rich, full-bodied, and rounded on the
mellow palate, with caramel, malt,
corn, rye, and a hint of smoke. Sweet
oak, liquorice, and vanilla dominate
the finish.

ELMER T. LEE

USA

*Buffalo Trace Distillery,
1001 Wilkinson Boulevard,
Frankfort, Kentucky
www.buffalotrace.com*

Elmer T. Lee is a former Master
Distiller at Buffalo Trace *(see p66)*,
having joined what was then the
George T. Stagg Distillery in the
1940s. During his time there, the
name changed first to the Albert
B. Blanton Distillery (1953),
then to the Ancient Age Distillery
(1962), and finally to the Buffalo
Trace Distillery in 2001. Lee
is credited with creating the
first modern single barrel
bourbon in 1984.

◀ **ELMER T. LEE
SINGLE BARREL
BOURBON 45% ABV**
Aged from six to eight years, this
expression offers citrus, vanilla, and
sweet corn merging on the fragrant
nose, with a full and sweet palate,
where honey, lingering caramel,
and cocoa notes are also evident.

THE ENGLISH WHISKY CO.

England
*St George's Distillery,
Harling Road, Roudham, Norfolk
www.englishwhisky.co.uk*

According to Alfred Barnard, in his 1887 tome *Distilleries of the United Kingdom and Ireland*, England had at least four distilleries in the 1800s. These had all gone by the turn of the 20th century and it was not until 2006 that pot stills produced malt spirit in England again, thanks to The English Whisky Co., which hired distilling legend Iain Henderson to set things up.

**ENGLISH WHISKY CO.
CHAPTER 3 ▶**
NEW MAKE 40% ABV
It's not whisky, as it has not been matured for 3 years, but the new make is very fruity. Iain Henderson also made some peaty spirit in 2007.

117

EVAN WILLIAMS

USA
Heaven Hill Distillery,
1701 West Breckinridge Street,
Louisville, Kentucky
www.heaven-hill.com

The second biggest-selling bourbon after Jim Beam, Evan Williams takes its name from the person considered by many experts to be Kentucky's first distiller.

Evan Williams was born in Wales but emigrated to Virginia, moving to what would become Kentucky in around 1780. He set up a distillery at the foot of what is now Fifth Street in Louisville.

◀ EVAN WILLIAMS BLACK LABEL
BOURBON 43% ABV
Aromatic, with vanilla and mint notes. The palate is initially sweet, with caramel, malt, and developing leather and spice notes.

EVAN WILLIAMS SINGLE BARREL 1998 VINTAGE
BOURBON 43.3% ABV
Aromatic nose of cereal, dried fruit, caramel, and vanilla. Maple, molasses, cinnamon, nutmeg, and berry notes on the palate. Then a whiff of smoke, plus almonds and honey in the spicy finish.

THE FAMOUS GROUSE

Scotland
Owner: Edrington Group
www.thefamousgrouse.com

The bestselling blend in Scotland
was created by the Victorian
entrepreneur Matthew Gloag in
1896. At first, it was known
simply as The Grouse Brand, but
it evolved to become The Famous
Grouse. The company was passed
down through the generations
until 1970, when death duties
forced the family to sell out to ☞

THE FAMOUS GROUSE FINEST ▶
BLEND 40% ABV
Oak and sherry on the nose, well
balanced with a citrus note. Easygoing,
and full of bright Speyside fruit. Clean
and medium-dry finish.

THE FAMOUS GROUSE BLENDED MALT RANGE
BLENDED MALTS 43% ABV
Aged at 10-, 12-, 15-, 18-, and 30-years-
old, each expression is a blend of malt
whiskies from Edrington's distilleries.
These are all fruity, spicy whiskies,
with vanilla and more tannic, sherry
influences becoming increasingly
marked through the age range.

119

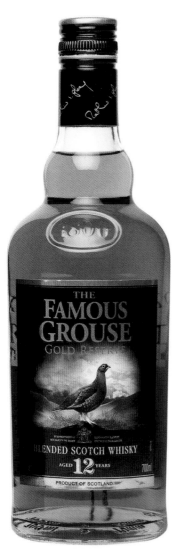

THE FAMOUS GROUSE

Highland Distillers, today part of the Edrington Group, which also owns some of Scotland's finest single malt distilleries – Highland Park, Macallan, and Glenrothes among them. Naturally, there are high proportions of these whiskies in The Famous Grouse blend.

Since 2007 there has been a number of interesting initiatives. The Black Grouse contains more strongly-flavoured Islay malt in the blend, while Snow Grouse is a grain whisky intended to be drunk cold from the freezer, like vodka – a creamy mouth-coating effect results. The Famous Grouse also produces a range of blended malts, aged from 10 to 30 years.

◀ GOLD RESERVE 12-YEAR-OLD
BLEND 40% ABV
Floral and oaky, with a fruity palate, and spicy taste. Rounded off by a long, medium-dry finish.

THE BLACK GROUSE
BLEND 40% ABV
Cream teas, peaches, apples, and jammy aromas. Soft peat and smoke notes on the palate (more so with water), plus vanilla, pepper, and spices, then a gentle finish.

FECKIN IRISH WHISKEY

Ireland
www.feckinwhiskey.com

As Irish whiskey sales continue
to buck the trend and sail
upwards, it's not surprising that
bright entrepreneurs continue
to pour new products onto the
market. From its name to the
label, this offering is aimed at the
younger end of the spectrum, and
there's not a tweed jacket in sight.
"Feck", by the way, is a very mild
and very Irish swear word that
was popularized on the TV
show *Father Ted*.

FECKIN IRISH WHISKEY ▶
BLEND 40% ABV
Made using whiskey from the Cooley
Distillery, this is light, approachable,
and totally inoffensive. It's clearly a
young whiskey and lacks much in
the way of depth.

FETTERCAIRN

Scotland
Fettercairn, Laurencekirk, Kincardineshire

While the northeastern flank of the Grampians is full of distilleries spilling down to the Spey, the southern slopes are now depleted. Fettercairn stands as their sole survivor. The distillery was established in 1824 as a farm distillery on the Fasque Estate, which was soon bought by Sir John Gladstone, father of the Victorian prime minister William Gladstone. It remained in family hands until 1939, since when it has been bought, sold, and mothballed several times. Today Fettercairn is part of Whyte & Mackay, but their main priorities are in the shape of Dalmore and Jura.

◀ **FETTERCAIRN 12-YEAR-OLD**
SINGLE MALT: HIGHLANDS 40% ABV
A relatively closed nose gives way to a nutty toffee flavour in the mouth, which dries on the finish.

FORTY CREEK

Canada
*Kittling Ridge Distillery,
Grimsby, Ontario
www.fortycreekwhisky.com*

Kittling Ridge was named 2008
Canadian Distillery of the Year
by *Whisky Magazine*. Unusually,
it uses pot stills as well as column
stills, and a mashbill of rye, barley,
and corn. Built in 1970, it is part
of a well-respected winery and
was originally designed to make
eau de vie. John Hall, its owner
since 1992, brings the skills of
a winemaker to distilling: "I am
not so bound by tradition as
inspired by it". Whisky critic
Michael Jackson called Forty
Creek "the most revolutionary
whisky in Canada".

FORTY CREEK
BARREL SELECT ▶
BLEND 40% ABV

A complex, fragrant nose, with soft
fruit, honeysuckle, vanilla, and some
spice. A similar palate, with traces of
nuts and leather, and a smooth finish
with lingering fruit and vanilla.

FOUR ROSES

USA
1224 Bond Mills Road,
Lawrenceburg, Kentucky
www.fourroses.us

Built to a striking Spanish Mission-style design in 1910, Four Roses Distillery near Lawrenceburg takes its name from the brand first trademarked by Georgia-born Paul Jones Jr in 1888. Legend has it that the southern belle with whom he was in love wore a corsage of four red roses to signify her acceptance of his marriage proposal, hence the name he gave to his bourbon.

◄ FOUR ROSES SMALL BATCH
BOURBON 45% ABV
Mild and refined on the nose, with nutmeg and restrained honey. Bold and rich on the well-balanced palate, with spices, fruit, and honey flavours. The finish is long and insinuating, with developing notes of vanilla.

FOUR ROSES SINGLE BARREL
BOURBON (VARIABLE ABV)
Rich, complex nose, comprising malt, fruits, spices, and fudge. Long and mellow in the mouth, with vanilla, oak, and a hint of menthol. The finish is long, spicy, and decidedly mellow.

FRYSK HYNDER

The Netherlands
Us Heit distillery, Snekerstraat 43,
8701 XC Bolsward, Friesland
www.usheitdistillery.nl

Us Heit (Frisian for "Our Father")
was founded as a brewery in 1970.
In 2002, owner Aart van der
Linde, an avid whisky enthusiast,
decided to start distilling whisky
with barley from a local mill. It
is the same barley from which Us
Heit beer is made and it is malted
at the distillery. A 3-year-old single
malt whisky, Frysk Hynder, has
been released in limited quantities
every year since 2005. Us Heit uses
different types of cask for maturing
its whisky, from ex-bourbon barrels
to wine casks and sherry butts.

FRYSK HYNDER
SHERRY MATURED ▶
SINGLE MALT 43% ABV
Sweetish and remarkably soft for a
young whisky. Tasty, with a beautiful,
full body and distinct sherry notes.

GEORGE DICKEL

USA
*1950 Cascade Hollow Road,
Normandy, Tennessee*
www.dickel.com

Along with Jack Daniel's,
George Dickel is the last licensed,
full-scale distillery in Tennessee,
though a century ago there were
around 700 operating there.

The Dickel operation was
moved to Kentucky after
Prohibition arrived in Tennessee
in 1910, but later returned to its
roots at a new distillery close to
the location of the original.

◀ **GEORGE DICKEL NO. 12**
TENNESSEE WHISKEY 45% ABV
Aromatic, with fruit, leather,
butterscotch, and a whiff of charcoal
and vanilla. Rich palate with rye,
chocolate, fruit, and vanilla. The finish
offers vanilla toffee and drying oak.

**GEORGE DICKEL
BARREL SELECT**
TENNESSEE WHISKEY 43% ABV
Aromas of rich corn, honey, nuts,
and caramel lead into a full body
with soft vanilla, spices, and roast
nuts. The long, creamy finish boasts
almond and spices.

GEORGE T. STAGG

USA
Buffalo Trace Distillery,
1001 Wilkinson Boulevard,
Frankfort, Kentucky
www.buffalotrace.com

Part of the Buffalo Trace Antique
Collection, George T. Stagg takes
its name from the one-time owner
of what is now the Buffalo Trace
Distillery. In the early 1880s the
distillery was owned by Edmund
Haynes Taylor Jr. During tough
economic times he obtained a loan
from his friend Stagg – who later
foreclosed on Taylor, taking over
his company in the process.

GEORGE T. STAGG
2008 EDITION ▶
BOURBON 72.4% ABV
Distilled in the spring of 1993, this
high-strength whiskey boasts a rich
nose of butterscotch, marzipan, sweet
oak, and glacé cherries. The palate
features corn, roasted coffee beans,
leather, spice, and mature oak, with
a long toffee and spice finish.

GEORGIA MOON

USA

Heaven Hill Distillery,
1701 West Breckinridge Street,
Louisville, Kentucky
www.heaven-hill.com

Corn whiskey is distilled from
a fermented mash of not less
than 80 per cent corn, and no
minimum maturation period
is specified. One of the best-
known examples is Heaven Hill's
Georgia Moon. With a label that
promises the contents are less
than 30 days old, and available
bottled in a mason jar, Georgia
Moon harks back to the old days
of moonshining.

◄ **GEORGIA MOON**
CORN WHISKEY 40% ABV
The nose commences with an
initial tang of sour liquor, followed
by the smell of sweet corn. The palate
suggests cabbage water and plums,
along with emerging sweeter, candy-
corn notes. The finish is short.
Drinkers should not expect
anything sophisticated.

128

GIRVAN

Scotland

*Grangestone Industrial Estate,
Girvan, Ayrshire*

The distillery at Girvan was
established in 1964 by William
Grant & Sons in response to a
perceived threat to their grain-
whisky supplies. Today it includes
a grain-whisky distilling complex,
a gin distillery, and the recently
opened Ailsa Bay single malt
distillery. Girvan is rarely bottled
by the proprietors as a single grain,
but limited numbers of third-party
bottlings are occasionally seen.
Older expressions are generally
dominated by the maize component
and are greatly softened by age
to provide a delicate and refined
whisky of some subtlety and
delightful complexity.

GIRVAN 1964 ▶
SINGLE GRAIN 43% ABV
Sweet vanilla nose and a deliciously
creamy mouthfeel. Bittersweet caramel
palate, with a note of ripe banana.

GLEN BRETON

Canada
*Glenora Distillery, Route 19,
Glenville, Cape Breton, Nova Scotia
www.glenoradistillery.com*

This is North America's only malt whisky distillery. Cape Breton Island has a strong Scottish heritage, but the Scotch Whisky Association has criticized the name for sounding too much like a Scotch.

Production began in June 1990, halting within weeks due to lack of funds. The distillery was later bought by Lauchie MacLean, who has re-distilled earlier, inconsistent spirit, and bottles at 8 or 9 years.

Glenora has its own maltings and uses Scottish barley that is given a light peating. The two stills it uses are made by Forsyths of Rothes.

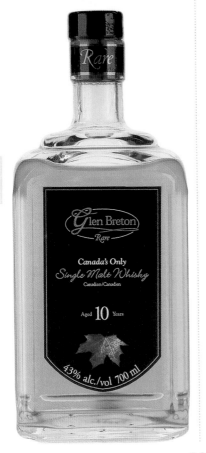

◀ GLEN BRETON RARE
SINGLE MALT 43% ABV
Butterscotch, heather, ground ginger, and honey nose. Light to medium body, with a creamy mouthfeel and notes of wood, almonds, caramel, and peat.

GLEN DEVERON

Scotland
Macduff Distillery, Banff, Aberdeenshire

While the single malt is Glen Deveron (named after the water source – the River Deveron in eastern Speyside), the distillery is called Macduff. It was founded in 1962 by a consortium led by the Duff family. Much of the malt was used in blends, particularly William Lawson, whose owners bought the distillery in 1972. Since then it has changed hands twice, increased its number of stills to five, and now belongs to Bacardi. Various age statements are produced, and, just to confuse matters, there are occasional independent bottlings under the name Macduff.

**GLEN DEVERON
10-YEAR-OLD ▶**
SINGLE MALT: HIGHLANDS
40% ABV
Although it is described as a "Pure Highland Single Malt" on the bottle's label, in style this is a classic, clean, gentle Speyside whisky.

GLEN ELGIN

Scotland
Longmorn, Morayshire
www.malts.com

The Glen Elgin distillery was
founded in 1898, when demand
for Speyside malt from the
blenders was at its peak. But boom
soon turned to bust, the industry
entered a prolonged slump, and
production at Glen Elgin was
intermittent during its first three
decades, as the business passed
from one owner to the next.

After many years of appearing
only in blends (notably White
Horse), a first distillery bottling of
Glen Elgin was released in 1977.

◀ GLEN ELGIN 12-YEAR-OLD
SINGLE MALT: SPEYSIDE
43% ABV

This is one of the most floral and
perfumed Speyside malts, with a nutty,
honey-blossom aroma and a balanced
flavour that goes from sweet to dry.

GLEN ELGIN 16-YEAR-OLD
SINGLE MALT: SPEYSIDE
58.5% ABV

The 16-year-old is a non chill-filtered,
cask-strength malt with a deep
mahogany colour and a ripe, fruitcake
flavour from its years in European oak.

GLEN GARIOCH

Scotland
*Oldmeldrum, Inverurie,
Aberdeenshire
www.glengarioch.com*

This small Aberdeenshire distillery
was founded in 1798, yet the first
distillery bottling of Glen Garioch
as a single malt was not until
1972. It survived the long years
in between thanks to its
popularity among blenders.

Glen Garioch is now part of
Morrison Bowmore, which bottles
most, if not all of, the distillery's
limited production as a single malt
in a range of age statements, from
8 to 21 years old.

GLEN GARIOCH 15-YEAR-OLD ▶

**SINGLE MALT: HIGHLANDS
43% ABV**

A floral, heathery nose offers notes
of Lapsang tea. On the palate, a malty
flavour dries to a spicy finish.

GLEN GARIOCH 21-YEAR-OLD

**SINGLE MALT: HIGHLANDS
43% ABV**

A smooth, well-rounded malt with a
luscious syrupy texture and a mellow,
ripe fruit character that shows some
influence from sherry casks.

GLEN GRANT

Scotland
Rothes, Morayshire
www.glengrant.com

Glen Grant, built in 1840, was the first of the five distilleries in the town of Rothes. It was a very good site for a distillery, with the Glen Grant burn supplying water for the mash and to power the machinery, and plentiful supplies of grain from the barley fields of nearby Moray.

Having passed through the hands of Pernod Ricard in 2001–2006, it is now with the Italian Campari drinks group. Though it receives little attention at home, it is one of the top five bestselling malts in the world.

◀ GLEN GRANT SINGLE MALT
SINGLE MALT: SPEYSIDE
40% ABV

Light, spirity, and floral on the nose. Initially dry on the palate, but softer, nut flavours develop. A herby finish rounds off this aperitif-style whisky.

GLEN GRANT 10-YEAR-OLD
SINGLE MALT: SPEYSIDE
40% ABV

A relatively dry nose with the scent of orchard fruit. Light to medium body with a cereal, nutty flavour.

GLEN KEITH

Scotland
Keith, Banffshire

Having bought Strathisla in 1950, Seagram built Glen Keith on the site of an old corn mill seven years later. Both are in Keith and were part of Seagram's whisky arm, Chivas Brothers (now part of Pernod Ricard). Both also shared a simple function – to supply the company's bestselling blended brands. Glen Keith began life using triple distillation and later pioneered the use of computers in its whisky-making at a time when some distilleries had only recently joined the national grid.

Glen Keith was mothballed in 2000 and, while independent bottlings are available, its 10-year-old is increasingly hard to find.

GLEN KEITH 10-YEAR-OLD ▶
SINGLE MALT: SPEYSIDE
43% ABV
This relatively rare official bottling is a mix of grassy Speyside aromas and some toffee sweetness on the tongue.

135

GLEN ORD

Scotland
Muir of Ord, Ross-shire
www.malts.com

Despite its name, Glen Ord is
not in a valley, but on the fertile
flatlands of the Black Isle, north
of Inverness. It was founded in
1838, close to the alleged site of
the Ferintosh Distillery, which
was established in the 1670s.
In 1923 Glen Ord was bought
by John Dewar & Sons, shortly
before they joined the Distiller's
Company Limited (DCL).

With six stills and 3.4
million litres (750,000 gallons) of
production, it has plenty to spare
for a single malt. Confusingly, this
has been called Ord, Glenordie,
and Muir of Ord at various times.
Recent bottlings are called The
Singleton of Ord, aiming at the
US market.

◀ **GLEN ORD 12-YEAR-OLD**
SINGLE MALT: HIGHLANDS
43% ABV
This citrussy, orange-peel-scented malt
has a gentle apple-pie flavour and some
spicy ginger notes on the finish.

GLEN SCOTIA

Scotland
Campbeltown, Argyll
www.lochlomonddistillery.com

Strung-out at the far end of the
Mull of Kintyre, Campbeltown's
rise and fall as "whiskyopolis" has
been well-documented, as has the
story of the Springbank Distillery,
which managed to pull through
and now enjoys cult status *(see
p321)*. But, it was not the only
one, for the much lesser known
Glen Scotia also survived. With its
single pair of stills, Campbeltown's
"other" distillery was founded in
the 1830s by the Galbraith family,
who retained control for the rest
of the century. After various
owners followed, it was bought
by Glen Catrine (Loch Lomond
Distillers) in 1994.

GLEN SCOTIA 12-YEAR-OLD ▶
SINGLE MALT: CAMPBELTOWN
40% ABV
This distillery bottling replaced the
8-year-old and has a spicy aroma with
sweeter, richer notes on the palate.

G

GLEN SPEY

Scotland

Rothes, Aberlour, Banffshire
www.malts.com

James Stuart was an established
distiller with Macallan and the key
partner in building the Glenrothes
Distillery in 1878, although he
quickly pulled out of that venture.
A few years later, he decided to
convert an oat mill he owned into
Glen Spey, on the opposite bank of
the Rothes burn from Glenrothes.
The project inevitably led to
disputes over water rights. In
1887, Glen Spey was sold to the
London-based gin distiller
Gilbey's, who later merged with
Justerini & Brooks. Its J&B blend
has contained Glen Spey ever
since. The current owners, Diageo,
have just one malt bottling in their
Flora & Fauna range.

◀ **GLEN SPEY FLORA & FAUNA
12-YEAR-OLD**
**SINGLE MALT: SPEYSIDE
43% ABV**
A light, grassy nose and brisk, nutty
flavour. Very dry, with a short finish.

GLENALLACHIE

Scotland
Aberlour, Banffshire

This modern gravity-flow distillery
was established by a subsidiary
of the giant Scottish & Newcastle
Breweries in 1967. The architect
was William Delmé-Evans, who
had earlier designed and part-
owned Tullibardine and Jura.
With the capacity to produce
2.8 million litres (615,000 gallons)
of pure alcohol a year, there
should be plenty available for a
single malt. And yet, so far there
have only been a few independent
bottlings and a 16-year-old cask
strength expression from the
distillery's current owners,
Chivas Brothers (Pernod Ricard).

**GLENALLACHIE
16-YEAR-OLD 1990** ▶
**SINGLE MALT: SPEYSIDE
56.9% ABV**
A dark, heavily sherried whisky
matured in first-fill Oloroso casks,
which can be hard to find.

GLENBURGIE

Scotland
Glenburgie, Forres, Morayshire

Glenburgie began life as the
Kilnflat Distillery in 1829. It
was renamed Glenburgie in
1878 and, after various changes
in ownership, became part of
Canada's Hiram Walker in the
1930s. From then on, the primary
role of this distillery was to supply
whisky for Ballantine's Finest. Yet,
as early as 1958, long before most
of Speyside began thinking of
single malt, Glenburgie released
its own bottling under the name
Glencraig. In 2004, its then
owners, Allied Distillers,
demonstrated their faith in
Glenburgie by investing £4.3m.
The distillery was completely
rebuilt and only the stills and
milling equipment were kept.

◀ **GLENBURGIE 15-YEAR-OLD**
SINGLE MALT: SPEYSIDE
46% ABV
On the fruitier side of Speyside, with
a relatively luscious texture and notes
of stewed plums.

GLENCADAM

Scotland
Brechin, Angus
www.glencadamdistillery.co.uk

With the demise of Lochside in
2005, Glencadam became the
only distillery left in Angus. It was
founded in 1825 by George Cooper
and, despite various changes in
ownership, remained in private
hands until 1954, when it became
part of Hiram Walker and later
Allied Distillers. While there was
some safety in numbers on
Speyside, Glencadam looked
increasingly isolated. When it
shut down in 2000 – a victim of
overproduction in the industry –
its prospects looked bleak. But it
slipped back into independent
hands in 2003 when bought by
Angus Dundee *(see p17)*.

GLENCADAM 10-YEAR-OLD ▶
SINGLE MALT: HIGHLANDS
46% ABV
The nose is fresh and grassy, with
citrus notes and a trace of spicy oak.
Rounded on the palate, citrussy and
crisp. Well-balanced, with a long finish.

GLENDRONACH

Scotland
Forgue, Huntly, Aberdeenshire

This distillery is the spiritual sister to Ardmore, and fellow contributor to the Teacher's blend. Although William Teacher & Sons did not buy Glendronach until 1960, the firm had sourced Glendronach malts for years. After Teacher's was swallowed up by Allied Distillers, Glendronach was picked, in 1991, to be one of the "Caledonian Malts" – the company's belated riposte to UDV's Classic Malts. A decade later, after five years in mothballs, the distillery re-opened. By that time the single malts had become less peaty and were matured in American oak ex-bourbon casks rather than sherry casks.

◀ **GLENDRONACH
12-YEAR-OLD**
**SINGLE MALT: SPEYSIDE
40% ABV**
This dense, heavily sherried malt replaced the 15-year-old and is best suited to after-dinner sipping.

GLENDULLAN

Scotland
Dufftown, Keith, Banffshire
www.malts.com

There were already six distilleries
in Dufftown when the Aberdeen-
based blenders William Williams
& Sons decided to build a seventh.
Work on Glendullan began in 1897,
and within five years its whisky
had secured a royal warrant
from the new king, Edward VII.
It has been in almost continual
production ever since, and for
years was a key filling in the
deluxe Old Parr blend *(see p277)*.
In the 1960s, a modern distillery
was erected next door, and for the
following 20 years the two sides
of Glendullan worked in tandem.
Today, the modern distillery
carries on alone.

GLENDULLAN FLORA & FAUNA
12-YEAR-OLD ▶
SINGLE MALT: SPEYSIDE
43% ABV

A crisp, aperitif-style malt with a
sweeter palate than you would expect.

GLENFARCLAS

Scotland
Ballindalloch, Banffshire
www.glenfarclas.co.uk

The oldest family-owned distillery in Scotland has belonged to the Grants since 1865, when John Grant and son George took over the tenancy of Rechlarich farm, near Ballindalloch. It gradually assumed importance in the family business, and went on to become the Glenfarclas-Glenlivet Distillery Company in partnership with the Pattison Brothers of Leith, whose bankruptcy at the end of the 19th century almost dragged the Glenfarclas distillery down with it.

◀ GLENFARCLAS 105
SINGLE MALT: SPEYSIDE
60% ABV
A cask strength 10-year-old. Water dampens the fiery edge and brings out a sweet, nutty-spicy character.

GLENFARCLAS 10-YEAR-OLD
SINGLE MALT: SPEYSIDE
40% ABV
This rich, malty whisky with a smoky, aromatic nose is a nod to the Highlands.

Surrounded by 10 large dunnage warehouses, Glenfarclas is no boutique distillery. It boasts a modern mill and six stills. It also claims to be the first malt distillery to have offered a cask strength expression – Glenfarclas 105 was released in 1968. At that time, the industry doubted that single malts, let alone something that was 60 per cent pure alcohol, would catch on with the whisky buyer.

Recently, Glenfarclas offered 10 vintage expressions, ranging from 1952 to 1989. The house style is a robust, outdoors take on Speyside, with a greater affiliation to sherry butts than bourbon barrels.

GLENFARCLAS 12-YEAR-OLD ▶
SINGLE MALT: SPEYSIDE
43% ABV
A distinct sherry nose, with spicy flavours of cinnamon and stewed fruit.

GLENFARCLAS 15-YEAR-OLD
SINGLE MALT: SPEYSIDE
46% ABV
Described by writer Dave Broom as "George Melly in a glass", for its fruity, over-the-top exuberance. It is intensely perfumed, sherried, and powerful.

145

GLENFIDDICH

Scotland
Dufftown, Keith, Banffshire
www.glenfiddich.com

With a wife and nine children to support on a salary of £100 a year, William Grant had to scrimp and save until he raised the funds to start Glenfiddich in 1886. Using stones from the bed of the River Fiddich, and second-hand stills from neighbouring Cardhu, he was able to produce his first spirit on Christmas Day 1887. From these humble beginnings, Glenfiddich has grown into the biggest malt distillery in the world. By the time William Grant died in 1923, his

◀ GLENFIDDICH 12-YEAR-OLD
SINGLE MALT: SPEYSIDE
40% ABV
A gentle aperitif-style whisky with a malty, grassy flavour and a little vanilla sweetness. Quite soft.

GLENFIDDICH 15-YEAR-OLD SOLERA RESERVE
SINGLE MALT: SPEYSIDE
40% ABV
After 15 years in American oak, this is finished off in Spanish casks for an extra-soft layer of fresh fruit and spice.

firm was already producing its own blends, which were sold as far afield as Australia and Canada. The company also pioneered today's market for single malts in the 1960s – there was no big brand before Glenfiddich.

Today Glenfiddich has 29 stills and a capacity of 10 million litres (2.2 million gallons) of pure alcohol a year. In time this will be matched by Diageo's new Roseisle Distillery, but it is believed that Roseisle will supply malt for the likes of Johnnie Walker. For the moment, Glenfiddich's pole position as the most popular malt whisky in the world looks secure.

GLENFIDDICH 18-YEAR-OLD SOLERA RESERVE ▶
SINGLE MALT: SPEYSIDE
40% ABV
A big step up from the 12-year-old: ripe tropical fruit flavours, a pleasant oaky sweetness, and a trace of sherry.

GLENFIDDICH 21-YEAR-OLD CARIBBEAN RUM CASK
SINGLE MALT: SPEYSIDE
40% ABV
Rich, toffee-flavoured malt with flavours of bananas, caramel, spice, and chocolate orange.

Whisky Tour: Speyside

Speyside boasts the greatest concentration of distilleries in the world. Distillery tours were pioneered here, when William Grant & Sons first opened Glenfiddich to the public in 1969. Its competitors laughed – but soon opened their own centres. Speyside hosts two whisky festivals each year, in May and September. Convenient accommodation options include the Highlander Inn in Craigellachie and The Mash Tun in Aberlour.

SCOTLAND

DAY 1: GLENFIDDICH, THE BALVENIE

1 Begin at Dufftown's **Glenfiddich**, the ultimate home of whisky tourism. The distillery offers a free tour or an extended option with tastings at extra cost. You need to pre-book for the extended tour, which lasts two and a half hours.

2 After lunch at Glenfiddich, take in sister distillery **The Balvenie**. The three-hour guided tour here, which must also be pre-booked, includes the floor maltings and tastings of exclusive vintages.

THE BALVENIE

FORRES

NAIRN

A96

A940

MILL BUIE

A939

B9007

A939

CÀRN NA LÒINE

GRANTOWN-ON-SPEY **7**

A95

DAY 2: COOPERAGE, ABERLOUR, THE MACALLAN, CARDHU

3 Head to Craigellachie to start the day at the **Speyside Cooperage**. There you can watch a film about cask-making and see the coopers at work from a viewing gallery.

ABERLOUR CASKS

4 Afterwards, take the A95 road towards **Aberlour** Distillery, which is the next stop. Again, pre-booking is advisable. The tour culminates in a tasting and the chance to bottle your own whisky from the cask.

A95

A95

Spey

NETHY BRIDGE

BOAT OF GARTEN

AVIEMORE

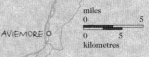

miles
0   5

0   5
kilometres

5 Head over the Spey, pausing to admire the Thomas Telford bridge (built in 1812), then take the B9102 to **The Macallan**. Its "Precious Tour" is the one to pre-book for its tutored nosing and tasting of a range of Macallan whiskies.

6 **Cardhu** Distillery is further along the B9102, which you can visit without pre-booking. The malt made here is used in the Johnnie Walker blends.

DAY 3: GRANTOWN-ON-SPEY, THE WHISKY CASTLE, THE GLENLIVET, GORDON & MACPHAIL

7 **Grantown-on-Spey** is the gateway to the Cairngorms National Park. It's a handy place to pick up provisions, and has a good little whisky shop on the High Street called the Wee Spey Dram.

8 Head east from Grantown to get to Tomintoul, where **The Whisky Castle** shop has an excellent selection of Scotch malts.

9 Pre-register on **The Glenlivet** website (*www.theglenlivet.com*) as a "Guardian" to gain access to a secret room where you can enjoy some unusual drams. The free tour is a good introduction to the oldest legal distillery on Speyside; better still is its three-day Whisky School.

10 The final stop is a place of pilgrimage for serious whisky fans: the **Gordon & MacPhail** shop in Elgin. Here you'll find all your favourites, some rare bottles, and exceptional value in G&M's own bottlings from their vast stock of whiskies.

GORDON & MACPHAIL

TOUR STATISTICS

DAYS: 3
LENGTH: 90 miles (145km)
TRAVEL: Car, or bus and taxi
DISTILLERIES: 8

GLENGOYNE

Scotland

Dumgoyne, Stirlingshire
www.glengoyne.com

The Campsie Fells were once a hotbed of whisky smuggling. Before the Excise Act of 1823, there were at least 18 illicit distillers in this corner of Stirlingshire. Among them was probably George Connell, who finally took out a licence for his Burnfoot Distillery in 1833. It went on to become Glenguin and eventually Glengoyne in 1905.

◀ GLENGOYNE 10-YEAR-OLD
SINGLE MALT: HIGHLANDS
40% ABV
This unpeated whisky has a clean, grassy aroma, with a nutty sweetness that comes through on the palate.

GLENGOYNE 12-YEAR-OLD CASK STRENGTH
SINGLE MALT: HIGHLANDS
57.2% ABV
Non chill-filtered and bottled at cask strength, this 12-year-old is the purest representation of the distillery. Lightly sweet nose, with notes of heather, pear drops, and marzipan. Malty, cereal palate, seasoned with black pepper.

By then the distillery was owned by the blending house of Lang Brothers, who were bought out in the 1960s by Robertson & Baxter, now the Edrington Group.

In 2001 it released a novel expression of Glengoyne, involving the first ever use of Scottish oak casks. Two years later, the distillery was sold to the blender and bottler Ian MacLeod & Co. The number of single malts has grown dramatically and includes single cask bottlings alongside the core range.

GLENGOYNE 21-YEAR-OLD ▶
SINGLE MALT: HIGHLANDS
43% ABV
Now matured entirely in first-fill sherry casks, this is a rich, after-dinner malt, with notes of brandy butter, cinnamon, and sweet spice.

GLENGOYNE 17-YEAR-OLD
SINGLE MALT: HIGHLANDS
43% ABV
This whisky has a rich, sherried nose with Christmas-pudding aromas; butterscotch and treacle flavours, with some citrus notes.

GLENKINCHIE

Scotland

Pencaitland, Trenent, East Lothian
www.malts.com

Robert Burns described the rolling farmland south of Edinburgh as "the most glorious corn country I have ever seen", and it was here at Pencaitland that John and George Rate founded Glenkinchie in 1825.

In more recent history, the Glenkinchie 10-year-old was picked as one of the original Classic Malts by Diageo in 1988. New expressions have recently been added and the 10 has been replaced by a 12-year-old.

◀ GLENKINCHIE 12-YEAR-OLD
SINGLE MALT: LOWLANDS
43% ABV

The nose reveals a sweet, grassy aroma with a faint wisp of smoke. In the mouth it has a firm, cereal flavour and a touch of spice at the end.

GLENKINCHIE 20-YEAR-OLD
SINGLE MALT: LOWLANDS
58.4% ABV

Aged in bourbon casks and then re-racked into brandy barrels, the 20-year-old has a luscious, mouth-coating texture and plenty of spicy, stewed fruit flavours.

GLENLIVET

Scotland
Ballindalloch, Banffshire
www.theglenlivet.com

In the early 19th century, Glen Livet was a glen dedicated to making moonshine after the harvest – there were at least 200 illicit stills in this small corner of Speyside. Among them was George Smith, who in 1824 established Glenlivet as a licensed distillery. But breaking ranks with the smuggling fraternity meant that Smith had to carry revolvers for his protection.

Smith began supplying Andrew Usher in Edinburgh who

THE GLENLIVET
12-YEAR-OLD ▶
SINGLE MALT: SPEYSIDE
40% ABV
Citrussy and heathery, with a scent of fresh wood and soft fruit, a light to medium body, and a dry, clean finish.

THE GLENLIVET FRENCH OAK
RESERVE 15-YEAR-OLD
SINGLE MALT: SPEYSIDE
40% ABV
A smoother, richer take on the 12-year-old, with a malty, strawberries-and-cream flavour laced with spice.

G

GLENLIVET

 bottled a prototype blend, Old Vatted Glenlivet, in 1853. As blended Scotch took off, demand for "Glenlivet-style" malts to feed the blends soared. Distillers all down the Spey bolted the magic name "Glenlivet" to their distillery and hoped the blenders would beat a path to their door.

Glenlivet's current owner – the French giant Pernod Ricard – seems keen to seize poll position among top selling malts. In 2008 it announced plans to boost capacity to 10 million litres (2.2 million gallons), the same as Glenfiddich.

◀ THE GLENLIVET XXV
SINGLE MALT: SPEYSIDE
43% ABV
This 25-year-old is a sumptuous after-dinner malt of real complexity, with flavours of candied orange peel and raisins and an intense nutty, spicy character.

THE GLENLIVET 18-YEAR-OLD
SINGLE MALT: SPEYSIDE
43% ABV
This whisky has far more depth and character than the standard 12-year-old. Honeyed, fragrant, and dries to a long, nutty finish.

GLENLOSSIE

Scotland
Elgin, Morayshire
www.malts.com

Glenlossie was built in 1876 by
John Duff, the former manager
of Glendronach. For a century
it was a single entity, and part
of DCL from 1919. Its role was
simply to pump out malt whisky
for blends. Yet, within the
industry, the quality of Glenlossie
was appreciated and it was one
of only a dozen to be designated
"top class". It now shares its
site with Mannochmore, a
new distillery built in 1971.

Glenlossie has produced a
10-year-old since 1990, although
there have been a fair number
of independent bottlings from
Gordon & MacPhail, among others.

**GLENLOSSIE FLORA & FAUNA
10-YEAR-OLD ▶**
**SINGLE MALT: SPEYSIDE
43% ABV**
Grassy and heathery, with a smooth,
mouth-coating texture and a long
spicy finish.

GLENMORANGIE

Scotland

Tain, Ross-shire
www.glenmorangie.com

Glenmorangie started life as an old farm distillery, but was licensed in 1843 by William Matheson, who was already involved with Balblair. It remained a rustic operation for years. In the 1880s Alfred Barnard described Glenmorangie as "the most ancient and primitive we have seen" and "almost in ruins".

Outside investors were brought in just in time and the distillery was rebuilt. For much of the 20th century its key role was to supply malt for blends such as Highland Queen and James Martin's. In

◀ GLENMORANGIE ORIGINAL
SINGLE MALT: HIGHLANDS
40% ABV
This is the ever-popular 10-year-old. It has honeyed flavours with a hint of almonds.

GLENMORANGIE 18-YEAR-OLD
SINGLE MALT: HIGHLANDS
43% ABV
A rich, well-rounded whisky, with dried fruit notes and a distinctive nuttiness from its finishing in sherry butts.

the 1970s, though, Glenmorangie started laying down casks for a 10-year-old single malt. It was the best decision the company ever took – by the late 1990s, this had become the best-selling single malt in Scotland.

Glenmorangie's stills are tall and thin, and produce a light, very pure spirit. The real skill of the distillery has been in the way it has combined this elegant spirit with wood – indeed, Glenmorangie has been a pioneer of wood finishes. After endless experiments with increasingly exotic barrels, it is an expert in how particular casks can twist and refocus a mature malt before bottling.

GLENMORANGIE 25-YEAR-OLD ▶
SINGLE MALT: HIGHLANDS 43% ABV
Packed with flavour, this produces dried fruit, berries, chocolate, and spice. An intense and complex whisky.

GLENMORANGIE NECTAR D'OR
SINGLE MALT: HIGHLANDS 46% ABV
Here, the Glenmorangie honeyed floral character is given a twist of spice and lemon tart from Sauternes casks.

GLENROTHES

Scotland
Rothes, Morayshire
www.glenrotheswhisky.com

After Dufftown, Rothes is the
second busiest whisky town on
Speyside. Not that you would
know it: the distilleries are tucked
discreetly out of sight, including
Glenrothes, which sits quietly in
a dip beside the Rothes burn.

After its founding in 1878,
Glenrothes began to build a
reputation among blenders for
the quality of its malt. It seemed
as if there was never any to spare
– until 1987, when the first single

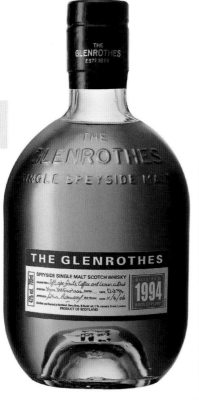

◀ THE GLENROTHES 1994
SINGLE MALT: SPEYSIDE
43% ABV
A satisfyingly complex malt with
a fruity, toffee-scented bouquet
that leads to a soft citrus flavour
and long, gentle finish.

THE GLENROTHES 1978
SINGLE MALT: SPEYSIDE
43% ABV
A very rare expression, released
in 2008, with a concentrated plum
pudding and treacle character, a silky,
honeyed texture, and great length.

158

malt, a 12-year-old was released. At first, Glenrothes failed to stand out: it had entered the 12-year-old stakes late in the day and there was plenty of competition, particularly on Speyside.

This all changed with the launch of the highly acclaimed Glenrothes Vintage malt in 1994. The brand owners, wine merchants Berry Brothers & Rudd, realized that vintage variation might be appreciated by malt-whisky-lovers as well as wine-lovers. In 2004, Glenrothes Select Reserve was released to provide continuity between vintages.

THE GLENROTHES SELECT RESERVE ▶
SINGLE MALT: SPEYSIDE 43% ABV

Like non-vintage Champagne, this is a vatting of different ages to produce a complex whisky with notes of barley sugar, ripe fruit, vanilla, and spice. Sweeter on the nose than in the mouth.

THE GLENROTHES 1975
SINGLE MALT: SPEYSIDE 43% ABV

Increasingly hard to find, this vintage offers big, rich flavours – stewed fruits, toffee, bitter chocolate, and orange peel. Medium-sweet, satisfying finish.

GLENTAUCHERS

Scotland
Mulben, Keith, Banffshire

Many late-Victorian distilleries
sprang up in the hope of finding
a market among whisky blenders
but, in 1897, Glentauchers was
built explicitly to supply
Buchanan's blend, which evolved
into the top-selling Black & White.
The distillery was a joint venture
between James Buchanan and
the Glasgow-based blender W. P.
Lowrie. They chose an ideal site,
right by a main road that
connected to the east-coast rail
line from Aberdeen to Inverness.
Now owned by Pernod Ricard,
Glentauchers has the same
principal role it always had –
supplying malt for blends.

◀ **GLENTAUCHERS
GORDON & MACPHAIL 1991**
**SINGLE MALT: SPEYSIDE
43% ABV**
This 16-year-old Gordon & MacPhail
bottling has a sweet, sherried
character, with a subtle smoky flavour.

GLENTURRET

Scotland
Crieff, Perthshire
www.thefamousgrouse.com

This small Perthshire distillery, first licensed in 1775, claims to be the oldest working distillery in Scotland. Glenturret is known as the spiritual home of The Famous Grouse *(see p119)*, an association showcased at its visitor centre and its Famous Grouse Whisky School, which offers a one-day malt whisky course, including an in-depth distillery tour.

Glenturret's other claim to fame is Towser, the distillery cat, who won a place in *The Guinness Book of Records* for killing nearly 30,000 mice.

GLENTURRET 10-YEAR-OLD ▶
SINGLE MALT: HIGHLANDS
40% ABV
Replacing the 12-year-old, this floral, vanilla-scented malt is now the main Glenturret expression.

GLENTURRET 14-YEAR-OLD
SINGLE MALT: HIGHLANDS
59.7% ABV
This limited-edition, cask-strength bottling has a molasses-like sweetness and notes of liquorice.

GOLD COCK

Czech Republic

Jelinek Distillery,
Razov 472, 76312 Vizovice
www.rjelinek.cz

Jelinek Distillery was founded
at the end of the 19th century,
and acquired the Gold Cock brand
from Tesetice, a Czech distillery
that no longer exists. For its two
expressions – Red Feathers and
a 12-year-old – Jelinek uses
Moravian barley and water sourced
from an underground well that is
rich in minerals. The type of cask
used is not specified.

◀ **GOLD COCK RED FEATHERS**
BLEND 40% ABV
Light and grainy, slightly metallic,
and sweetish.

GOLDEN HORSE

Japan
Toa Shuzo, Chichibu
www.toashuzo.com

The Golden Horse brand is still owned by Toa Shuzo, the firm which used to own the Hanyu distillery *(see p175)*, and the whiskies are drawn from its last remaining stocks. There are bottlings at 8, 10, and 12 years. They are rarely seen on the export markets and at the time of writing it is unclear what will happen to the Golden Horse brand once the Toa Shuzo stocks have disappeared.

GOLDEN HORSE 8-YEAR-OLD ▶
SINGLE MALT 40% ABV
A quite vibrant nose with light malt extract notes and some oak. There's a basic sweetness to this lightly perfumed malt, which has just a wisp of smoke on the finish, but a nagging acidic touch in some bottlings.

GOLDLYS

Belgium

Graanstokerij Filliers,
Leernsesteenweg 5, 9800 Deinze
www.filliers.be

The Flemish distiller Filliers has
been making grain spirits since
1880. In 2008 it surprised the
whisky world by launching two
whiskies it had been maturing for
years. Their name comes from the
River Lys, which is nicknamed the
"Golden River" because of the flax
retted (soaked) in it. Goldlys uses
malt, rye, and corn, and is distilled
twice, first in a column still, then
in a pot still – a process that is
quite similar to that used to
make bourbon. The spirit is then
matured in former bourbon casks.

◀ **GOLDLYS 10-YEAR-OLD**
MIXED GRAIN WHISKY
40% ABV
Spicy, sweet fruit, liquorice, and a
touch of wood. Some pepper in the
short, dry finish.

GRAND MACNISH

Scotland
Owner: Macduff International

The long history of this brand
dates back to Glasgow and 1863,
when the original Robert McNish
(an "a" crept into the brand name
later), a grocer and general
merchant, took up blending.

Grand Macnish Original still
uses up to 40 whiskies in the
blend, as was Robert McNish's
practice. The distinctive bottle's
label is graced by the McNish clan
motto, *"Forti nihil difficile"* ("To
the strong, nothing is difficult").

GRAND MACNISH ORIGINAL ▶
BLEND 40% ABV
Old leather and ripe fruits on the
nose, giving way to a brandy-like
aroma. Noticeably sweet on the palate,
with strong vanilla (wood) influences.
A sustained and evolving finish, with
some gentle smoke.

GRAND MACNISH 12-YEAR-OLD
BLEND 40% ABV
The extra age shows here in a fuller,
rounder flavour with greater intensity
and a more sustained finish.

GRANT'S

Scotland
Owner: William Grant & Sons

This staunchly independent company has prospered on Speyside since 1887 and remains in private hands. Today it is famous for Glenfiddich and its sister single malt, Balvenie, but it also produces a third malt, Kininvie, which is reserved for blending. In addition, it built a grain distillery at Girvan and a new single malt distillery, Ailsa Bay, also reserved for blending.

◀ GRANT'S FAMILY RESERVE
BLEND 40% ABV
An unmistakably Speyside nose, with fluting malty notes. A firm mouthfeel; banana-vanilla sweetness balances sharper malty notes. Clean, but very complex with a long, smooth finish.

GRANT'S 12-YEAR-OLD
BLEND 40% ABV
A blend of fine single malt and grain whiskies, matured in oak casks before being finished in ex-bourbon barrels. A warm and full-bodied Scotch of great richness is the result.

The company is determined to maintain close control over their supplies of whisky, and with good reason: Grant's Family Reserve blend broke through the 1 million case barrier as long ago as 1979. Grant's now sells around 4 million cases of whisky a year and is one of the world's top five Scotch whisky brands, enjoyed in over 180 countries.

The blended range of whiskies continues to evolve, while still remaining true to the mark of quality associated with its distinctive triangular bottle.

GRANT'S ALE CASK RESERVE ▶
BLEND 40% ABV

Grant's has ventured into special wood finishes with great success. This is the only Scotch whisky to be finished in barrels that have previously held beer. Ale casks give the whisky a uniquely creamy, malty, and honeyed taste.

GRANT'S SHERRY CASK RESERVE
BLEND 40% ABV

Prepared in the same way as the ground-breaking ale cask version, but here the whisky is finished in Spanish Oloroso sherry casks, giving it a warm, rich, and fruity palate.

GREEN SPOT

Ireland
*Midleton Distillery, Midleton,
County Cork*

In the days before distillers in Ireland spent millions on building brands, they simply used to make the stuff, leaving the filthy job of selling the whiskey to bonders like Mitchell's. This, of course, was a terrible business plan: it allowed the Scots to build global brands, while the Irish were obsessed with an ever-shrinking domestic market. By the time the Irish got back into the race in the 1960s, Irish whiskey had a miserable 1 per cent of the global whiskey market. Green Spot is the last bonder's own label. Owned by Mitchell's of Dublin, it's a pure pot still whiskey, made in Midleton.

◀ **GREEN SPOT**
PURE POT STILL 40% ABV
Green Spot is matured for just six to eight years, but a glass of this is still bracing stuff, with a wonderful lightly sherried finish. One of a kind.

GREENORE SINGLE GRAIN

Ireland

*Cooley Distillery, Riverstown,
Cooley, County Louth
www.cooleywhiskey.com*

Greenore is the only Irish single
grain on sale. Produced in a
continuous still rather than in
a pot still, grain whiskey is lighter
in taste and rougher on the back
of the throat. For this reason, it is
usually kept for blending. Greenore
single grain whiskey is double-
distilled, then matured in bourbon
casks for at least eight years.

GREENORE SINGLE GRAIN 8-YEAR-OLD ▶
SINGLE GRAIN 40% ABV

This is a winner: a crackle of linseed
on the nose and a peppery bite of firm
cereal. No tell-tale "grain burn" at the
end, but rather a sophisticated sprinkle
of grated Bourneville chocolate.

GREENORE SINGLE GRAIN 15-YEAR-OLD
SINGLE GRAIN 43% ABV

It's even more difficult to spot that this
is a grain whiskey after fifteen years in
oak. With pronounced linseed notes
and a minty coolness, there's an almost
pot still quality to this classy whiskey.

GRÜNER HUND

Germany
Fleischmann, Bamberger Strasse 2,
91330 Eggolsheim-Neuses
www.fleischmann-whisky.de

The Fleischmann brandy
distillery was founded in 1980
on the premises of the original
family company – a grocery and
tobacco shop. In 1996, after nearly
14 years of experimentation with
whisky-distilling, the company
launched their first whisky
expression. There are now seven
single cask malt whiskies available
– Blaue Maus, Spinnaker,
Krottentaler, Schwarzer Pirat,
Grüner Hund, Austrasier, and
Old Fahr – all bottled at 40% ABV.

◄ **GRÜNER HUND**
SINGLE MALT 40% ABV
Roasted almonds and cocoa on the
nose. Dark chocolate, chilli, and
gingerbread on the tongue, with
a dry and medium-long finish.

GUILLON

France

Hameau de Vertuelle,
51150 Louvois, Champagne
www.whisky-guillon.com

The Guillon Distillery is located
in the Champagne region of
France, and was purpose-built in
1997 to produce whisky. It started
distilling in 1999, distinguishing
itself by the use of a variety of
ex-wine casks for maturation.
For the first maturation period,
ex-Burgundy casks are used. After
that, the whisky is finished for six
months in casks that used to
contain sweet wines like Banyuls,
Loupiac, and Sauternes. Guillon
bottles a premium blend at 40%
ABV. The various single malts are
bottled at 42, 43, and 46% ABV.

GUILLON NO. 1 ▶
SINGLE MALT 46% ABV
Highly aromatic, fruity, and elegant,
thanks to the unusual finish in
sweet-wine casks.

HAIG

Scotland
Owner: Diageo

The distinguished name of Haig can trace its whisky-making pedigree back to the 17th century, when distilling began on the family farm. The company developed extensive interests in grain whisky distilling and was an early pioneer of blending. By 1919, however, it was absorbed into the DCL, where it continued to be a powerful force. The company's Dimple brand *(see p106)* was a highly successful deluxe expression, and Haig was once the bestselling whisky in the UK. But its glory days are far behind it: today, under the control of Diageo, it is found mainly in Greece and the Canary Islands.

◄ **HAIG**
BLEND 40% ABV
Some sweetness on the nose, with faint smoky notes. Light and delicate, with soft wood notes and some spice on the finish, where a hint of smoke returns.

HANCOCK'S RESERVE

USA

Buffalo Trace Distillery,
1001 Wilkinson Boulevard,
Frankfort, Kentucky
www.buffalotrace.com

This whiskey, which is usually
created from barrels of spirit
aged for around 10 years, takes
its name from Hancock Taylor,
great-uncle of US president
Zachary Taylor, and an early
surveyor of Kentucky. He
was shot and killed by Native
Americans in 1774, and it is
said that his deathbed will was
one of the first legal documents
executed in the region.

HANCOCK'S RESERVE
PRESIDENT'S SINGLE
BARREL ▶
BOURBON 44.45% ABV
Oily on the nose, with liquorice,
caramel, and spicy rye. Sweet in the
mouth, with malt, fudge, and vanilla
notes. Drying in the finish, with
notable oak notes, but the whiskey's
residual sweetness remains to the end.

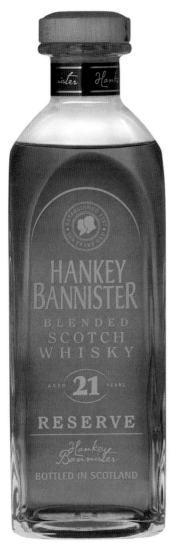

HANKEY BANNISTER

Scotland
Owner: Inver House Distillers

Founded by Messrs Hankey and Bannister in 1757, the brand now is owned by Inver House Distillers, giving it access to single malts from some of Scotland's most distinguished but lesser-known distilleries, such as Balblair, Balmenach, and Knockdhu. Key markets for Hankey Bannister include Latin America, Australia, and South America, but it is exported to 47 countries.

◄ HANKEY BANNISTER 21-YEAR-OLD
BLEND 43% ABV
A fresh and quite youthful nose. Soft and smooth, creamy toffee, with the vanilla house style coming through. Greater depth on the palate, with malty overtones and a warm finish.

HANKEY BANNISTER 40-YEAR-OLD
BLEND 43.3% ABV
Warm and fragrant aromas of raisin, chocolate, and citrus combine with spicy notes, leading to an exceptionally long-lasting, smooth, full-bodied finish.

HANYU

Japan

*Distribution: Number One Drinks,
Netherconesford, King Street,
Norwich, UK
www.one-drinks.com*

The Hanyu distillery was built by
the Akuto family in the 1940s for
producing shochu. Full production
of whisky began in 1980, and
Hanyu enjoyed success until the
financial crisis of 1996 triggered
the end of the whisky boom in
Japan. The distillery had to close
in 2000. When the firm was bought
out in 2003, Ichiro Akuto was
given a few months to buy back
as much stock as he could before
the distillery was demolished *(see
Ichiro's Malt p187)*.

HANYU 1988 CASK 9501 ▶
SINGLE MALT 55.6% ABV
Vibrant and intense, with vanilla, some
citrus, and a delicate cocoa-butter
character. The Japanese oak adds a
bitter-sweet edge. On the palate there's
a rich depth. The finish shows smoke.

Single Cask

NUMBER
ONE 番

DRINKS
COMPANY

Distilled at
Hanyu Distillery
Distilled 1988
Bottled 2007
Cask No .... #9501
Number of bottles 352bts
Cask Type... Bourbon hogshead
finished in Japanese oak

Volume
700ml

Japanese Single Malt Whisky
www.onedrinks.co.uk

Alc/vol
55.6%

HAZELBURN

Scotland

Springbank Distillery, Well Close, Campbeltown, Argyll
www.springbankdistillers.com

Springbank Distillery is the great survivor of the Campbeltown whisky boom, which saw a staggering 34 distilleries in town in the 19th century. Today, Springbank is a mini-malt-whisky industry on its own, with three separate distillations under one roof: Springbank itself, the pungently smoky Longrow, and the light, gentle Hazelburn. As well as using no peat in its malt, Hazelburn – which was named after an old, abandoned distillery in Campbeltown – is triple-distilled. The first spirit was produced in 1997 and bottled as an 8-year-old in 2005. The 6,000 bottles released sold out within weeks.

◀ **HAZELBURN 8-YEAR-OLD**
SINGLE MALT: CAMPBELTOWN
46% ABV
Lowland in style, clean and refreshing, with a subtle, malty flavour.

HEAVEN HILL

USA
*1701 West Breckinridge Street,
Louisville, Kentucky
www.heaven-hill.com*

Heaven Hill is the USA's largest independent producer of distilled spirits to remain in family ownership. When in 1996 the distillery and warehouses were almost completely destroyed by fire, the company purchased Diageo's technologically advanced Bernheim Distillery in Louisville, and all production was moved to that site.

Heaven Hill's speciality is older, higher proof bourbons, traditional in character, full-bodied, and complex, such as Evan Williams (*see p118*) and Elijah Craig (*p115*), but its diverse portfolio also includes Bernheim Original (*p48*), Pikesville (*p288*) and Rittenhouse Rye (*p300*).

HEAVEN HILL ▶
BOURBON 40% ABV
An excellent and competitively priced "entry-level" bourbon, with a nose of oranges and corn bread, a sweet, oily mouth-feel, and vanilla and corn featuring on the well-balanced palate.

HELLYERS ROAD

Australia
153 Old Surrey Road,
Burnie, Tasmania
www.hellyersroaddistillery.com.au

Hellyers Road opened in 1999 and is owned by the Betta Milk Cooperative. It now has about 3,000 ex-bourbon casks under maturation, and also produces a Tasmanian barley-based, pot-still vodka. The experience gained in running a milk processing plant has provided owner Laurie House with all the knowledge he needs to run this modern and highly automated plant.

The distillery is named after Henry Hellyer who, in the 1820s, built the first road into the interior of Tasmania, the same road that now leads to the distillery.

◀ **HELLYERS ROAD ORIGINAL**
SINGLE MALT 46.2% ABV
A light-bodied, pale-coloured malt, un-tinted and non chill-filtered. The nose is fresh and citric, with vanilla notes.

HIGHLAND PARK

Scotland
Kirkwall, Orkney
www.highlandpark.co.uk

Today Highland Park's far-flung Orkney island location is a great asset for the marketing of its whiskies but, for much of its history, the distance from its core market – the big blenders on the mainland – represented a major challenge for the distillery. It survived, and now produces a Highland malt that is highly regarded. Having invested

HIGHLAND PARK 12-YEAR-OLD ▶
SINGLE MALT: ISLANDS
40% ABV

This whisky has all-round quality. There are soft heather-honey flavours, some richer spicy notes, and an enveloping wisp of peat smoke that leaves the finish quite dry.

HIGHLAND PARK 18-YEAR-OLD
SINGLE MALT: ISLANDS
43% ABV

This is a touch sweeter than the 12-year-old, with notes of heather, toffee, and polished leather. The peat smoke flavour comes through stronger on the finish than on the palate.

HIGHLAND PARK

 in the brand, its owners have ambitious plans to reach the top ten.

Highland Park distillery was first licensed to David Roberston in 1798, but since 1937 it has been part of Highland Distilleries (now the Edrington Group). To this day, a proportion of the barley is malted using the distillery's original floor maltings. The malt is then dried in a kiln, using local peat, which has a slightly sweeter aroma than that from Islay.

◀ HIGHLAND PARK 30-YEAR-OLD
SINGLE MALT: ISLANDS 48.1% ABV
The flagship of the range. Caramel sweetness, aromatic spices, dark chocolate, and orange notes. A long, drying, smoky finish, tinged with salt.

HIGHLAND PARK 25-YEAR-OLD
SINGLE MALT: ISLANDS 48.1% ABV
Its deep amber colour reveals plenty of contact with European oak. In fact, half of it was matured in first-fill sherry butts. Despite its age, it has a rich, nutty flavour, with dried fruits and scented smoke.

HIGHWOOD

Canada
*114 10th Avenue Southeast,
High River, Alberta
www.highwood-distillers.com*

Unusually for Canada, Highwood, founded in 1974, is independently owned. It makes a range of spirits and is the only distillery in Canada using just wheat in its column stills as the base spirit for its blends. In 2005, it bought the Potter's and Cascadia distilleries. Potter's is a separate brand from Highwood. It is mixed with sherry, which adds another dimension to its flavour.

HIGHWOOD ▶
CANADIAN RYE 40% ABV
A blend of wheat and rye spirits. The oaky, vanilla-scented nose has traces of rye spice, orange blossom, and honey. The palate balances sweetness with oak tannins and nuts.

HIRSCH

Canada

*Distribution: Preiss Imports Inc,
San Diego, USA*

This whisky is no longer being
made, but is still available via a
US distributor. Although Canadian
whisky is often referred to as
"rye", only a few brands contain
more than 50 per cent rye spirit,
which is what makes it a true
rye whisky. Hirsch is one, and
connoisseurs claim it rivals the
best Kentucky ryes. The whiskies
are bottled in small batches,
made in column stills, aged in
ex-bourbon barrels, selected by
Preiss Imports, and bottled by
Glenora Distillers, Nova Scotia,
which also produces a single malt
called Glen Breton *(see p130).*

**◄ HIRSCH SELECTION
8-YEAR-OLD**

CANADIAN RYE 43% ABV
Solvent and pine essence, then sweet
maple sap on the nose. The taste is
sweet, with caramel, dry coconut, and
oak-wood; full-bodied. A bittersweet
finish with a few earthy notes.

HIRSCH RESERVE

USA
Distributor: Preiss Imports
www.hirschbourbon.com

Hirsch Reserve is a drop of US whiskey history. The spirit itself was distilled in 1974 at Michter's Distillery, the last surviving one in Pennsylvania. Michter's closed in 1988, but one Adolf H. Hirsch had acquired a considerable stock of the spirit some years previously and, after it had been matured for 16 years, it was put into stainless steel tanks to prevent further ageing. This whiskey is now available from Preiss Imports but, once gone, is gone forever.

HIRSCH RESERVE ▶
BOURBON 45.8% ABV
Caramel, honey, and rye dominate the complex nose, with a whiff of smoke also coming through. Oily corn, honey, and oak on the rich palate, with rye and more oak in the drying finish.

HOLLE

Switzerland
Hollen 52, 4426 Lauwil, Basel
www.single-malt.ch

Until 1st July 1999 it was strictly
forbidden in Switzerland to distil
spirit from grain, which was
considered a food staple. After
a change in the law, the Bader
family, who had been making fruit
spirits for a long time, started to
distil from grains, and became the
country's first whisky producer.

◀ **HOLLE**
SINGLE MALT 42% ABV
Delicate aromas of malt, wood, and
vanilla, with a flavour of wine. There
are two varieties: one is matured in
a white-wine cask, the other in a
red-wine cask. A cask strength
version is bottled at 51.1% ABV.

HUDSON

USA

*Tuthilltown Distillery, 14 Gristmill
Lane, Gardiner, New York
www.tuthilltown.com*

In 1825, New York State had more
than 1,000 working distilleries and
produced a major share of the
nation's whiskey. These days,
Tuthilltown is New York's only
remaining distillery. It was
founded in 2001 by Brian Lee
and Ralph Erenzo, and produces
a quartet of "Hudson" bottlings,
including a rich and full-flavoured
four-grain whiskey and a rich,
caramel single malt, intended as
an American "re-interpretation"
of traditional Scottish whiskies.

HUDSON MANHATTAN RYE ▶
RYE WHISKEY 46% ABV
The first whiskey to be distilled in
New York State for more than 80 years.
Floral notes and a smooth finish on the
palate, with a recognizable rye edge.

HUDSON BABY BOURBON
BOURBON 46% ABV
Made with 100 per cent New York State
corn, this is the first bourbon ever to
be made in New York. It is a mildly
sweet, smooth spirit with subtle hints
of vanilla and caramel.

I.W. HARPER

USA

Four Roses Distillery,
1224 Bond Mills Road,
Lawrenceburg, Kentucky
www.fourroses.us

The historic and once bestselling I.W. Harper brand was established by Jewish businessman Isaac Wolfe Bernheim (1848–1945), a major figure in the bourbon business at the turn of the 20th century. It was made at the Bernheim Distillery *(see p48)* in Louisville. It is now produced for current owners Diageo by Four Roses Distillery and is one of the leading bourbons in the Japanese market.

◀ I.W. HARPER
BOURBON 43% ABV

A big-bodied bourbon in which pepper combines with mint, oranges, caramel, and quite youthful charring on the nose, while caramel, apples, and oak feature on the elegant palate. The finish is dry and smoky.

ICHIRO'S MALT

Japan

*Distribution: Number One Drinks,
Netherconesford, King Street,
Norwich, UK
www.one-drinks.com*

Ichiro's Malt is a range of bottlings from Ichiro Akuto, who was the former president of Hanyu *(see p175)*, and the grandson of the founder Isouji Akuto. The whiskies are drawn from the 400 casks of Hanyu single malt that Akuto managed to obtain after the Hanyu distillery was closed down.

The bulk of Hanyu's remaining stock is being released by ☞

KING OF DIAMONDS, DISTILLED 1988, BOTTLED 2006 ▶
SINGLE MALT 56% ABV
Complex and nutty, with some dry sacking notes, sandalwood, citrus, pineapple, and pine. Spicy yet floral on the palate with subtle smoke. One of the most highly complex in the series.

ACE OF DIAMONDS, DISTILLED 1986, BOTTLED 2008
SINGLE MALT 56.4% ABV
Mature nose, with Seville orange, furniture polish, rose, pipe tobacco, and when diluted, sloe and Moscatel. Spicy and chocolatey on the tongue.

ICHIRO'S MALT

🌿 Akuto in a series of 53 whiskies named after playing cards. This Card Series, as it is known, is memorable not only for its distinctive branding but also for the high quality of many of its expressions.

The Card Series will be eked out until Akuto's new Chichibu single malt is fully established *(see p80)*. All of the bottlings are very limited, but some are available on export markets through distributors.

◀ FIVE OF SPADES, DISTILLED 2000, BOTTLED 2008
SINGLE MALT 60.5% ABV
A sweet nose of sandalwood, light raisin, mint, dark chocolate, and some smoke. Water brings out baked muffins, an incense-like note, and white pepper.

ACE OF SPADES, DISTILLED 1985, BOTTLED 2006
SINGLE MALT 55% ABV
Sometimes called the Motorhead malt, after the band who sang *Ace of Spades*, this is one of the oldest in the Card Series. Bold, rich, and fat with masses of raisin, some tarry notes, and treacle. The palate is chewy and toffee-like, with some prune and a savoury finish.

IMPERIAL BLUE

India
Owner: Pernod Ricard
www.pernod-ricard.com

Imperial Blue is Pernod Ricard's
second bestselling brand in India,
at over 3.8 million cases a year.
Previously a Seagram's brand (and
still labelled as such), it benefited
hugely from Pernod Ricard's
acquisition of Seagram in 2001,
jumping from producing under
half a million cases to over a
million by 2002. Imperial Blue hit
the headlines in 2008 when some
bottles in Andhra Pradesh were
found to be under-strength. It later
transpired that they had been
sabotaged by disgruntled workers.

IMPERIAL BLUE ▶
BLEND 42.8% ABV
In spite of the "grain" in its name,
Imperial Blue is a blend of imported
Scotch malt and locally made neutral
spirit. It is light, sweet, and smooth.

INCHGOWER

Scotland
Buckie, Banffshire
www.malts.com

This is Speyside, but only just – the Inchgower Distillery sits near the mouth of the Spey and the fishing port of Buckie. It was established in 1871 by Alexander Wilson, using equipment from the disused Tochieneal Distillery, which had been founded in 1824 by his father, John Wilson, a short distance down the coast at Cullen. It remained a family business until 1930, when the stills went cold. Six years on, the local town council bought it for just £1,000, selling it on to Arthur Bell & Sons in 1938. Bell's blends swallow up most of the malt.

◀ INCHGOWER FLORA & FAUNA 14-YEAR-OLD
SINGLE MALT: SPEYSIDE 43% ABV
Brisk and fresh, with a floral nose, sweet-and-sour flavour, and quite a short finish.

INISHOWEN

Ireland
Cooley Distillery, Riverstown,
Cooley, County Louth
www.cooleywhiskey.com

Inishowen is the kind of concept
an accountant would come up
with. It's brand economics by
numbers. The Scotch industry
is worth billions, with blended
Scotch making up 90 per cent
of sales. So if an Irish brand could
create a similar product, it would
have to be a sure-fire success
– wouldn't it? There's nothing
much wrong with Inishowen – it
is well-made and nicely blended
– it's just that it will never be…
well, Scotch.

INISHOWEN ▶
BLEND 40% ABV
You won't find any other blended Irish
whiskey that has a nose like this: it's
both peaty and floral. However, it's the
fine grain whiskey and not the malt
that gives Inishowen some real charm.

I

INVER HOUSE GREEN PLAID

Scotland
Owner: Inver House Distillers

Controlled today by Thai Beverage, Inver House is one of the smaller but more dynamic Scotch whisky companies and, in 2008, was named International Distiller of the Year by *Whisky Magazine*. Its Green Plaid label was originally launched in 1956 in the US, where it remains among the top ten bestselling whiskies. More than 20 malts and grains are used to blend Green Plaid, which is available as a competitively priced non-aged version and as 12- and 21-year-olds. Inver House's Speyburn, anCnoc, Balblair, Old Pulteney, and Balmenach single malts undoubtedly feature strongly in the blend.

◄ **INVER HOUSE GREEN PLAID**
BLEND 40% ABV
A light, pleasant, undemanding dram, with notes of caramel and vanilla.

INVERGORDON

Scotland

Cottage Brae, Invergordon, Ross-shire
www.whyteandmackay.com

Located on the shores of the
Moray Firth, the Invergordon grain
distillery is owned by Whyte &
Mackay. It was established in 1961
and expanded in 1963 and 1978.
The distillery issued its pioneering
official bottling of Invergordon
Single Grain as a 10-year-old in
1991, but this was subsequently
withdrawn. As a consequence,
the only supplies now available
are independent bottlings, many
of which are very highly regarded
by independent tasters.

INVERGORDON CLAN DENNY 1966 ▶

SINGLE GRAIN 49.8% ABV

The independent bottlings of
Invergordon are uniformly old
(typically 38–42 years), and are
characterized by a sweet nose and
creamy texture. Expect notes of
vanilla and wood, and spices such
as cinnamon and nutmeg.

THE IRISHMAN

Ireland
www.hotirishman.com

Bernard Walsh's The Irishman
range includes two core offerings
and a special release. The single
malt uses whiskey from Bushmills,
and is a vatting of whiskey matured
in bourbon and sherry casks.
The second core release is the
Irishman 70, which is a more
innovative concoction. The 70 in
the title refers to the percentage
of Bushmills malt in the bottle.
The remaining 30 per cent is pure
pot still from Midleton. There is no
grain whiskey used in this range.

◄ THE IRISHMAN
SINGLE MALT
SINGLE MALT 40% ABV
Bushmills tends to keep all the best
whiskey for itself, which means this
malt has great cereal character but will
never be outstanding. There is a hint
of sherry on the palate, but this could
have done with a bit longer in the cask.

THE IRISHMAN 70
**PURE POT STILL/MALT BLEND
40% ABV**
The combination of malt and pot still is
intriguing, offering a direct hit of dried
fruit and rich, almost-burnt sugar.

ISLAY MIST

Scotland
Owner: MacDuff International

Created in 1922 for the 21st
birthday of the son of the Laird
of Islay House, Islay Mist is a
highly awarded blend of single
malts from the Hebridean island.
The strongly flavoured Laphroaig
is predominant, but is tempered
with Speyside and Highland malts.
Naturally, Islay Mist is favoured by
lovers of peat-flavoured whiskies,
but it also offers an excellent
alternative to less characterful
blends. It is produced by MacDuff
International, and is available in
standard, deluxe, 8-year-old, and
17-year-old versions. The latter
two use identical blend recipes;
the difference is the age.

ISLAY MIST DELUXE ▶
BLEND 40% ABV
A great smoky session whisky that
some will find easier to drink than
full-on Islay malt. Sweet and complex
under all the peat.

J&B

Scotland
Owner: Diageo

A Diageo brand widely sold in Spain, France, Portugal, Turkey, South Africa, and the US, J&B is one of the world's top-selling blended whiskies.

The founding firm dates from 1749. In 1831 it was bought by the entrepreneurial Alfred Brooks, who renamed it Justerini and Brooks. The company began blending in the 1880s, and developed J&B Rare in the 1930s, when the end of Prohibition in the US created a demand for lighter-coloured whisky with a more delicate favour.

◀ J&B RARE
BLEND 40% ABV
Top-class single malts such as Knockando, Auchroisk, and Glen Spey are at its heart; delicate smokiness suggests an Islay influence. Apple and pear sweetness, vanilla, and honey against a background of restrained peat.

J&B JET
BLEND 40% ABV
A very mellow, smooth whisky, with Speyside malt at its core.

JACK DANIEL'S

USA
280 Lynchburg Road,
Lynchburg, Tennessee
www.jackdaniels.com

Jack Daniel's has become an iconic brand worldwide. Its founder, Jasper Newton "Jack" Daniel reputedly started to make whiskey as a child, and by 1860 was running his own distilling business at the tender age of 14.

Today, Jack Daniel's is owned by the Kentucky-based Brown-Forman Corporation.

JACK DANIEL'S OLD NO. 7 ▶
TENNESSEE WHISKEY 40% ABV
Powerful nose of vanilla, smoke, and liquorice. On the palate, oily cough-mixture and treacle, with a final kick of maple syrup and burnt wood lingering in the finish. Not particularly complex, but muscular and distinctive.

JACK DANIEL'S SINGLE BARREL
TENNESSEE WHISKEY 47% ABV
Charming and smooth on the nose, with notes of peach, vanilla, nuts, and oak. The comparatively dry palate offers depth, richness, and elegance, with oily corn, liquorice, malt, and oak. Malt and oak linger in the lengthy finish, along with a touch of rye spice.

JAMES MARTIN'S

Scotland
Owner: Glenmorangie

The James Martin name relates to the Leith blenders MacDonald Martin Distillers (now Glenmorangie) and dates back to 1878, when the original James Martin set up in business. Presented in stylish Art Deco bottles, the blend was always highly regarded, as it contained a healthy share of Glenmorangie single malt with some richer components.

Currently there are 12- and 20-year-old versions of James Martin's, while bottles of the 30-year-old can still be bought from specialist retailers.

◀ JAMES MARTIN'S 20-YEAR-OLD
BLEND 40% ABV

Citrus on the nose initially, then honey, vanilla, and a rich mead liqueur. With water, hints of coconut and vanilla appear. Very soft on the palate at the start, with cereal (grain) notes to the fore. Complex, lively spice and soft, sweet grain notes. Well-balanced with a soft finish.

JAMESON

Ireland

Midleton Distillery,
Midleton, County Cork
www.jamesonwhiskey.com

This is the biggest selling Irish whiskey. The standard blend is a 50:50 blend of medium-bodied pot still and grain whiskey. It's a light, approachable spirit that lacks character. Beyond the standard bottling, though, are some cracking whiskeys. Gold Reserve was originally launched as a premium, duty-free blend, but it is now widely available. Some of the whiskeys used in it are more ☞

JAMESON ▶
BLEND 40% ABV
The malty smell is promising but the drink itself is a let-down. The grain is unruly and overwhelms the pot-still, leaving some citrus notes. There is a gentle buzz of sherry – nothing more.

JAMESON GOLD RESERVE
BLEND 43% ABV
This is a viscous, oily, syrupy mouth-coater of a whiskey. Finer, lighter flavours find it hard to fight their way through the fug of sugars. The finish is buzzy and long, in rather the same way as a cough medicine.

JAMESON

🥄 than 20 years old, but they are cut with younger pot still whiskey, matured in first-fill oak casks. This is the only Irish whiskey to feature virgin wood, and it lends the blend a really sweet, vanilla-like flavour.

Jameson's Special Reserve 12-year-old spends 12 years in Oloroso sherry butts and has won several awards. Six extra years in the cask doesn't change the flavour profile of the 18-year-old premium offering too much, but what it does do is double the price.

◀ JAMESON SPECIAL RESERVE 12-YEAR-OLD
BLEND 40% ABV

A world-beating whiskey. Hints of leather and spice on the nose and an incredibly silky quality in the mouth. Dried fruits wrapped in milk chocolate round off a master-class in how to make a great whiskey.

JAMESON LIMITED RESERVE 18-YEAR-OLD
BLEND 40% ABV

The pot still here has taken old age well. The body is firm and yielding and the Oloroso wood has to be very fine not to dominate a blend this old. Sweet almond and spiced fudge notes complement the oiliness of the pot still.

JEFFERSON'S

USA
*McLain & Kyne Ltd (Castle Brands),
Louisville, Kentucky*
www.mclainandkyne.com

The Louisville company of McLain
& Kyne Ltd was formed by Trey
Zoeller to carry on the distilling
traditions of his ancestors. McLain
& Kyne specializes in premium,
very small-batch bourbons, most
notably Jefferson's and Sam
Houston *(see p309)*.

JEFFERSON'S SMALL BATCH 8-YEAR-OLD ▶
BOURBON (VARIABLE ABV)
This bourbon has been aged in the
heart of metal-clad warehouses to
accentuate the extreme temperatures
of Kentucky, forcing the bourbon to
expand deep into the barrel and
extract desirable flavours from the
wood. The nose is fresh, with vanilla
and ripe peach notes, while the
smooth, sweet palate boasts more
vanilla, caramel, and berries. The
finish is quite delicate, with toasted
vanilla and cream.

Whisky Tour: Ireland

In 1887, when the Victorian travel and drinks writer Alfred Barnard visited Ireland, he had 28 different distilleries to visit. Nowadays, the range is more limited, but every bit as enjoyable. Several historic whiskey distilleries have facilities for tourists, and there are other attractions and the beautiful Irish landscape to explore.

DAY 1: GIANTS CAUSEWAY, BUSHMILLS

1 Start your journey at the magnificent **Giants Causeway**, a World Heritage Site near the town of Bushmills, where extraordinary hexagonal basalt columns stretch out along the rugged coast.

2 Of all the Irish distilleries that are open to the public, **Bushmills** is the only one that is still in production. Enjoy the tour, sample some fine whiskeys, then stay at the nearby Bushmills Inn for some great food and a good night's sleep.

GIANTS CAUSEWAY

DAY 2: COOLEY, OLD JAMESON DISTILLERY

COOLEY DISTILLERY

3 Although **Cooley** Distillery is not open to the public, the nearby hills and the seaside town of Greenore are worth seeing on the way to Dublin.

4 Avoid the Dublin traffic by taking the LUAS tram from Junction 9 of the M50 to Smithfield in the city centre. This is near the **Old Jameson Distillery**, which offers guided tours and the chance to sample Jameson whiskey.

FINISH
CORK **7—8**
THE JAMESON
EXPERIENCE

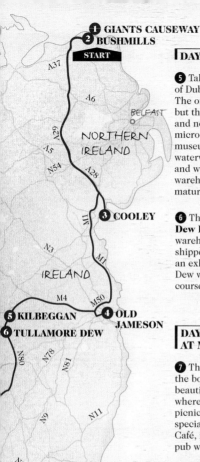

1 GIANTS CAUSEWAY
2 BUSHMILLS
START

A37

A6

BELFAST

NORTHERN
IRELAND

A29
A5
N54
A28

M1

3 COOLEY

N3

M1

IRELAND

M4
M50

5 KILBEGGAN
4 OLD
JAMESON
6 TULLAMORE DEW

N78
N81
N80

N9
N11

N24
N25
WATERFORD

TOUR STATISTICS

DAYS: 4
LENGTH: 375 miles (600km)
TRAVEL: Car, tram, walking
DISTILLERIES: 1 working,
3 converted

DAY 3: KILBEGGAN, TULLAMORE DEW

5 Take Junction 7 of the M50 and head west out of Dublin to the old Locke's building at **Kilbeggan**. The original distillery fell silent in 1957, but the site has been revived by locals and now houses the Kilbeggan micro-distillery and a whiskey museum with working waterwheel, restaurant, shop, and whiskey bar. Cooley leases warehouses at this site and matures some whiskeys here.

KILBEGGAN

6 The vibrant town of Tullamore is home to the **Tullamore Dew Heritage Centre**. This building used to be a bonded warehouse for storing whiskey casks before they were shipped downstream to Dublin, and is now the setting for an exhibition about traditional whiskey-making. Tullamore Dew whiskey is distilled at Midleton these days, but is, of course, available for tasting at the heritage centre.

DAY 4: CORK, THE JAMESON EXPERIENCE AT MIDLETON

7 The cross-country trip from Tullamore to Cork traverses the boggy heart of Ireland – a bleak landscape that is strangely beautiful at any time of the year. **Cork** city is a food haven, where you can visit the historic English Market to buy a picnic lunch, or perhaps try the Market Café for local specialities. For a drink, stop at the South County Bar & Café, in Douglas Village, a suburb of Cork. It's a traditional pub with its own "whiskey corner" to celebrate Irish whiskey.

POT STILL AT MIDLETON

8 The Jameson Experience is set in the beautifully restored 18th-century distillery at Midleton, and boasts the world's largest pot still, which now stands outside the buildings. For refreshment, try the restaurant at nearby Ballymaloe House, which is overseen by Darina Allen, the doyen of Irish foodies.

JIM BEAM

USA

*Clermont Distillery, 149 Happy
Hollow Road, Clermont, Kentucky
www.jimbeam.com*

Jim Beam is the bestselling
bourbon brand in the world, and
its origins date back to the 18th
century, when German-born
farmer and miller Jacob Boehm
travelled west into Bourbon
County, Kentucky, from Virginia,
carrying with him his copper pot
still. He is reputed to have sold his
first barrel of whiskey for cash in
1795, and subsequently moved

◄ JIM BEAM WHITE LABEL 4-YEAR-OLD
BOURBON 40% ABV
Vanilla and delicate floral notes on the
nose. Initially sweet, with restrained
vanilla, then drier, oaky notes develop,
fading into furniture polish and soft
malt in the finish.

JIM BEAM CHOICE 5-YEAR-OLD
BOURBON 40% ABV
Charcoal-filtered in the style of
Tennessee whiskeys after maturation.
Soft and silky in character, with more
caramel notes than other expressions.

his distilling operation into Washington County when he inherited land there.

Jim (James Beauregard) Beam himself was Jacob Boehm's great-grandson. He joined the family business at the age of 16, in 1880, and trade prospered in the years before Prohibition forced the closure of the distillery.

Jim Beam founded the present Clermont Distillery soon after the repeal of Prohibition in 1933, despite being 70 years old at the time. He died in 1947, five years after "Jim Beam" first appeared on the bottle label, and two years after the firm had been sold to Harry Blum of Chicago, previously a partner in the company.

JIM BEAM BLACK LABEL 8-YEAR-OLD ▶
BOURBON 43% ABV
Greater depth than White Label, with more complex fruit and vanilla notes, plus liquorice and sweet rye.

JIM BEAM RYE
RYE WHISKEY 40% ABV
Light, perfumed, and aromatic on the nose, with lemon and mint. Oily in the mouth, with soft fruits, honey, and rye. Drying and spicy in the finish.

JOHNNIE WALKER

Scotland
Owner: Diageo

While the original firm can be traced back to the purchase of a Kilmarnock grocery store in 1820, Walker's did not enter the whisky business in a serious way until the 1860s. Then, John Walker's son and grandson progressively launched and developed their range of whiskies. These were based around the original Walker's Old Highland blend, which was launched in 1865 and is the

◀ JOHNNIE WALKER BLACK LABEL
BLEND 40% ABV
The flagship, classic blend, recognizable by the smoky kick contributed by Talisker, Caol Ila, and Lagavulin. Glendullan and Mortlach add some Speyside malt.

JOHNNIE WALKER GREEN LABEL
BLENDED MALT 43% ABV
Complex, rich, and powerful. Pepper and oak, fruit aromas, a malty sweetness, and some smoke.

ancestor of today's Black Label. In 1925 the firm joined DCL and, by 1945, Johnnie Walker was the world's bestselling brand of Scotch.

The range comprises Johnnie Walker Red, Black, Gold, Blue, Blue Label King George V, and Green Label. From time to time the firm also releases one-off, limited, or regional expressions. In recent years there has been a trend to move the brand upmarket. When Blue Label was launched in 1992 it set new price records for blended whisky. This was followed by the King George V Edition, which cost three times as much as the Blue, and the ultra-exclusive 1805, sold at £1,000 a single glass.

JOHNNIE WALKER
GOLD LABEL ▶
BLEND 40% ABV
Honey, fresh fruit, and toffee notes, with smoke in the background. Diageo recommends chilling this in the freezer before serving.

JOHNNIE WALKER
BLUE LABEL
BLEND 40% ABV
Smooth and mellow, with traces of spice, honey, and the signature hint of smoke.

JOHNNY DRUM

USA

*Kentucky Bourbon Distillers,
1869 Loretto Road,
Bardstown, Kentucky
www.kentuckybourbonwhiskey.com*

Johnny Drum is said to have
been a Confederate drummer
boy during the American Civil
War, and later a pioneer farmer
and distiller in Kentucky. Johnny
Drum bourbon was formerly
produced in the Willet Distillery
near Bardstown, but this closed
in the early 1980s when the last
of the Willet family members
retired. The plant was acquired
by Kentucky Bourbon Distillers
Ltd, for whom a range of whiskeys
is distilled under contract.

◀ **JOHNNY DRUM**
BOURBON (VARIABLE ABV)
Smooth and elegant on the nose, with
vanilla, gentle spices, and smoke. This
is a full-bodied bourbon, well-balanced
and smooth in the mouth, with vanilla
and a hint of smoke. The finish is
lingering and sophisticated.

JURA

Scotland
Isle of Jura, Argyllshire
www.isleofjura.com

When two estate owners on Jura resurrected the Jura distillery in the late 1950s, half a century after it had fallen into disuse, the profile of the whisky changed. Gone was the strong, phenolic malt of the past, and in came something more Highland in style, with less peat and a more subtle touch, although in recent years Jura has also produced an array of limited-edition bottlings, some of which have been quite heavily peated.

JURA 10-YEAR-OLD ▶
SINGLE MALT: ISLANDS
40% ABV
A lightly peated island malt that seems to have improved in recent years.

JURA SUPERSTITION
SINGLE MALT: ISLANDS
43% ABV
A mix of heavily peated, young Jura with older whisky, to produce an intensely smoky, smooth-textured malt.

KAVALAN

Taiwan
*King Car Kavalan Distillery,
Yuanshan, Yi-lan County
www.kavalanwhisky.com*

Situated on Yi-lan Plain, in the
north east of Taiwan, Kavalan
is proudly named by the founder,
Mr T.T. Lee, after the indigenous
people of the plain.

The distillery was built in
2006 and has the capacity to
produce 3.9 million litres (858,000
gallons) per annum. The intense
heat and humidity of the site
greatly speeds up maturation and
increases evaporation. Under such
circumstances, the whisky is fully
mature after two to three years.

Kavalan was first bottled in 2008.
There are now four expressions
available, and they are all excellent.

◀ KAVALAN CLASSIC
SINGLE MALT 40% ABV
Light and fruity on the nose, led by
tropical fruits (mango, papaya) and
ripe peaches. Light bodied, the taste is
sweet, with fresh acidity, drying in the
medium-length finish. With water a
trace of fennel appears, and peach-
cream and chocolate in the aftertaste.

KENTUCKY GENTLEMAN

USA

Tom Moore Distillery, 1 Barton Road, Bardstown, Kentucky

Kentucky Gentleman is offered both as a blended whiskey and as a straight bourbon. According to its producers, the blended version is created from a blend of Kentucky straight bourbon whiskey and spirits from the finest grains.

The popular straight expression enjoys a notably loyal following in the southern states, particularly Florida, Alabama, and Virginia. It is produced at the Tom Moore Distillery, Bardstown, which was controlled by Barton Brands until 2009, when it was sold to the New Orleans-based Sazerac Company.

KENTUCKY GENTLEMAN ▶
BOURBON 40% ABV
Made with a higher percentage of rye than most whiskeys made at Tom Moore, this offers caramel and sweet oak aromas, and is oily, full-bodied, spicy, and fruity in the mouth. Rye, fruits, vanilla, and cocoa figure in the lingering, flavourful, and comparatively assertive finish.

KESSLER

USA

Jim Beam Distillery,
149 Happy Hollow Road,
Clermont, Kentucky
www.jimbeam.com

One of the best-known and most highly regarded blended American whiskeys, Kessler traces its origins back to 1888, when it was first blended by one Julius Kessler, who travelled from saloon to saloon across the West, selling his whiskey as he went.

◀ KESSLER
BLEND 40% ABV

Kessler has carried the slogan "Smooth as Silk" for more than half a century, and it certainly lives up to its name. The nose is light and fruity, and the palate sweet, with just enough complexity of liquorice and leather to highlight the fact that the bourbon in this blend was aged for a minimum of four years.

KILBEGGAN

Ireland

The Old Kilbeggan Distillery, Main Street, Kilbeggan, County Westmeath
www.kilbegganwhiskey.com

In the mid-1950s the most famous of the Kilbeggan distilleries, John Locke & Sons, fell silent. Although the two remaining Locke family members – sisters Flo and Sweet – had warehouses full of raw ingredients, they had no interest in whiskey-making. With post-war whiskey prices on the rise, they decided to sell the distillery.

Nowadays, Kilbeggan whiskeys are Cooley blends, distilled in County Louth, but the spirits are still matured and bottled on site.

KILBEGGAN ▶
BLEND 40% ABV

A grainy blend, with strong notes of honey and porridge. The end note is a pleasing combination of coffee and dark chocolate.

KILBEGGAN 15-YEAR-OLD
BLEND 40% ABV

Age can thin and fracture a whiskey, or it can be its making. The Kilbeggan 15-year-old blend is spectacular. Expect the usual Cooley honey and biscuit notes, distilled to perfection.

KILCHOMAN

Scotland
Rockside Farm, Bruichladdich, Islay
www.kilchomandistillery.com

Whisky-making began here in 2005, and this is as quintessential a farm distillery as you'll find. The barley is grown on Rockside Farm, and malting, fermenting, distilling, and maturing all take place on-site; a dam on the farm creates a supply of fresh water. At the time of writing, Kilchoman was yet to bottle its first whisky, but they do sell New Spirit. Matured in bourbon casks for about five months, this isn't technically new make, but then neither is it whisky yet either. It does, though, offer a signpost to the kind of whisky that will one day issue forth from the Kilchoman warehouse.

◀ KILCHOMAN NEW SPIRIT
NEW MAKE SPIRIT 63.5% ABV
A light wave of peat on the nose, but essentially fruity and fresh. There's a butterscotch sweetness too.

KIRIN GOTEMBA

Japan
Shibanta 970, Gotembashi, Shizuoka
www.kirin.co.jp

Kirin's Gotemba distillery was
built in 1973 as part of a joint
venture with the former Canadian
giant Seagram (*see p313*). Its
output is much in line with the
light flavours preferred by the
Japanese consumer in the 1970s.
That said, the distillery had to
supply all the needs of Kirin's
blends, so it made three grain
whiskies and three styles of malt.

GOTEMBA FUJISANROKU 18-YEAR-OLD ▶
SINGLE MALT 40% ABV
More floral and restrained than the
"old" Fuji Gotemba 18-year-old, with
less of the oakiness. Some peach, lily,
and a zesty grapefruit note. The honey
found in the grain reappears here.

FUJI GOTEMBA 15-YEAR-OLD
SINGLE GRAIN 40% ABV
A very sweet and concentrated nose,
almost liqueur-like in its syrupy,
honeyed unctuousness. There are
touches of sesame, coconut, and
orange zest. The palate is soft and
gentle with a melting butter quality.
The finish balances oak and sweetness.

KIRIN WHISKY
SINGLE
MALT
18 Years Old
Silky smoothness
and spreading aroma,
the gift from Mt. Fuji

富士山麓

DISTILLED AND BOTTLED BY
KIRIN DISTILLERY CO.,LTD

KIRIN KARUIZAWA

Japan
*Maseguchi 1795–2, Oaza,
Miyotamachi, Kitasakugun, Nagano
www.kirin.co.jp*

This former winery was converted
to whisky-production in the 1950s.
To achieve its robust, big-hitting,
and smoky style it retains
techniques that are rare now even
in Scotland: the heaviness of the
Golden Promise strain of barley
used is accentuated by the small
stills, while maturation in ex-sherry
casks adds a dried-fruit character.

◀ KARUIZAWA 1995: NOH SERIES, BOTTLED 2008
SINGLE MALT 63% ABV
Hugely resinous nose that mixes tiger
balm, geranium, boot polish, prune,
and oiled woods. Lightly astringent
palate that needs water to release the
tannic grip. An exotic and floral whisky.

KARUIZAWA 1986: CASK NO. 7387, BOTTLED 2008
SINGLE MALT 60.7% ABV
Incense on the nose along with wax,
crystallized fruits, dried fig, cep, cassia,
tamarind paste, smoke, and spice. The
palate needs water to bring forth dried
fruits, rosewood, and coffee.

KNAPPOGUE CASTLE

Ireland
Bushmills Distillery, 2 Distillery Road, County Antrim

After World War II, the owner of Knappogue Castle took to buying casks of whiskey, which he would store in a cellar. These whiskeys would then be bottled and given away to family and friends over time. The last of these original casks, filled with Tullamore whiskey, was bottled in 1987.

In the 1990s, the son of the castle's owner, Mark Andrews, decided to follow suit and bottle single vintages of his own, also labelled Knappogue Castle. The first of these were created from whiskey produced at Cooley Distillery, but the more recent vintages come from Bushmills.

KNAPPOGUE CASTLE 1995 ▶
SINGLE MALT 40% ABV
Clearly originates from a Bushmills malt, and a classy one to boot. There are notes of toasted nuts, while a juicy, honey sweetness lingers on the palate. It is still too young, though, to display the full potential of its characteristics.

217

KNOB CREEK

USA

*Jim Beam Distillery,
149 Happy Hollow Road,
Clermont, Kentucky*
www.jimbeam.com

Knob Creek is the Kentucky town where Abraham Lincoln's father, Thomas, owned a farm and worked at the local distillery. This bourbon is one of three introduced in 1992, when Jim Beam launched its Small Batch Bourbon Collection. It is made to the same high-rye formula as the Jim Beam-distilled Basil Hayden's *(see p39)* and Old Grand-Dad *(p276)* brands.

◀ **KNOB CREEK 9-YEAR-OLD**
BOURBON 50% ABV
Knob Creek has a nutty nose of sweet, tangy fruit and rye, with malt, spice, and nuts on the fruity palate, drying in the finish with notes of vanilla.

KNOCKANDO

Scotland
Knockando, Morayshire
www.malts.com

Knockando was launched as a single malt in the late 1970s. Most of the distillery's production has tended to go into J&B.

Established in 1898, the distillery was only run on a seasonal basis and soon fell victim to the speculative crash that hit the industry at the beginning of the 20th century. Knockando was snapped up by the London gin distillers Gilbey's, who, via a series of acquisitions, became part of what is now Diageo. In 1968, the floor maltings were stopped and the old malt barns converted to host meetings for J&B salesmen.

KNOCKANDO 12-YEAR-OLD ▶
SINGLE MALT: SPEYSIDE
43% ABV
This gentle, grassy malt has a cereal character and a light, creamy texture.

KNOCKANDO 18-YEAR-OLD
SINGLE MALT: SPEYSIDE
43% ABV
A slightly more fulsome expression, with a smooth, mellow texture.

KNOCKEEN HILLS

Ireland
www.irish-poteen.com

Poteen (or poitín) is a clear spirit that was traditionally distilled in homemade pot stills throughout Ireland. It was originally made with malted barley or any other available grain, though potatoes were also used. One of the few to survive is Knockeen Hills. Its spirit is bottled at three strengths: triple-distilled at 60% and 70% ABV, and quadruple-distilled at 90% ABV. It should not be drunk neat.

◀ KNOCKEEN HILLS 60
POTEEN 60% ABV
Clean, fresh, and fruity on the nose. Creamy textured, with tantalizing sweet and juicy fruit notes on the palate. Crisp, mouth-cleansing finish.

KNOCKEEN HILLS 70
POTEEN 70% ABV
Stronger on the nose than the 60. With a large measure of water (almost 50:50), it becomes fruity, with tangerine-skin aromas and a sweet perfumed note. Warming in the mouth, sweet and sour on the palate, with a dry, fruit-tinged finish.

LADYBURN

Scotland

Owner: William Grant & Sons

Now long-since closed, Ladyburn
was a malt distillery within a huge
grain distillery in Girvan on the
Ayrshire coast. Its owners, William
Grant & Sons, moved into grain
whisky in 1964, when DCL
threatened to stop supplying them
with grain spirit for its blends. Two
years later, in 1966, it created
Ladyburn on the site. It only ran
for nine years before being
converted into a vodka distillery
in 1975, so single malt bottlings
are very rare. Despite this, official
bottlings, as well as independents,
continue to be eked out of the
remaining stocks, and there are
rumours that the owners kept
back 30 casks to release as and
when they choose.

LADYBURN 1973 ▶
**SINGLE MALT: LOWLANDS
50.4% ABV**
A limited-release bottling, with a
mellow, oaky character and delicious
vanilla sweetness.

LAGAVULIN

Scotland
Port Ellen, Isle of Islay
www.malts.com

Lagavulin is said to have evolved into a distillery from various illicit smuggling botheys in 1817. In 1836 its lease was taken over by Alexander Graham, who sold the island's whiskies through his shop in Glasgow. Peter Mackie, the nephew of Graham's partner, worked for the business and went on to create the famous White Horse blend based on Islay malt. When Laphroaig refused to supply him, he built Malt Mill Distillery in the grounds of Lagavulin, which he inherited after his uncle's death.

◀ LAGAVULIN 16-YEAR-OLD
SINGLE MALT: ISLAY
43% ABV
Intensely smoky nose with the scent of seaweed and iodine and a sweetness in the mouth that dries to a peaty finish.

LAGAVULIN 12-YEAR-OLD
SINGLE MALT: ISLAY
56.4% ABV
An initial sweetness gives way to scented smoke and a malty, fruity flavour ahead of the dry, peaty finish.

Malt Mill was demolished in the 1960s, but Lagavulin rode on the back of the White Horse until its iconic 16-year-old became a founding member of the "Classic Malts" in 1988.

During the slump in demand for Scotch in the 1980s, Lagavulin was working a two- to three-day week. Sixteen years down the line, the managers were having to juggle the short supply with booming demand. To try and meet demand, production at Lagavulin was cranked up to a seven-day week, and less and less was made available for blends. It is said that over 85 per cent of Lagavulin is now bottled as a single malt.

LAGAVULIN DISTILLERS EDITION ▶
SINGLE MALT: ISLAY
43% ABV

A richer, fuller-flavoured take on the 16-year-old, still with plenty of dense smoke and seaweed.

LAGAVULIN 21-YEAR-OLD
SINGLE MALT: ISLAY
56.5% ABV

Pungent and smoky on one hand, a sherried, golden-syrup warmth on the other. The two sides live in harmony.

LAMMERLAW

New Zealand
Bottled by Cadenhead
www.wmcadenhead.com

In 1974, the Wilson Brewery and
Malt Extract Company produced
New Zealand's first legal whisky
for 100 years. Unfortunately, its
pot stills were made from stainless
steel, and the spirit was horrible.
In 1981, the distillery was
acquired by Seagram, who vastly
improved quality and produced
a 10-year-old single malt –
Lammerlaw – named after the
nearby mountain range. The
distillery was dismantled in 2002,
and the casks passed to Milford's
owners *(see p256)*. Cadenhead has
bottled Lammerlaw in its World
Whiskies series.

◀ CADENHEAD'S LAMMERLAW
10-YEAR-OLD
SINGLE MALT 47.3% ABV
Light-bodied and somewhat "green"
and cereal-like, but pleasant to taste.

LANGS

Owner: Ian MacLeod
www.ianmacleod.com

At the heart of this blend is
Glengoyne single malt, from the
distillery just outside Glasgow. This
was bought in 1876 by two local
merchants, Alexander and Gavin
Lang. Brand and distillery were
later sold to Robertson & Baxter.

The subsequent sale to Ian
MacLeod marked an important
transition for that business, from
blender and bottler to full-blown
distiller. Today, the principal
Langs products are Langs Select
12-year-old and Langs Supreme.

LANGS SUPREME ▶
BLEND 40% ABV

A rich malt aroma on the nose,
well-matured, with just a hint of sherry.
A full-flavoured, medium-sweet blend,
with the Glengoyne heart evident.

LANGS SELECT 12-YEAR-OLD
BLEND 40% ABV

Rhubarb, cooking apples, and plenty
of vanilla on the nose. Richer on the
palate, with lots of fruity notes and a
lemon-tart sweetness that build towards
a spicy finish with hints of peat smoke.

225

LAPHROAIG

Scotland

Port Ellen, Isle of Islay
www.laphroaig.com

Laphroaig has always revelled in its pungent smokiness – a mix of hemp, carbolic soap, and bonfire that is about as a far from the creamy, cocktail end of whisky as it is possible to get. Its intense medicinal character is said to be one reason it was among the few Scotch whiskies allowed into the US during Prohibition – it was accepted as a "medicinal spirit",

◄ LAPHROAIG 10-YEAR-OLD CASK STRENGTH

SINGLE MALT: ISLAY
57.3% ABV

Tar, seaweed, and salt, and some sweet wood too. Iodine and hot peat rumble through a long, dramatic finish.

LAPHROAIG 10-YEAR-OLD

SINGLE MALT: ISLAY
40% ABV

The 10-year-old is also very popular. Beneath the dense peat smoke and salty sea spray is a refreshing, youthful malt with a sweet core.

and could be obtained on prescription from a doctor.

Laphroaig was founded in 1810 by Alexander and Donald Johnston, although official production did not begin for five years. Living beside the equally famous Lagavulin has not always been easy, and there were the usual fights over water access, but today the feeling is more one of mutual respect.

Laphroaig is one of the very few distilleries to have retained its floor maltings, which supply about a fifth of its needs.

LAPHROAIG QUARTER CASK ▶
SINGLE MALT: ISLAY
48% ABV

The Quarter Cask is at the heart of Laphroaig's core range. Small casks speed up the maturation process and lead to a sweet, woody taste that succumbs to a triumphal burst of peat smoke.

LAPHROAIG 25-YEAR-OLD
SINGLE MALT: ISLAY
50.9% ABV

A spicy, floral character, with smoke and sea spray taking over only in the finish. Also available in cask strength.

LARK

Australia
14 Davey Street, Hobart, Tasmania
www.larkdistillery.com.au

The modern revival of whisky-making in Australia began in Tasmania, with the opening of this small distillery in Hobart in 1992. It was the brainchild of Bill Lark, who realized that the island has all the right ingredients: plenty of rich barley fields, abundant pure soft water, peat bogs, and a perfect climate for maturation.

Lark is now assisted by his wife Lyn and daughter Kristy. They use locally grown Franklin barley, 50 per cent of it re-dried over peat. The malt is bottled from single casks at three to five years.

◀ LARK'S SINGLE MALT
SINGLE MALT 58% ABV
Malty and lightly peated, with peppery notes. A smooth mouthfeel, with rich malt, apples and oak-wood, and some spice in the finish.

LARK'S PM
BLENDED MALT 45% ABV
Sweet and smoky on the nose and palate; clean and lightly spicy. Consider this a well-made "barley schnapps".

THE LAST DROP

Scotland
www.lastdropdistillers.com

This unusual super-premium blend is the brainchild of three industry veterans – Tom Jago, James Espey, and Peter Fleck. Allegedly, a random discovery of very old whiskies pre-vatted at 12 years of age and then allowed to mature for a further 36 years in sherry casks, The Last Drop would appear to have been something of an accident and cannot be repeated. Included in the blend are whiskies from long-lost distilleries, the youngest reputed to have been distilled in 1960. Savour the tasting notes – at £1,000 or so a bottle and with only 1,347 bottles available, it may be the closest you'll get to tasting it.

THE LAST DROP ▶
BLEND 54.5% ABV
Exceptionally complex nose, with figs, chocolate, and vanilla. An unusual combination of new-mown hay, dried fruit, herbs, and buttery biscuits.

L

LAUDER'S

Scotland
Owner: MacDuff International

Between 1886 and 1893, Lauder's Royal Northern Cream scooped up a total of six gold medals in international competitions – a tribute to the meticulous research and repeated trials undertaken by the original proprietor, Archibald Lauder, a Glasgow publican. The development of the blend is said to have taken him two years. Today Lauder's is once again blended in Glasgow, by MacDuff International, and Lauder's Bar on Sauchiehall Street remains to commemorate Lauder himself. His blend has largely slipped from public view in its homeland, but is imported by Barton Brands of Chicago to the US, where it remains popular among value-conscious consumers.

◀ **LAUDER'S**
BLEND 40% ABV
A light and fruity blend designed for session drinking and mixing.

LEDAIG

Scotland
*Tobermory Distillery,
Tobermory, Isle of Mull*

Tobermory, the capital of Mull and the island's main port, was originally called Ledaig, and this was the name chosen by John Sinclair when he began distilling here in 1798. Quite when the Ledaig Distillery became Tobermory is unclear, as it has had an incredibly interrupted life, spending more time in mothballs than in production. In recent years the distillery adopted a similar approach to Springbank, producing a heavily peated robust West Coast malt called Ledaig and a lightly peated malt called Tobermory. At present there is a 10-year-old Ledaig, first released in 2008, and a 10- and a 15-year-old Tobermory *(see p346)*.

LEDAIG 10-YEAR-OLD ▶
**SINGLE MALT: ISLANDS
43% ABV**
Slightly medicinal, but full of dry, slightly dusty peat smoke.

L

LIMEBURNERS

Australia
Great Southern Distilling Company,
252 Frenchman Bay Road, Albany,
Western Australia
www.distillery.com.au

The Great Southern Distillery was
built in 2007, the brainchild of
lawyer and accountant Cameron
Syme. Its location was chosen for
Albany's cool, wet winters and
enough breeze to provide 75 per
cent of its energy needs by wind
power. It is close to the Margaret
River wineries, which supply the
ingredients for schnapps and
liqueur-making. Limeburners
whisky is offered in single barrel
bottlings: the first bottling, Barrel
M2, launched in April 2008, won
an award.

◀ LIMEBURNERS BARREL M11
SINGLE MALT 43% ABV
The fourth bottling (M11), nicknamed
"The Dark One", is from a French oak
ex-brandy cask, re-racked into a
second-fill ex-bourbon barrel.

LINKWOOD

Scotland
Elgin, Morayshire
www.malts.com

From the outset, Linkwood was
a well-conceived distillery. It
was surrounded by barley fields
to supply the grain, and cattle
to feed on the spent draff. The
building you see today dates back
to the 1870s, when the original
Linkwood was demolished and
a new distillery was built on the
same site. It remained in private
hands until 1933, when it became
part of DCL.

LINKWOOD FLORA & FAUNA 12-YEAR-OLD ▶
**SINGLE MALT: SPEYSIDE
43% ABV**
On the lighter side of the Speyside
style, with a fresh, grassy, green-apple
fragrance and faint notes of spice. In
the mouth it has a delicate sweet-and-
sour flavour and a slow finish.

LINKWOOD RARE MALTS 26-YEAR-OLD
**SINGLE MALT: SPEYSIDE
56.1% ABV**
Bright and breezy for a 26-year-old.
Lightly smoky with caramelized sugar
notes. Spicy and warm in the finish.

LOCH FYNE

Scotland
Owner: Richard Joynson
www.lfw.co.uk

Created by Professor Ronnie
Martin, a former production
director at United Distillers
(now Diageo), Loch Fyne is the
exclusive and eponymous house
blend of Loch Fyne Whiskies of
Inverary. It is blended and bottled
under licence for this famous
Scottish whisky specialist.

Slightly sweet and smoky,
Loch Fyne is an easy-drinking,
well-flavoured blend, which has
been praised by leading critics
and won awards in international
competition. Also available is a
full-strength 12-year-old liqueur.

◀ **LOCH FYNE
PREMIUM SCOTCH
BLEND 40% ABV**
Apple dumplings on the nose,
enlivened by orange and tangerine
notes. Subtle, with nutty, oil-related
aromas and hints of smoke. The palate
is smooth and well-balanced: acidic,
salty, sweet, and dry. The finish is
surprisingly warming.

LOCH LOMOND

Scotland

Alexandria, Dumbartonshire
www.lochlomonddistillery.com

Within the confines of the Loch Lomond Distillery, on the southern end of Loch Lomond, all manner of Scotch whiskies are produced, although originally it was just malt. The distillery was built in 1965 as a joint venture between Barton Brands of America and Duncan Thomas. Twenty years later it was bought by Alexander Bulloch and his company, Glen Catrine Bonded Warehouse Ltd. Today, grain whisky is produced alongside the malt. The distillery's stills have rectifying columns that can be adjusted to produce a lighter or heavier spirit.

LOCH LOMOND ▶
SINGLE MALT: HIGHLANDS
40% ABV
With no age statement and a competitive price, this is likely to be a fairly young single malt. It has a light, fresh flavour and no great influence of wood.

LOCHRANZA

Scotland

Isle of Arran Distillers,
Lochranza,
Isle of Arran
www.arranwhisky.com

This blended whisky is named
after the picturesque village
where the Isle of Arran Distillery
is based. This was established as
recently as 1995 by industry
veteran Harold Currie, but has
subsequently changed hands.
Lochranza is a pleasant, easy-
drinking standard blend. It may
well see further development in
future years as a proportion of
the distillery's own mature stock
of single malts can find its way
into the recipe. Arran Distillers
also produce the Robert Burns
blend *(see p.301)*.

◀ LOCHRANZA
BLEND 40% ABV

The initial impression is of melted
toffee, followed by pears, oak, and
hints of lime. Smooth and sweet,
lightly sherried and oaky, with a
medium finish. A dash of water
helps the flavours.

LOCKE'S

Ireland
*Cooley Distillery, Riverstown,
Cooley, County Louth
www.cooleywhiskey.com*

It's hard to believe that, just 30
years ago, this truly remarkable
distillery was almost derelict.
Since the early 1950s, when the
Locke's whiskey business initially
folded, the abandoned buildings
had been used to house pigs and
farm machinery. Then, in the late
1970s, the local community got
together and restored the
distillery. After the renovation was
completed, a deal was made with
Cooley and, after decades of dusty
silence, whiskey barrels once more
trundled into the warehouses.

LOCKE'S 8-YEAR-OLD MALT ▶
SINGLE MALT 40% ABV
A vatting of Cooley's unpeated malt,
with a top dressing of peated malt. It
is not a bad whiskey; just a bit dull.

LOCKE'S BLEND
BLEND 40% ABV
This is a pleasant enough dram. It
would be particularly good in a hot
whiskey, where its limited range
doesn't have to sing out.

LONG JOHN

Scotland
Owner: Chivas Brothers

Despite reasonably healthy sales
in France, Scandinavia, and some
Spanish-speaking markets, Long
John appears very much the poor
relation in the Chivas Brothers'
stable, dominated as it is by
Chivas Regal and Ballantine's.
The brand has passed through
a number of owners since it was
founded in the early 19th century
by the eponymous "Long" John
MacDonald. The Scottish Whisky
Association's Directory of
Member's Brands lists a non-age
version as well as a 12- and
15-year-old.

◀ LONG JOHN 12-YEAR-OLD
BLEND 40% ABV
The blend is said to contain 48
different malts, including Laphroaig
and Highland Park. A deluxe blend,
Long John 12-year-old is a dark,
traditional style of whisky, noted for
its distinctive character.

12 Years Old

Long John

BLENDED SCOTCH WHISKY

LONG JOHN DISTILLERIES
GLASGOW : SCOTLAND

LONGMORN

Scotland
Elgin, Morayshire

John Duff, George Thomson, and Charles Shirres went into partnership in 1894 and built the Longmorn distillery. With its four stills, it was conceived on a grand scale at a cost of £20,000 (around £2m in today's money). Within five years Duff had bought out his partners and built another distillery, BenRiach, next door.

Since 2000, the 15-year-old bottling has been replaced by one a year older, clearly aimed at the super-premium category of malts.

LONGMORN 16-YEAR-OLD ▶
SINGLE MALT: SPEYSIDE
48% ABV
Its cereal aroma is sweetened with coconut from ageing in bourbon casks. The mouthfeel is smooth and silky and dries on the tongue to give a crisp, slightly austere finish.

LONGMORN CASK STRENGTH 17-YEAR-OLD 1991
SINGLE MALT: SPEYSIDE
49.4% ABV
Richly floral on the nose and palate. Vanilla and ripe pears combine beautifully with tantalizing oaky notes.

LONGROW

Scotland

Springbank Distillery,
Well Close, Campbeltown, Argyll
www.springbankdistillers.com

In 1973, the Springbank
Distillery decided to distil a
pungent, heavily smoked whisky
alongside its main malt. The new
whisky was christened Longrow
after a distillery that had once
stood next door. It was released as
an experiment in 1985 and finally
became a regular fixture in 1992.

Today, the core range includes
the 10-year-old, its cask strength
sibling – the 10-year-old 100 Proof
– and the 14-year-old.

◀ LONGROW 10-YEAR-OLD
SINGLE MALT: CAMPBELTOWN
46% ABV

This dense, phenolic whisky has plenty
of smoky complexity, alongside some
sweetness from maturing in a mix
of ex-bourbon and sherry casks.

LONGROW 14-YEAR-OLD
SINGLE MALT: CAMPBELTOWN
46% ABV

Coal smoke on the nose and coal dust
on the palate – to phenol-lovers this is
manna. An industrial-tasting mix of
hot tar, brine, and coke.

MACALLAN

Scotland
Easter Elchies, Craigellachie,
Morayshire
www.themacallan.com

The Macallan was first licensed
in 1824 as the Elchies Distillery.
It was a small-scale operation:
annual production was still only
180,000 litres (40,000 gallons)
when it was sold to Roderick
Kemp in 1892. The distillery was
expanded and remained in family
control until 1996, when it was
bought by Highland Distillers
(now part of the Edrington
Group), for £180 million. ☞

THE MACALLAN
10-YEAR-OLD ▶
SINGLE MALT: SPEYSIDE
40% ABV
The signature Macallan, matured in
sherry butts. This popular whisky has
a dried-fruit, slightly toffee-scented
nose and a well-rounded flavour.

THE MACALLAN
FINE OAK 10-YEAR-OLD
SINGLE MALT: SPEYSIDE
40% ABV
With less sherry influence than the
standard 10-year-old, more of the
fresh, brisk, malty distillery character
comes through.

MACALLAN

In the intervening years, the distillery was rebuilt in the 1950s and the number of stills grew to 21. More importantly, The Macallan 10-year-old established itself as one of the leading single malts on Speyside. The distillery had always used sherry casks, which were shipped in from Spain. A deep amber colour and fruitcake character came to symbolize the whisky. So the launch of the Fine Oak series in 2004, which uses bourbon casks alongside sherry butts, marked a radical departure. It has clearly widened The Macallan's appeal, however.

◀ THE MACALLAN 30-YEAR-OLD
SINGLE MALT: SPEYSIDE 43% ABV
A big, post-prandial malt with a sweet, sherried nose and spicy flavours of orange peel, cloves, and dates that linger on the finish.

THE MACALLAN 25-YEAR-OLD
SINGLE MALT: SPEYSIDE 43% ABV
Spicy citrus notes accompany the ripe dried-fruit character from the sherry casks, which lead to a little wood-smoke on the tongue.

MACARTHUR'S

Scotland
Owner: Inver House Distillers

The MacArthur clan of Argyllshire fought nobly alongside Robert the Bruce in the struggle for Scottish independence and subsequently gave their name to this standard blend. Like so many others, it has its roots in the upsurge of blending from independent merchants in the late-Victorian era and can be traced to the 1870s. Today it is owned by Inver House Distillers, who describe it as having a "light, smooth flavour with toffee and vanilla from cask ageing". MacArthur's is not to be confused with single malts bottled independently under the label James MacArthur.

MACARTHUR'S ▶
BLEND 40% ABV
Fragrant, barley-malt nose with sweet, citrus aftertones. A medium-bodied, uncomplicated whisky, softly aromatic, with a smooth, mellow palate and a fresh, lingering finish.

MACKMYRA

Sweden
Mackmyra, Bruksgatan 4,
81832 Valbo
www.mackmyra.se

Founded in 1999, Mackmyra
launched Preludium 01, the first
bottling in a limited series, in
2006. Preludiums 02, 03, 04, and
05 followed in rapid succession.
Preludium 06 was released in
December 2007, followed by
Special 01 in June 2008. The
distillery also offers single cask
Reserve bottlings.

◄ MACKMYRA PRELUDIUM 06
SINGLE MALT 50.5% ABV
Fruity, with aromas of lemon, pear,
banana, and honey. Gentle hints of
caramel, roast oak, and pepper. A
distinctive smoky character, with
undertones of juniper. The finish
brings sweetness, charred oak cask,
smoke, and a touch of salt.

MACKMYRA PRELUDIUM 05
SINGLE MALT 48.4% ABV
Marzipan, custard, and a light citrus
note on the nose. Flavours of crème
brûlée, bitter chocolate, and lemon
zest. A bit oily; slightly metallic
and grainy in the finish – creamier
with water.

MAGILLIGAN

Ireland
Cooley Distillery, Riverstown,
Cooley, County Louth

This is a confusing whiskey. It may
well say pure pot still on the label,
but you are actually buying a
young, Cooley-produced single
malt (though the Magilligan brand
is not part of Cooley's own stable).
The fault lies with Irish legislature;
it has not legally defined what
constitutes a "pure pot still". At
the moment, any whiskey that is
made in a pot still can be called
pot still whiskey. So, buyers
should beware.

   Magilligan comes in various
guises, including a limited-edition
1991 vintage bottled at 46% ABV.

MAGILLIGAN ▶
SINGLE MALT 43% ABV
This is a thin young malt, with hints
of greatness, but it has been bottled
as an adolescent. An 8-year-old version
is available, but the regular Magilligan
offering tastes like a vatting of
whiskeys between three and five
years old.

MAKER'S MARK

USA

3350 Burks Springs Road,
Loretto, Kentucky
www.makersmark.com

Maker's Mark Distillery is located
on the banks of Hardin's Creek,
near Loretto. Established in 1805,
it is the USA's oldest working
distillery remaining on its original
site. The Maker's Mark brand was
developed during the 1950s by Bill
Samuels Jr, and today is owned by
Fortune Brands Inc.

◀ MAKER'S MARK
BOURBON 45% ABV

A subtle, complex, clean nose, with
vanilla and spice, a delicate floral note
of roses, plus lime and cocoa beans.
Medium in body, it offers a palate of
fresh fruit, spices, eucalyptus, and
ginger cake. The finish features more
spices, fresh oak with a hint of smoke,
and a final flash of peach cheesecake.

MANNOCHMORE

Scotland
Elgin, Morayshire
www.malts.com

From conception, Mannochmore's simple role in life was supplying malt for Haig, then the top-selling blend in the UK. Fourteen years later it fell victim to the chronic oversupply in the industry and was mothballed, as the big distillers sought to drain the whisky loch. It was back in production by 1989 and launched its first official malt as part of the Flora & Fauna range three years later.

MANNOCHMORE FLORA & FAUNA 12-YEAR-OLD ▶
SINGLE MALT: SPEYSIDE
43% ABV
An aperitif-style malt, with a light, floral nose but, in the mouth, a more luscious, spicy character, with hints of liquorice and vanilla, comes through.

MANNOCHMORE RARE MALTS 22-YEAR-OLD
SINGLE MALT: SPEYSIDE
60.1% ABV
Distilled in 1974, this limited edition exudes fragrant, flowery aromas. Herbaceous and peppery, with a touch of peat in the mix.

MASTERSTROKE

India

Owner: Diageo Radico
www.radicokhaitan.com
www.diageo.com

Masterstroke De Luxe Whisky, an IMFL (Indian Made Foreign Liquor) priced for the "prestige" category, was launched by Diageo Radico in February 2007. The company is a joint 50:50 venture between Radico Khaitan Ltd, "India's fastest-growing liquor manufacturer", and the world's largest drinks company, Diageo. It is their first joint venture. Within three months the brand was being endorsed by Bollywood superstar Shah Rukh Khan.

◀ **MASTERSTROKE**
BLEND 42.8% ABV

A rich nose and mouthfeel, lent by a liberal amount of Blair Athol single malt. Well-balanced, with the light finish characteristic of IMFLs.

MCCARTHY'S

USA

Clear Creek Distillery,
2389 NW Wilson Street,
Portland, Oregon
www.clearcreekdistillery.com

Steve McCarthy established Clear
Creek Distillery more than 20
years ago and has been distilling
whiskey for over a decade. He is
of the opinion that, since it is
made from peat-malted barley
brought in from Scotland, "our
whiskey would be a single malt
Scotch if Oregon were Scotland".

MCCARTHY'S OREGON ▶
SINGLE MALT 40% ABV
McCarthy's is initially matured in
former sherry casks for two or three
years, then for six to twelve months
in barrels made from air-dried Oregon
oak. Kippery and spicy on the nose,
with a hint of sulphur, peat, and
vanilla, it is big-bodied and oily,
smoky-sweet on the meaty palate,
and with dry oak, malt, spice, and
salt in the long finish.

CLEAR CREEK DISTILLERY

McCARTHY'S

OREGON SINGLE MALT

POT DISTILLED
WHISKEY

Distilled from a Fermented Mash
of Peat-Malted Scottish Barley,
Barrel-Aged 3 Years and Bottled by
Clear Creek Distillery
PORTLAND, OREGON, U.S.A.
ALC. 40% BY VOL. (80 PROOF)
750 ML

MCCLELLAND'S

Scotland
Owner: Morrison Bowmore

The range of McClelland's single malts offers a chance to explore Scotland and four of its key whisky-distilling regions. It was first launched in 1986, with a Highland, Lowland, and Islay expression. These proved so successful that a Speyside expression was introduced in 1999. According to the company, each one is carefully selected to reflect the true essence and

◀ MCCLELLAND'S HIGHLAND
SINGLE MALT: HIGHLANDS 40% ABV
Delicate wood notes on the nose, with sweet buttercream and fresh vanilla. Some initial sweetness, giving way to fresh fruit and lime hints.

MCCLELLAND'S ISLAY
SINGLE MALT: ISLAY 40% ABV
The nose is unmistakably Islay: wood smoke and cinders, tar, vanilla, and citrus hints. Forceful sea salt, burnt oak, and peat smoke, with vanilla undertones on the palate.

character of the region in which it is produced.

The brand currently claims to be number four in the US market, where it competes against Glenlivet, Glenfiddich, and The Macallan. It is also distributed to global markets, including Taiwan, Austria, South Africa, Japan, Canada, France, Russia, and the Netherlands. A Speyside 12-year-old was launched in November 2008 and will be joined by Highland, Lowland, and Islay 12-year-olds.

MCCLELLAND'S LOWLAND ▶
SINGLE MALT: LOWLANDS
40% ABV
A richly floral nose with hints of nutmeg, ginger, and citrus fruits. Very clean and delicate on the palate, with floral notes.

MCCLELLAND'S SPEYSIDE
SINGLE MALT: SPEYSIDE
40% ABV
Fresh mint, cut pine, hints of dark chocolate, and sweet malt on the nose. Initially sweet, developing nutty flavours and floral hints.

MCDOWELL'S

India
Owner: United Spirits
www.unitedspirits.in

Scotsman Angus McDowell founded McDowell & Co in Madras in 1826 as a trading company specializing in liquor and cigars. McDowell's No.1 was launched in 1968.

A malt whisky distillery was commissioned by McDowell & Co at Ponda, Goa, in 1971. The spirit is matured in ex-bourbon casks for around three years. It is claimed that the heat and humidity of Goa leads to a more rapid maturation. The product is described as "the first-ever indigenously developed single malt whisky in Asia".

◀ MCDOWELL'S NO.1 RESERVE
BLEND 42.8% ABV
"Blended with Scotch and Select Indian Malts", this has a nose of dried figs and sweet tobacco and, later, prunes and dates. A sweet taste initially, then burnt sugar and a short finish.

MCDOWELL'S SINGLE MALT
SINGLE MALT 42.8% ABV
With fresh cereal and fruit on the nose and a sweet, pleasantly citric taste, this is not unlike a young Speyside.

MELLOW CORN

USA
Heaven Hill Distillery,
1701 West Breckinridge Street,
Louisville, Kentucky
www.heaven-hill.com

According to Heaven Hill, "The forerunner and kissing cousin to Bourbon, American straight corn whiskey is defined by the US Government as having a recipe or mashbill with a minimum of 81 percent corn, the rest being malted barley and rye".

Today, Heaven Hill is the sole remaining national producer of this classic whiskey style, bottling Georgia Moon *(see p128)* in addition to Mellow Corn.

MELLOW CORN ▶
CORN WHISKEY 50% ABV
Wood varnish and vanilla, with floral and herbal notes on the nose. The palate is big and oily, and fruity, with toffee apples. More fruit, cinder toffee, and understated vanilla complete the finish. Young and boisterous.

253

MICHAEL COLLINS

Ireland
www.michaelcollinswhiskey.com

Despite the fame of General Michael Collins among the Irish people, most of them have never heard of this whiskey.

The reason for this is that it was initially formulated for the American market by Cooley Distillery in conjunction with US importer Sidney Frank. However, it can now be bought on both sides of the Atlantic.

Unusually for an Irish whiskey, the Michael Collins malt is double-distilled and lightly peated. The blend is a mix of the malt and a younger grain whiskey.

◄ MICHAEL COLLINS SINGLE MALT
SINGLE MALT 40% ABV
Soft and drinkable, with plenty of biscuity flavours. Vanilla notes emerge, with a hint of light smoke.

MICHAEL COLLINS BLEND
BLEND 40% ABV
Less impressive than the malt. It is thin, with the scent of woody embers at its core, but it lacks a decent finish.

MIDLETON

Ireland
Midleton, County Cork
www.irishdistillers.ie

Among all the spirits produced
at Midleton – Jameson, Powers,
Paddy, and all of the Irish Distillers'
portfolio of whiskeys – there is just
one regularly appearing whiskey
that carries the actual Midleton
moniker. Launched in 1984,
Midleton Very Rare is aimed at
the premium market and the price
reflects whatever that market can
bear. A new vintage is released late
every year.

MIDLETON VERY RARE ▶
BLEND 40% ABV
On the nose, classy oak and bold cereal
notes dance on a high wire made of
pure beeswax. The body is full and
yielding, and the finish breaks on the
tongue in waves of silky, walnut whip.

MIDLETON MASTER DISTILLER'S PRIVATE COLLECTION 1973
PURE POT STILL 56% ABV
A bottling of pure pot still whiskey
from the old Midleton Distillery. Just
800 bottles were released. Its taste is
said to be spicy, fruity, and honeyed,
with some dry, sherry nuttiness.

MILFORD

New Zealand

The New Zealand Malt Whisky
Company & Preston Associates,
14–16 Harbour St, Oamaru
www.milfordwhisky.co.nz

Milford whisky was originally
made at Willowbank Distillery
in Dunedin, South Island, which
was owned by the Wilson Brewery
(*see Lammerlaw, p224*). The New
Zealand Malt Whisky Company
now owns the Milford label (and
also the less prestigious Prestons
label) and is building a new
distillery at Bannockburn,
Central Otago. It has also
opened a retail warehouse at
Oamaru, where the new Milford
malt will be matured and bottled.

◀ MILFORD 10-YEAR-OLD
SINGLE MALT 43% ABV

Often compared to a Scottish Lowland
malt, Milford's 10-year-old has a light,
dry, and fragrant nose; the taste is
sweet, then dry, with a slightly
woody, short finish.

MILLARS

Ireland

Cooley Distillery, Riverstown,
Cooley, County Louth
www.cooleywhiskey.com

Once upon a time, every single
drop of Irish whiskey was bottled
by bonders. Gilbey's, Mitchell's,
or Millars would buy whiskey in
bulk and sell it to their customers,
often straight from the cask. This
method died out over the latter
part of the 20th century, and
Adam Millars & Co in Dublin was
one of the only bonders to survive.

The Millars brand is now owned
by Cooley, and this hard-to-find
whiskey is a grain-heavy blend.

MILLARS SPECIAL RESERVE ▶
BLEND 40% ABV

This is a superb little whiskey. It is
a perky dram, with a real sense of fun.
A peppery character on the nose is
underpinned by a luxurious, spicy
body in the glass.

MILLBURN

Scotland
Inverness, Inverness-shire

It was Millburn's misfortune to be located on the outskirts of Inverness on the road to Elgin. When the whisky industry suffered one of its big periodic downturns in the 1980s, the distillery was in the wrong place at the wrong time – not remote enough to simply be mothballed when there was the prospect of redevelopment instead. And so it shut down for good in 1985 and was turned into a steakhouse; today, it's a hotel and restaurant called The Auld Distillery. Limited-edition bottlings are still released intermittently by the owner of its stocks, Diageo.

◀ MILLBURN RARE MALTS 25-YEAR-OLD
SINGLE MALT: SPEYSIDE 61.9% ABV
This Rare Malts bottling is a big, meaty whisky that is dry and chewy in the mouth, with damp wood, smoke, and orange skins.

MILLSTONE

The Netherlands
*Zuidam, Weverstraat 6, 5111 PW,
Baarle Nassau*
www.zuidam-distillers.com

What started as a gin distillery
some 50 years ago is now a
company with a second generation
of the Zuidam family at the helm.
It produces beautifully crafted
single malts, alongside excellent
young and old *jenevers*, as the
Dutch call their gin. The Millstone
5-year-old single malt whisky was
introduced in 2007, to be followed
by an 8-year-old sibling. Zuidam
uses ex-bourbon as well as
ex-sherry casks to mature its
whisky. A 10-year-old expression
is in the making.

MILLSTONE 5-YEAR-OLD ▶
SINGLE MALT 40% ABV
Delicate aromas of fruit and honey
combined with vanilla, wood, and a
hint of coconut. Rich honey sweetness
in the mouth, delicate spicy notes,
and a long vanilla-oak finish.

MILTONDUFF

Scotland
Miltonduff, Elgin, Morayshire

Once one of the illicit stills that were rife in Speyside in the 19th century, Miltonduff has been owned by Pernod Ricard since 2005. Much of the 5.5 million litre (1.2 million gallon) production is used to supply malt for its top-selling blend, Ballantine's Finest. An official 15-year-old malt is now available, although a wider range of bottlings exists among the independents, particularly Gordon & MacPhail.

◄ MILTONDUFF 15-YEAR-OLD
SINGLE MALT: SPEYSIDE
46% ABV
This non chill-filtered distillery bottling is hard to find. It has a gentle Speyside character with a honeyed, leathery aroma and a nutty, herbal flavour.

MILTONDUFF GORDON & MACPHAIL 1968
SINGLE MALT: SPEYSIDE
40% ABV
This rare Gordon & MacPhail bottling has a rich sherried character with notes of liquorice, menthol, and crystallized ginger.

MONKEY SHOULDER

Scotland
Owner: William Grant & Sons

The name may seem contrived, but this blended malt from William Grant & Sons refers to a condition among workers in the maltings – turning the damp grain by hand, they often incurred a repetitive strain injury.

Three metal monkeys decorate the shoulder of the bottle and just three single malts go into the blend – Glenfiddich, Balvenie, and Kininvie. At the launch, great play was made of the whisky's mixability, and you're as likely to encounter it on a cocktail menu as you are in your local off-licence.

MONKEY SHOULDER ▶
BLEND 40% ABV
Banana, honey, pears, and allspice on the nose. Vanilla, nutmeg, citrus hints, and generic fruit on the palate. A dry finish, then a short burst of menthol.

MORTLACH

Scotland
Dufftown, Keith, Banffshire
www.malts.com

The six stills at Mortlach are
configured in a uniquely complex
manner, with a fifth of the spirit
being triple-distilled in an
intermediate still called
"Wee Witchie". This process
is intended to add richness
and depth to the spirit, which
is then condensed in traditional
worm tubs outdoors, to create
a more robust style of whisky.

◀ MORTLACH FLORA & FAUNA 16-YEAR-OLD
SINGLE MALT: SPEYSIDE 43% ABV
As suggested by the rich amber colour,
there is a strong sherry influence at
play, although not enough to unbalance
this beguiling, complex malt with notes
of dark mint-chocolate on the nose.

MORTLACH 21-YEAR-OLD
SINGLE MALT: SPEYSIDE 43% ABV
Caramel and soft fruits on the nose.
The palate is drier, with the sherry
wood influence bringing resinous,
oaky flavours.

MURREE

Pakistan

Murree Distillery,
National Park Road, Rawalpindi
www.murreebrewery.com

With a dispensation having been granted to the non-Muslim owners of Muree to distil alcoholic drinks "for visitors and non-Muslims", this is the only distillery of alcoholic beverages in a Muslim country.

The barley comes from the UK and is malted in floor maltings and Saladin boxes. Some of the spirit is filled into cask, most into large vats (some made from Australian oak), and matured in cellars equipped with a cooling system.

MURREE'S CLASSIC 8-YEAR-OLD ▶
SINGLE MALT 43% ABV
A flowery, buttery nose and finish, somewhat green, with a boiled-sweets taste. Unlikely to be pure malt whisky.

MURREE'S RAREST 21-YEAR-OLD
SINGLE MALT 43% ABV
This is the oldest whisky to have been produced in Asia. The Murree key notes have developed and deepened with a big dose of wood-extractive flavours.

ESTB 1861

MURREE'S
MALT WHISKY
CLASSIC
8
Years old
43% Vol   75° Proof

Single Malt Whisky
matured in oak casks

Matured & Bottled at the
Murree Brewery Co. Ltd. Rawalpindi-Pakistan
ISO 9001 Certified Company

WHISKIES

M

GREAT

NANT

Australia

The Nant Estate, Bothwell, Tasmania
www.nantdistillery.com.au

The Nant estate in Tasmania, founded in 1821, was bought by Keith and Margaret Batt in 2004 with a view to building a distillery on the historic working farm. With the expert guidance of Bill Lark (*see page 228*), the distillery went into production in April 2008. The plan is to produce a limited number of casks each year. The barley and water for the distillery come from the estate, while a restored mill provides the grist. There is also an elegant new visitor centre.

◄ NANT DOUBLE MALT
BLENDED MALT 43% ABV

This is a vatting of two casks selected from other Tasmanian distilleries, and gives an idea of what Nant's own whisky will taste like in the future. Sweet and fruity, with plums and cream soda, it is medium-bodied and smooth.

NIKKA – GRAIN & BLENDS

Japan
Nikka 1, Aobaku, Sendaishi, Miyagiken; Kurokawacho 7–6, Yoichimachi, Yoichigun, Hokkaido
www.nikka.com

Japan's second-largest distillery company was founded in 1933 by Masataka Taketsuru. This charismatic distiller had learned whisky-making in Scotland – at Longmorn on Speyside and Hazelburn in Campbeltown. ☞

NIKKA WHISKY FROM THE BARREL ▶
BLEND 51.4% ABV
Nikka's award-winning blend of malts and grain is given further ageing in first-fill bourbon casks. The nose is upfront, and slightly floral, with good intensity, peachiness, and a lift akin to rosemary oil and pine sap. The palate is lightly sweet, with some vanilla, a hint of cherry, and plenty of spiciness on the finish. This is a top blend.

NIKKA ALL MALT
BLENDED MALT 40% ABV
A blend of pot still malt and 100 per cent malt from a Coffey still. Sweet and dry oak on the nose alongside some banana. The palate is soft and unctuous.

NIKKA – GRAIN & BLENDS

His company, Nikka, operates two malt distilleries at Yoichi and Miyagikyo. It also has grain plants and a growing portfolio of styles including blends and single malts.

In recent years, Nikka has been focusing on the export market. Although its blends are available overseas, its commercial push has been through its single-malt range branded as Nikka Miyagikyo and Nikka Yoichi.

◀ NIKKA PURE MALT RED
BLENDED MALT 43% ABV
Nikka produces a blended malt range called the Pure Malt Series. The Red is light and fragrant, with faint hints of pineapple, fresh apple, pear, and a gentle almond-like oakiness.

NIKKA SINGLE COFFEY MALT
MALTED BARLEY MASH 55% ABV
This unusual whisky is made by distilling a 100 per cent malted-barley mash in a Coffey still. As a result, no one is sure if it is a malt or a grain. The nose is gentle, sweet, and rounded, with notes of banana, honey, coconut, persimmon, and dry grass. On the palate it is chewy and sweet, with nutmeg, cinnamon, peach, and vanilla.

NIKKA MIYAGIKYO

Japan
*Nikka 1, Aobaku, Sendaishi,
Miyagiken*
www.nikka.com

Also known as Sendai after its
nearest town, Miyagikyo was the
second distillery built by Nikka.
Today, it has a malt distillery with
eight stills, a grain plant with two
different set-ups, and extensive
warehousing. The predominant
style is lightly fragrant and softly
fruity. That said, there are some
peaty examples, too.

NIKKA MIYAGIKYO
10-YEAR-OLD ▶
SINGLE MALT 45% ABV
Typical of the main distillery character,
this has an attractive floral lift – lilies,
hot gorse, lilac – with a touch of anise
in the background. The palate shows
balanced, crisp oak, some butterscotch
notes, and a pine-like finish.

NIKKA MIYAGIKYO 12-YEAR-OLD
SINGLE MALT 45% ABV
The extra two years fill out the nose
with flowers, giving way to soft tropical
fruits, such as mango and persimmon,
as well as a richer vanilla pod character.
Good structure, with a wisp of smoke.

NIKKA TAKETSURU

Japan
*Nikka 1, Aobaku, Sendaishi,
Miyagiken; Kurokawacho 7–6,
Yoichimachi, Yoichigun, Hokkaido
www.nikka.com*

This small range of blended
(vatted) malts is named after
the founder of Nikka, Masataka
Taketsuru. Like the Pure Malt
Series, it is made up of component
whiskies from the firm's two sites.

◀ NIKKA TAKETSURU 17-YEAR-OLD
BLENDED MALT 43% ABV
There's obvious smoke at work here:
some cigar-box aromas, varnish, and
light leather. When diluted, a fresh
tropical-fruit character comes out.
This is what leads on the palate, before
the peat smoke begins to assert itself.

NIKKA TAKETSURU 21-YEAR-OLD
BLENDED MALT 43% ABV
With this multi-award winner, the
smoke is immediate while the spirit
behind is thicker, richer, and darker:
ripe berries, cake mix, oak, and
a touch of mushroom or truffle
indicative of age. Fruit syrups,
figs, prunes, and smoke.

NIKKA YOICHI

Japan

*Kurokawacho 7–6, Yoichimachi,
Yoichigun, Hokkaido
www.nikka.com*

Although Yoichi's malts are most
definitely Japanese, they do have
close resemblances to their cousins
in Scotland – the whiskies of Islay
and Campbeltown in particular. A
wide range of styles is made, but
Yoichi is famous for its complex,
robust, oily, and smoky malts.

NIKKA YOICHI 10-YEAR-OLD ▶
SINGLE MALT 45% ABV

There's a hint of maltiness in here.
Salt spray and light smoke on the nose
initially, with some caramelized fruit
notes. Yoichi's oiliness coats the tongue
while the smoke changes from fragrant
to sooty with dried flowers in the finish.

NIKKA YOICHI 12-YEAR-OLD
SINGLE MALT 45% ABV

This is classic Yoichi – big, deep, robust,
and complex. The peatiness adds an
earthy character to the coal-like
sootiness. Poached pear and baked
peach give a balancing sweetness,
offset by smoke, liquorice, and heather.

THE NOTCH

USA

Triple Eight Distillery,
5&7 Bartlett Farm Rd,
Nantucket, Massachusetts
www.ciscobrewers.com

Dean and Melissa Long started up
their Nantucket Winery in 1981,
and added the Cisco Brewery in
1995. Two years later they founded
the region's only micro-distillery,
Triple Eight. The first single malt
whiskey was distilled in 2000
and is called The Notch Whiskey,
because it is "not Scotch", though
it is produced in the Scottish style.
It is matured in former bourbon
barrels before being finished in
French oak Merlot barrels.

◀ THE NOTCH
SINGLE MALT 44.4% ABV

Sweet aromas of almonds and fruit
on the nose, backed by vanilla and
toasted oak. Mellow honey and pear
notes are present on the palate, which
also contains a suggestion of Merlot.
The finish is lengthy and herbal.

OBAN

Scotland
Oban, Argyll
www.malts.com

Oban Distillery dates back to
1793, when Oban itself was a tiny
West Coast fishing village. Since
then the town – which is dubbed
"The Gateway to the Isles" – has
grown up around it, preventing
the distillery from growing.

Since 1988 Oban has been one of
Diageo's "Classic Malts", albeit the
smallest of them. Given the success
of the range in America, its owners
may wonder whether it should
have picked a larger distillery.

OBAN 14-YEAR-OLD ▶
**SINGLE MALT: HIGHLANDS
43% ABV**
The brisk, maritime distillery
character is mellowed by the years
in wood. The influence of sherry
adds a rich, dried-fruit character.

OBAN DISTILLERS
EDITION 1992
**SINGLE MALT: HIGHLANDS
43% ABV**
A 15-year-old malt, aged in different
casks during maturation. Spicy and
oaky flavours dominate from the
strong sherry-wood effect.

GREAT WHISKIES

O

271

OLD CHARTER

USA

Buffalo Trace Distillery,
1001 Wilkinson Boulevard,
Frankfort, Kentucky
www.buffalotrace.com

The Old Charter brand dates back to 1874, and the name is a direct reference to the Charter Oak tree, where Connecticut's colonial charter was hidden from the British in 1687. The Buffalo Trace Distillery itself dates back to the early 1900s and is listed on the National Register of Historic Places.

◀ **OLD CHARTER 8-YEAR-OLD**
BOURBON 40% ABV
Initially dry and peppery on the nose, with sweet and buttery aromas following through. Mouth-coating, with fruit, vanilla, old leather, and cloves on the palate. The finish is long and sophisticated.

OLD CROW

USA

Jim Beam Distillery,
149 Happy Hollow Road,
Clermont, Kentucky
www.jimbeam.com

Old Crow takes its name from
the 19th-century Scottish-born
chemist and Kentucky distiller
James Christopher Crow. Along
with Old Grand-Dad and Old
Taylor, this brand was acquired by
Jim Beam from National Distillers
in 1987, and the three distilleries
associated with these bourbons
were closed. All production now
takes place at Jim Beam's distilleries
in Boston and Clermont.

OLD CROW ▶
BOURBON 40% ABV
Complex on the nose, with malt,
rye, and sharp fruit notes combining
with gentle spice. The palate follows
through with spicy, malty, and citric
elements, with citrus and spice notes
to the fore.

O

WHISKIES

GREAT

273

OLD FITZGERALD

USA

Heaven Hill Distillery,
1701 West Breckinridge Street,
Louisville, Kentucky
www.heaven-hill.com

Old Fitzgerald was named by
John E. Fitzgerald, who founded
a distillery at Frankfort in 1870.
The brand moved to its present
home of Louisville when the
Stitzel brothers, Frederick and
Philip, merged their company
with that of William Larue Weller
& Sons, and subsequently opened
the new Stitzel-Weller distillery
at Louisville in 1935.

◄ VERY SPECIAL OLD FITZGERALD 12-YEAR-OLD
BOURBON 45% ABV

A complex and well-balanced bourbon,
made with some wheat in the mashbill,
rather than rye. The nose is rich, fruity,
and leathery, while the palate exhibits
sweet and fruity notes balanced by
spices and oak. The finish is long and
drying, with vanilla fading to oak.

OLD FORESTER

USA

Brown-Forman Distillery,
850 Dixie Highway,
Louisville, Kentucky
www.brown-forman.com

The origins of the Old Forester
brand date back to 1870, when
George Garvin Brown established
a distillery in Louisville, Kentucky.
The whiskey initially used the
spelling "Forrester", and some
say the name was selected to
honour Confederate army officer
General Nathan Bedford Forrest.

OLD FORESTER ▶
BOURBON 43% ABV
Complex, with pronounced floral
notes, vanilla, spice, pepper, fruit,
chocolate, and menthol on the nose.
Full and fruity in the mouth, where rye
and peaches vie with fudge, nutmeg,
and oak. The finish offers more rye,
toffee, liquorice, and drying oak.

OLD FORESTER
BIRTHDAY BOURBON (2007)
BOURBON 47% ABV
The 2007 release is sweet on the nose,
with cinnamon, caramel, vanilla, and
mint. The palate is full and complex,
with caramel, apples, and vanilla oak.
The finish is lengthy, warm and clean.

OLD GRAND-DAD

USA

Jim Beam Distillery,
149 Happy Hollow Road,
Clermont, Kentucky
www.jimbeam.com

Old Grand-Dad was established in 1882 by a grandson of distiller Basil Hayden (*see p39*). The brand and its distillery eventually passed into the hands of American Brands (now Fortune Brands Inc) which subsequently closed the distillery. Production now takes place in the Jim Beam distilleries in Clermont and Boston.

◀ **OLD GRAND-DAD**
BOURBON 43–57% ABV
Made with a comparatively high percentage of rye, the nose of Old Grand-Dad reveals oranges and peppery spices. Quite heavy-bodied, the taste is full, yet surprisingly smooth, considering the strength. Fruit, nuts, and caramel are foremost on the palate, while the finish is long and oily.

OLD PARR

Scotland
Owner: Diageo

The original "Old Parr" was one Thomas Parr, who lived from 1483 to 1635, making him 152 years old when he died. If that seems improbable, his tomb can be inspected in Poets' Corner, Westminster Abbey.

In 1871, Old Parr's name was borrowed by two famous blenders of their day, the Greenlees brothers, for their deluxe whisky. Now under the stewardship of industry giants Diageo, the brand has gone on to success in Japan, Venezuela, Mexico, and Colombia. By tradition, Cragganmore is the mainstay of the blend.

GRAND OLD PARR 12-YEAR-OLD ▶
BLEND 43% ABV
Pronounced malt, raisin, and orange notes on the nose, with some apple and dried-fruit undertones, and perhaps a hint of peat. Forceful on the palate, with flavours of malt, raisin, burnt caramel, and brown sugar.

O

OLD POTRERO

USA

Anchor Distilling Company,
1705 Marisposa Street,
San Francisco, California
www.anchorbrewing.com

Fritz Maytag is one of the pioneers of the American "micro-drinks" movement. In 1994 he added a small distillery to his brewery on San Francisco's Potrero Hill. Here, Maytag aims to "re-create the original whiskey of America", making small batches of spirit in traditional, open pot stills, using 100 per cent rye malt.

◀ OLD POTRERO
SINGLE MALT RYE 62.55% ABV
This "18th-century-style" whiskey displays a floral, nutty nose, with vanilla and spice. Oily and smooth on the palate, with mint, honey, chocolate, and pepper in the lengthy finish.

OLD POTRERO RYE
RYE WHISKEY 45% ABV
Aged for three years in new, charred-oak barrels, this 19th-century-style whiskey boasts nuts, buttery vanilla, sweet oak, and pepper on the nose. Complex in the mouth, oily, sweet, and spicy, with caramel, oak, and spicy rye notes in the finish.

OLD PULTENEY

Scotland

Pulteney Distillery, Wick, Caithness
www.oldpulteney.com

Wick was a tiny village when the
British Fisheries Society, under
the directorship of Sir William
Pulteney, resolved to turn it into
a model fishing port in the 1790s.
In 1826, with the trade in herring
booming, local distiller James
Henderson named his new
distillery in his honour.

The solitary wash still comes
with a giant ball, to increase reflux,
and a truncated top, supposedly
lopped off to fit the still room.

**OLD PULTENEY
12-YEAR-OLD ▶**
SINGLE MALT: HIGHLANDS
40% ABV
A brisk, salty, maritime malt with
a woody sweetness from ageing in
bourbon casks.

OLD PULTENEY 17-YEAR-OLD
SINGLE MALT: HIGHLANDS
46% ABV
The 17-year-old is partly matured in
sherry wood, to add fruity, butterscotch
notes to the flavour. Medium-full body
in the mouth, with a long finish.

OLD SMUGGLER

Scotland
Owner: Gruppo Campari

Reputedly, and appropriately, a big favourite during Prohibition, Old Smuggler was first developed by James and George Stodart in 1835. Although the firm is today largely forgotten, history records that it was the first to marry its whisky in sherry butts. The brand is now owned by Gruppo Campari, who acquired it along with its sister blend Braemar and the flagship Glen Grant Distillery from Pernod Ricard in 2006. It continues to hold a significant position in the US and Argentina, where it is the second-bestselling whisky, and is reported to be developing strong sales in Eastern Europe.

◀ OLD SMUGGLER
BLEND 40% ABV
Decent Scotch with no offensive overtones and some smoke hints. Blended for value, and for drinking with a mixer.

OLD TAYLOR

USA

Jim Beam Distillery,
149 Happy Hollow Road,
Clermont, Kentucky
www.jimbeam.com

Old Taylor was introduced by
Edmund Haynes Taylor Jr, who
was associated at various times
with three distilleries in the
Frankfort area of Kentucky,
including what is now Buffalo
Trace (*see p66*). He was the man
responsible for the Bottled-in-
Bond Act of 1897, which
guaranteed a whiskey's quality
– any bottle bearing an official
government seal had to be 100
proof (50% ABV) and at least four
years old. Old Taylor was bought
by Fortune Brands in 1987.

OLD TAYLOR ▶
BOURBON 40% ABV
Light and orangey on the nose, with
a hint of marzipan; sweet, honeyed,
and slightly oaky on the palate.

P&M

France
Domaine Mavela, Brasserie Pietra,
Route de La Marana,
20600 Furiani, Corsica
www.brasseriepietra.com

P&M is a fruitful cooperation
between two companies on the
Mediterranean island of Corsica.
Founded as a brewery in 1996,
Pietra produces the mash that
is distilled at Mavela. The pure
malt whisky is aged in casks made
of oak from the local forest. Other
spirits produced at Mavela include
P&M Blend and P&M Blend
Supérieur. Cask type and age
are not specified.

◀ P&M PURE MALT
MALT 42% ABV
This complex, aromatic whisky has
a subtle aroma of honey, apricot,
and citrus fruit, and a rich flavour.

PADDY

Midleton Distillery,
Midleton, County Cork
www.irishdistillers.ie

There was a time when Irish
whiskey was sold anonymously
from casks in pubs. What whiskey
a pub stocked was down to the
owner and his relationship with
the agent for the distillery.

Paddy Flaherty was an agent
for the Cork Distillers Company
of Midleton in the 1920s and 30s.
You knew when he was in town,
as he'd stand everyone free drinks
at the bar, and the whiskey he sold
– the CDC's Old Irish Whiskey –
became so synonymous with the
man himself that it was simply
known as Paddy's whiskey.

PADDY ▶
BLEND 40% ABV
This is a malty dram, which is both
solid and well matured. It offers
a satisfying, spicy, peppery kick.

PASSPORT

Scotland
Owner: Chivas Brothers

Passport was developed by
Seagram and acquired by
Pernod Ricard in 2002. Like
many brands that are invisible
in the UK, it enjoys conspicuous
success elsewhere: Passport's
main strongholds are the US,
South Korea, Spain, and Brazil,
where its fruity taste lends itself
to being served on the rocks, in
mixed drinks, and in cocktails.
Packaged in a distinctive retro,
rectangular green bottle, Passport
is "a unique Scotch whisky,
inspired by the revolution of
1960s Britain, with a young
and vibrant personality". Such
distinguished and famous malts
as Glenlivet are found in the blend.

◀ PASSPORT
BLEND 40% ABV
A fruity taste and a deliciously
creamy finish. It can be served
straight or, more usually, mixed
over ice. Medium-bodied, with
a soft and mellow finish.

PENDERYN

Wales

Penderyn, near Aberdare
www.welsh-whisky.co.uk

Currently the only whisky
distillery in Wales, Penderyn was
named "Microdistillery Whisky
of the Year" in 2008 by leading
American whisky magazine *Malt
Advocate*. It is indeed micro,
producing only one cask a day.
After a slow start, the distillery
is now acknowledged worldwide
as makers of exquisite whiskies.

Penderyn whisky is matured
in ex-bourbon casks, mainly from
Buffalo Trace and Evan Williams.
The contents are then re-casked
into ex-Madeira barrels – hence
the sweet taste. The label does
not state a specific age.

PENDERYN AUR CYMRU ▶
SINGLE MALT 46% ABV
Zesty and fresh, this malt is prickly,
fruity, and bitter-sweet.

PENDERYN PEATED
SINGLE MALT 46% ABV
Sweet, aromatic smoke followed by
vanilla, green apples, and refreshing
citrus notes.

PEREGRINE ROCK

USA

Saint James Spirits,
5220 Fourth Street,
Irwindale, California
www.saintjamesspirits.com

Saint James Spirits was founded
in 1995 by teacher Jim Busuttil,
who learnt the craft of distilling
in Germany and Switzerland.
He has been making single malt
whisky (note the Scottish spelling)
since 1997, and Peregrine Rock
is produced from peated Scottish
barley in a 40-US-gallon (150-
litre) alambic copper pot still
and put into bourbon barrels
for a minimum of three years.

◀ PEREGRINE ROCK CALIFORNIA PURE
SINGLE MALT 40% ABV
Floral on the nose, with fresh fruits
and a hint of smoke. The palate is
delicate and fruity, with a citric twist
to it, while sweeter, malty, and new-
mown-grass notes develop in the
slightly smoky finish.

PIG'S NOSE

Scotland
Owner: Spencerfield Spirits
www.spencerfieldspirit.com

Should you visit one of the UK's
many agricultural or county fairs,
you may well encounter this
whisky being sold from the back
of an old horse box. Do not walk
away: Pig's Nose has been re-
blended by Whyte & Mackay's
superstar master blender, Richard
Paterson, and launched back on
to the market in smart new livery.
Brother to the better-known blended
malt Sheep Dip (*see p315*), Pig's
Nose is a full-flavoured and
drinkable blend that more than
lives up to the claim that "our
Scotch is as soft and smooth
as a pig's nose".

PIG'S NOSE ▶
BLEND 40% ABV
The nose is delicate and refined, with
soft and sensual floral notes supported
by complex fruit flavours. On the
palate, there is a forceful array of
malty flavours from Scotland's four
distilling regions.

PIKESVILLE

USA
Heaven Hill Distillery,
1701 West Breckinridge Street,
Louisville, Kentucky
www.heaven-hill.com

Rye whiskeys fall into two
stylistic types, namely the
spicy, tangy Pennsylvania style,
as exemplified by Rittenhouse
(see p300), and the Maryland
style, which is softer in character.
Pikesville is arguably the only
example of Maryland rye still
being produced today. This
whiskey takes its name from
Pikesville in Maryland, where
it was first distilled during the
1890s, and last produced in
1972. A decade later the brand
was acquired by Heaven Hill.

◄ **PIKESVILLE SUPREME**
RYE WHISKEY 40% ABV
The crisp nose presents bubble
gum, fruit, and wood varnish, while
on the palate there is more bubble
gum, spice, oak, and overt vanilla.
The finish comprises lingering
vanilla and oranges.

PINWINNIE ROYALE

Scotland
Owner: Inver House Distillers

Pinwinnie Royale stands out from
the crowd, its label hinting at an
early ecclesiastical manuscript
and regal connections, though
there is little to support these
romantic suppositions. Given its
place in the Inver House stable,
it would seem likely that Old
Pulteney, Speyburn, anCnoc,
and Balblair single malts are
to be found in the blend, with
the emphasis on the lesser-known
names. As well as the standard
expression, there is a 12-year-old
version, which mixes a light
Speyside fruitiness with drier
background wood notes, and
a buttery texture.

PINWINNIE ROYALE ▶
BLEND 40% ABV
Young, spirity fruitiness on the
nose, smooth-textured but spicy
in the mouth, with burnt, sooty
notes in the finish.

POIT DHUBH

Scotland
Owner: The Gaelic Whisky Co.
www.gaelicwhisky.com

Pràban na Linne (also known as the Gaelic Whisky Co.) was established by Sir Iain Noble in 1976 to create employment in the south of Skye. The business has grown steadily since. Poit Dhubh (pronounced *Potch Ghoo*) is a non chill-filtered blended malt supplied as 8-, 12-, and 21-year-olds. A limited-edition 30-year-old was bottled for the company's 30th anniversary. Poit Dhubh makes much play of the possible bootleg nature of its whisky, stating, "We are unwilling either to confirm or deny that Poit Dhubh comes from an illicit still." This is, of course, complete fantasy.

◀ POIT DHUBH 8-YEAR-OLD
BLENDED MALT 43% ABV
Dried fruits and a light spiciness give a bittersweet character, with dry, woody notes and a trace of peat.

PORT ELLEN

Scotland
Port Ellen, Isle of Islay

Of all Islay malts, Port Ellen has possibly the largest cult following, owing to its rarity, which has increased every year since the distillery shut down in 1983. It was founded in 1825 by Alexander Kerr Mackay, and remained in family hands until the 1920s, when it became part of DCL (Distillers Company Ltd). Its misfortune was to be part of the same stable as Lagavulin and Caol Ila: when the downturn came, it was the weakest link. Today it remains active as a maltings plant, supplying Islay's distilleries with most of their malt.

PORT ELLEN DOUGLAS LAING 26-YEAR-OLD ▶

SINGLE MALT: ISLAY 50% ABV
Matured in refill bourbon casks, this bottling has a sweet and fruity nose, with some new leather. Sweetness on the palate, but overwhelmed by peat smoke. A long, tarry finish, with a dab of salt.

POWERS

Ireland
*Midleton Distillery,
Midleton, County Cork
www.irishdistillers.ie*

For longer than anyone could remember, Jameson and Powers used to stare each other down across the River Liffey in the heart of Dublin. The Powers family (on Dublin's south side) had been in the business since 1817, and a member of the family sat on the board of Irish Distillers until it was incorporated into the Pernod Ricard group, some 171 years later.

◀ POWERS GOLD LABEL
BLEND 40% ABV
This whiskey is something really special. The nose is classically Irish – at once bracing and brittle. At core, this whiskey is pure pot still, cut with just enough good grain. Powers Gold Label is an utterly captivating blend.

POWERS GOLD LABEL 12-YEAR-OLD
BLEND 40% ABV
An older, more layered expression of the same Powers formulation. Spice, honey, crème brûlée, with soft wood tones and sweet, fresh fruits.

PRIME BLUE

Scotland
Owner: Morrison Bowmore

Prime Blue is a blended malt available largely in Taiwan, where the market has developed in sensational style during the last decade. The colour blue is said to convey nobility and royalty, and the brand name was reputedly chosen to reflect sophistication in the whisky's taste. At their peak, sales exceeded 1 million cases a year, although the market for this style in the Far East has declined somewhat in recent years and competition in Taiwan and elsewhere has intensified. Standard, 12-, 17-, and 21-year-old versions are available.

PRIME BLUE ▶
BLENDED MALT 40% ABV
Aromas of vanilla and malted barley are soon followed by light cocoa, and then heathery, floral notes. Initially fruity on the palate, followed by a malty sweetness, and a long finish.

PRINTER'S

Czech Republic
*Stock Plzen, Palirenska 2,
32600 Plzen
www.stock.cz*

Stock Plzen was founded in the
1920s and is the best-known
spirits producer in the Czech
Republic, with a high-profile,
high-volume ethos. The company
makes 40 different spirits,
including Printer's Whisky, which
it claims is made using traditional
Scotch whisky production
methods. Another offering is
Whisky Cream Stock, which is a
cream liqueur made from Printer's
Whisky and bottled at 17% ABV.

◄ **PRINTER'S 6-YEAR-OLD**
BLEND 40% ABV
A delicate, peated whisky aged in small
oak barrels for a faster maturation.

QUEEN ANNE

Scotland
Owner: Chivas Brothers

A good example of an "orphan brand" that has found its way into the portfolio of a larger company and appears to lack any clear role and purpose, Queen Anne was once a leading name from the distinguished Edinburgh blenders Hill, Thomson & Co. It was first produced in 1884 and blended by one William Shaw. Today it belongs to Chivas Brothers. Like so many once-famous and proud brands, Queen Anne has been left bereft and isolated by consolidation in the Scotch whisky industry, steadfastly clinging on in one or more regions where once it was loved and popular.

QUEEN ANNE ▶
BLEND 40% ABV
Not especially characterful, as the flavours are so tightly integrated that it is difficult to discern individual aromas or tastes. A standard blend for mixing.

REBEL YELL

USA
Luxco, Bernheim Distillery,
St Louis, Missouri
www.luxco.com

Made at the Bernheim Distillery
in Louisville, Rebel Yell is distilled
with a percentage of wheat in its
mashbill, instead of rye. Whiskey
was first made to the Rebel Yell
recipe 1849 and, after enjoying
popularity in the southern states
for many years, the brand was
finally released on an international
basis during the 1980s. In addition
to the standard bottling, there is
also a limited-edition Rebel
Reserve expression.

◀ **REBEL YELL**
BOURBON 40% ABV

A nose of honey, raisins, and butter
leads into a big-bodied bourbon,
which again features honey and
a buttery quality, along with plums
and soft leather. The finish is long
and spicier than might be expected
from the palate.

REDBREAST

Ireland

*Midleton Distillery, Midleton,
County Cork*
www.irishdistillers.ie

Redbreast was the name that
wine merchants Gilbey's gave to
the Jameson whiskey that they
matured and bottled. The bonded
trade was finally phased out in
1968, but Redbreast was so
popular that it was allowed to
continue well into the 1980s.

In the 1990s, Irish Distillers
bought the brand from Gilbey's
and re-launched the drink as a
12-year-old pure pot still, part-
matured in sherry wood. There
is also a limited-edition 15-year-
old version.

REDBREAST 12-YEAR-OLD ▶
PURE POT STILL 40% ABV
This is, without doubt, one of the
world's finest whiskeys. Flavours range
from ginger to cinnamon, peppermint
to linseed, and liquorice to camphor.
A sherry note sets off an elegant finish.

WHISKIES

R

GREAT

REISETBAUER

Austria
Axberg 15, 4062 Kirchberg-Thening
www.reisetbauer.at

Hans Reisetbauer initially made
a name for himself as a quality
distiller of fruits. Then, in 1995,
he decided to start distilling single
malt whisky – growing his own
barley, malting, and fermenting
on his own premises. The wash is
distilled twice in copper pot stills.
For maturation, Reisetbauer uses
ex-wine casks that previously
contained Trockenbeerenauslese
and Chardonnay.

◄ REISETBAUER 7-YEAR-OLD
SINGLE MALT 43% ABV
Delicate and multi-layered on the
nose, with slightly roasted aromas
reminiscent of hazelnuts and dried
herbs. Pleasant notes of bread and
cereals on the palate. Slightly smoky,
with fine spice.

REISETBAUER 12-YEAR-OLD
MALT 48% ABV
Similar to the 7-year-old, with greater
emphasis on fruit notes from the wine
barrels used for maturation.

RIDGEMONT

USA

Tom Moore Distillery, 1 Barton Road, Bardstown, Kentucky

When this bourbon was introduced to the market in 2004, it was initially called Ridgewood Reserve but, after litigation between the distillers and Woodford Reserve's owners Brown-Forman, the name was changed. The "1792" element of the name pays homage to the year in which Kentucky became a state.

1792 RIDGEMONT RESERVE ▶
BOURBON 46.85% ABV
This comparatively delicate and complex 8-year-old small-batch bourbon boasts a soft nose with vanilla, caramel, leather, rye, corn, and spice notes. Oily and initially sweet on the palate, caramel and spicy rye develop along with a suggestion of oak. The finish is oaky, spicy, and quite long, with a hint of lingering caramel.

WHISKIES

R

GREAT

299

RITTENHOUSE RYE

USA

Heaven Hill Distillery,
1701 West Breckinridge Street,
Louisville, Kentucky
www.heaven-hill.com

Once associated with the rye whiskey-making heartland of Pennsylvania, Rittenhouse Rye now survives in Kentucky, and its mashbill comprises 51 per cent rye, 37 per cent corn, and 12 per cent barley.

◄ RITTENHOUSE RYE 21-YEAR-OLD
RYE WHISKEY 50% ABV
The nose is notably spicy, with nuts and oranges, while on the palate powerful spices and oak meet lemon and much sweeter notes of lavender and violet. The finish is a long, bitter, rye classic.

RITTENHOUSE RYE 100 PROOF
RYE WHISKEY 50% ABV
Marshmallow and lemon merge on the notably sweet nose, while the lemon carries over into the mouth, where it is joined by black pepper, liquorice, and caramel. The finish features dark chocolate and treacle toffee.

ROBERT BURNS

Scotland
Owner: Isle of Arran Distillers
www.arranwhisky.com

With the Scotch whisky industry generally apt to employ Scottish imagery and heritage associations at the drop of a tam-o'-shanter, it is a surprise to find that no one had previously marketed a brand named after Scotland's national bard. Independent distiller Isle of Arran has worked with the World Burns Federation to fill this gap, and now produces an officially endorsed Burns Collection of blended whiskies and malts.

ROBERT BURNS BLEND ▶
BLEND 40% ABV
Hints of oak on the nose give way to sherry, almonds, toffee, and ripe fruits. Plenty of toffee, cake, and dried fruits on the palate, with a light to medium, spicy finish.

ROBERT BURNS SINGLE MALT
SINGLE MALT 40% ABV
A nose of green apples, the acidity tempered by a note of vanilla. Apple and citrus notes on the palate, balanced by vanilla again. An aperitif whisky that is light in style and finish.

ROGUE SPIRITS

USA
*Rogue Brewery, 1339 NW Flanders,
Portland, Oregon*
www.rogue.com

Dead Guy Ale was created
in the early 1990s to celebrate
the Mayan Day of the Dead
(1 November, or All Souls' Day)
and, in 2008, the Oregon-based
producers launched their Dead
Guy Whiskey. It is distilled using
the same four malts used in the
creation of Dead Guy Ale, and
fermented wort from the brewery
is taken to the nearby Rogue
House of Spirits, where it is
double-distilled in a 150-US-
gallon (570-litre) copper pot
still. A brief maturation period
follows, in charred American
white-oak casks.

◄ **DEAD GUY**
BLENDED MALT 40% ABV
Youthful on the nose, with notes of
corn, wheat, and fresh, juicy orange.
The palate is medium-dry, fruity, and
lively. Pepper and cinnamon feature
in the finish.

ROSEBANK

Scotland
Camelon, Falkirk

Few Scottish distilleries have
managed to stay in continuous
production. Many closed during
the 1980s and '90s when the
industry was dealing with oversupply. Whether a distillery
survived when demand picked
up depended largely on location.
Rosebank, near Falkirk, was
closed in 1993 and has since been
redeveloped into offices and flats.
Founded in 1840, it was chosen to
be part of The Ascot Malt Cellar in
1982. Unfortunately for Rosebank,
when this became the 'Classic
Malts' series, Glenkinchie was
picked to represent the Lowlands
rather than Rosebank.

ROSEBANK DOUGLAS LAING 16-YEAR-OLD ▶
SINGLE MALT: LOWLANDS 50% ABV

This independent bottling from
Douglas Laing is part of its Old Malt
Cask collection. Despite its strength
and age, it is fresh and citrussy.

ROYAL BRACKLA

Scotland
Cawdor, Nairn, Nairnshire

Brackla was founded between the
River Findhorn and the Murray
Firth by Captain William Fraser
in 1812. He was soon complaining
that, although he was surrounded
by whisky-drinkers, he could only
sell 450 litres (100 gallons) a year.
By way of compensation, he
secured the first royal warrant
for a distillery in 1835. Whether
he would recognize Royal Brackla
today seems unlikely: it was fully
modernized in the 1970s and 1990s
and now belongs to Bacardi, who
launched a 10-year-old in 2004.

◀ ROYAL BRACKLA
10-YEAR-OLD
SINGLE MALT: HIGHLANDS
40% ABV
Aside from a limited-edition 25-year-
old, this is the only official bottling.
It has a grassy, floral nose and some
spicy, oily notes on the tongue.

ROYAL CHALLENGE

India
Owner: United Spirits
www.unitedspirits.in

This "blend of rare Scotch and matured Indian malt whiskies" is owned by Shaw Wallace, a part of United Spirits since 2005. It is described as "the iconic" premium Indian whisky and, until 2008, it was also the bestselling premium Indian whisky, but is now severely challenged by Blenders Pride *(see p56)*.

ROYAL CHALLENGE ▶
BLEND 42.8% ABV

A soft, rounded nose, with traces of malt, nuts, caramel, and a light rubber note. These aromas translate well in the taste at full strength. With water, it remains dense and full-bodied but the taste, diluted, is not as heavy. Very sweet, slightly nutty, and mouth-drying, but with a longish finish.

R

ROYAL LOCHNAGAR

Scotland
Ballater, Aberdeenshire
www.malts.com

This charming distillery sits alone on Deeside as the only whisky-making business in the area. It was founded in 1845 by John Begg, who wasted no time in asking his new neighbours at Balmoral Castle– Queen Victoria and Prince Albert – to look round his distillery. By the end of 1848, Lochnagar had become Royal Lochnagar. Today it is owned by Diageo.

◀ ROYAL LOCHNAGAR 12-YEAR-OLD
SINGLE MALT: HIGHLANDS 40% ABV
A subtle, leathery nose with a flavour that becomes drier and more acidic before a spicy, sandalwood finish.

ROYAL LOCHNAGAR SELECTED RESERVE
SINGLE MALT: HIGHLANDS 43% ABV
Deep, complex malt with a resinous, sweet, woody character and hints of apple pie and burnt sugar.

ROYAL SALUTE

Scotland
Owner: Chivas Brothers

Originally produced by Seagram in 1953 to commemorate the coronation of Queen Elizabeth II, Royal Salute claims to be the first super-premium whisky.

Historically, Chivas Brothers were noted for their exceptional stocks of rare, aged whiskies, and these formed the basis for the Royal Salute expressions. Now controlled by Pernod Ricard, the blenders, led by the highly respected Colin Scott, have access to single malts from well-known distilleries like Glenlivet, Aberlour, Strathisla, and Longmorn.

ROYAL SALUTE 21-YEAR-OLD ▶
BLEND 40% ABV
Soft, fruity aromas balanced with a delicate floral fragrance and mellow, honeyed sweetness.

ROYAL SALUTE, THE HUNDRED CASK SELECTION
BLEND 40% ABV
Elegant, creamy, and exceptionally smooth, with a mellow, oaky, slightly smoky finish.

RUSSELL'S RESERVE

USA
Boulevard Distillery,
Lawrenceburg, Kentucky

Master Distiller Jimmy Russell and his son Eddie, of Wild Turkey fame, developed this small-batch rye whiskey, launched in 2007.

According to Eddie Russell, "we knew the whiskey we wanted, but had never tasted it before. This one really makes the grade – deep character and taste and, at six years, aged to perfection."

◀ RUSSELL'S RESERVE RYE
RYE WHISKEY 45% ABV
Fruity, with fresh oak and almonds on the nose. Full-bodied and robust, yet smooth. Almonds, pepper, and rye dominate the palate, while the finish is long, dry, and characteristically bitter.

RUSSELL'S RESERVE 10-YEAR-OLD
BOURBON 45% ABV
This bourbon boasts a nose of pine, vanilla, soft leather, and caramel. More vanilla, toffee, almond, honey, and coconut in the mouth, and a slightly unusual note of chilli that continues through the lengthy, spicy finish.

SAM HOUSTON

USA

*McLain & Kyne Ltd (Castle Brands),
Louisville, Kentucky
www.mclainandkyne.com*

McLain & Kyne Ltd is best known
for what it terms "very small batch
bourbons", and the firm blends
whiskey from as few as eight to
twelve barrels of varying ages for
their Jefferson's *(see p201)* and
Sam Houston bourbon brands.

Sam Houston was introduced
in 1999 and is named after the
colourful 19th-century soldier,
statesman, and politician Samuel
Houston, who became the first
president of the Republic of Texas.

SAM HOUSTON SMALL BATCH 10-YEAR-OLD ▶
BOURBON (VARIABLE ABV)

The nose offers delicate aromas of red
berries, oak, and rye bread, while the
rich, tangy palate boasts resin, nutmeg,
rye bread, leather, and gentle spice.
Long, sweet, and textured in the finish.

SAZERAC RYE

USA
Buffalo Trace Distillery,
1001 Wilkinson Boulevard,
Frankfort, Kentucky
www.buffalotrace.com

Sazerac Rye is part of the
annually updated Buffalo Trace
Antique Collection and, having
been aged for 18 years, is the
oldest rye whiskey currently
available. Buffalo Trace says that
the 18-year-old 2008 release is
comprised of whiskey that has
been ageing in its warehouse
on the first floor – the first floor
enables the barrels to age slowly
and gracefully.

◀ **SAZERAC RYE 18-YEAR-OLD**
RYE WHISKEY 45% ABV
Rich on the nose, with maple syrup
and a hint of menthol. This expression
is oily on the palate, fresh, and lively,
with fruit, pepper, and pleasing oak
notes. The finish boasts lingering
pepper, with returning fruit and
a final flavour of molasses.

SCAPA

Scotland
St Ola, Orkney
www.scapamalt.com

Founded in 1885 on "Mainland",
the largest of the Orkney islands,
Scapa kept going more or less
continuously until 1994, when
it was shut down. Although
production resumed three
years later, it was only on a
seasonal basis, using staff from
its neighbour, Highland Park.
For years it seemed there was
only room for one viable distillery
on Orkney – that being Highland
Park – but Scapa's rescue came
in the form of Allied Domecq,
and over £2m was lavished on
it in 2004. The company has since
been bought by Chivas Brothers.

SCAPA 14-YEAR-OLD ▶
SINGLE MALT: ISLANDS
40% ABV
Compared to the robust, smoky
Highland Park, Scapa is softer and
a little sweeter. It has a heathery,
dried-fruit character with a
gentle spiciness.

SCOTTISH LEADER

Scotland
Owner: Burn Stewart Distillers

The owner describes Scottish Leader as an "international award-winning blend with a honey rich smooth taste profile. It has a growing presence in a number of world markets". The blend's heart is Deanston single malt, from the Perthshire distillery of the same name. Initially targeted at the value-conscious supermarket buyer, Scottish Leader has recently been repackaged and shows signs of an attempted move somewhat upmarket. The blends are now available in non-aged and 12-year-old expressions.

◀ **SCOTTISH LEADER**
BLEND 40% ABV
A standard blend in which the flavour characteristics are tightly integrated. Not much to mark it out, but okay for mixing or drinking on the rocks.

SEAGRAM'S

Canada
*Diageo Canada, West Mall,
Etobicoke, Ontario*
www.diageo.com

Joseph Emm Seagram ran a
flour mill in Ontario in the 1860s,
where he became interested in
distilling as a way of using surplus
grains. By 1883, distilling was the
core business and Seagram was
the sole owner. The brand 83
commemorates this. The VO
brand stands for "Very Own" and
was once the best-selling Canadian
whisky in the world. Diageo now
controls the Canadian Seagram's
labels, as well as Seagram's 7 Crown
(see p314), which is marketed as
an American whiskey.

SEAGRAM'S VO ▶
BLEND 40% ABV
The nose presents pear drops, caramel,
and some rye spice, along with butter.
Light-bodied, sweet, and lightly spicy,
with a slightly acerbic mouthfeel.

SEAGRAM'S 83
BLEND 40% ABV
At one time, this was even more
popular than VO. Now it is a standard
Canadian: smooth and easy to drink.

SEAGRAM'S 7 CROWN

USA
*Angostura Distillery,
Lawrenceburg, Indiana*

One of the best known and most characterful blended American whiskeys, Seagram's 7 Crown has survived the break-up of the Seagram distilling empire and is now produced by Caribbean-based Angostura (of Angostura Bitters fame). This relative newcomer to the US distilling arena has acquired the former Seagram distillery at Lawrenceburg, where 7 Crown is made, along with the long-shuttered Charles Medley Distillery in Owensboro Kentucky. The Lawrenceburg distillery is the largest spirits facility in the USA in terms of production capacity.

◄ SEAGRAM'S 7 CROWN
BLEND 40% ABV
This possesses a delicate nose with a hint of spicy rye, and is clean and well structured on the spicy palate.

SHEEP DIP

Scotland
Owner: Spencerfield Spirits
www.spencerfieldspirit.com

Sheep Dip is one of the better blended malts. The brand has been around since the 1970s but, under the ownership of Whyte & Mackay, was largely ignored. In 2005, it was taken on by Alex and Jane Nicol, who aim to rebuild the former glory of so-called "orphan brands". Since then, they've introduced new packaging, appointed a global network of agents and, most important of all, reformulated the whisky under the guidance of master blender Richard Paterson. It seems to be working. The whiskies are aged between 8 and 12 years in quality first-fill wood, producing a great dram.

SHEEP DIP ▶
BLENDED MALT 40% ABV
The nose is delicate and refined. Great finesse on the palate, then a majestic assertion of pure malty flavours.

SIGNATURE

India

Owner: United Spirits
www.unitedspirits.in

The recently introduced Signature Rare Aged Whisky comes from the McDowell's stable, owned by United Spirits, and has the slogan "Success is Good Fun". It is a blend of Scotch and Indian malt whiskies and is the fastest-growing brand in the company's portfolio. It has also won a clutch of international awards, including a gold in the Monde Selection 2006.

◀ SIGNATURE
BLEND 42.8% ABV

A rich nose, with a distinct medicinal note. Straight, the taste is surprisingly sweet, with smoky and medicinal undertones, becoming less sweet with water. Relatively light in body, with a distinct peaty, smoky edge.

SLYRS

Germany
Bayrischzellerstrasse 13 ,
83727 Schliersee, Ortsteil Neuhaus
www.slyrs.de

Slyrs was founded in 1999 and
makes a credible whisky, which
is distributed by Lantenhammer,
a schnapps distillery located in the
same village. Slyrs is bottled after
maturing for an unspecified time
in new American white-oak
barrels. In October 2008, Raritas
Diaboli, a special cask-strength
edition, was launched.

SLYRS ▶
SINGLE MALT 43% ABV
Some flowery aromas and spicy notes
deliver a nice and easy dram. The taste
varies according to the vintage.

SOMETHING SPECIAL

Scotland
Owner: Chivas Brothers

It's quite a name to live up to, but "something special" is a justifiable claim for this premium blend, which is the third bestselling whisky in South America, with sales of over half a million cases. The blend dates back to 1912, when it was created by the directors of Hill, Thomson & Co of Edinburgh. The primary component is drawn from Speyside malts, especially the highly regarded Longmorn, which is at the heart of the blend. A 15-year-old version was launched in 2006. The distinctive bottle is said to have been inspired by an Edinburgh diamond-cutter.

◀ **SOMETHING SPECIAL**
BLEND 40% ABV

A distinctive blend of dry, fruity, and spicy flavours, with a subtle, smoky, sweetness on the palate.

SPEYBURN

Scotland
Rothes, Aberlour, Morayshire
www.inverhouse.com

Whether she knew it or not, Queen Victoria's loyal subjects at the newly built Speyburn Distillery near Rothes laboured through the night to produce a whisky for her Diamond Jubilee in 1897. It was mid-December and, though the windows were not yet in place and snow was swirling in from outside, the distillery manager ordered the stills to be fired up. Speyburn has retained its Victorian charm and, since 1991, has been owned by Inver House.

SPEYBURN 10-YEAR-OLD ▶
SINGLE MALT: SPEYSIDE
40% ABV
Despite the release of older expressions, including a 25-year-old Solera, the core expression of Speyburn remains the 10-year-old, which has a flavour of vanilla fudge and a sweet, lingering finish.

SPEYSIDE

Scotland
Glen Tromie, Kingussie,
Inverness-shire
www.speysidedistillery.co.uk

With a production of just 600,000
litres (130,000 gallons), the distillery
named after Scotland's biggest
malt whisky region is no giant.
Nor is it all that old. Despite its
rustic appearance – only a
discreet modern smoke stack
belies its youth – Speyside was
commissioned in 1962 by the
blender and bottler George
Christie. Built stone-by-stone,
it was not finished until 1987.
Among its single malts have been
Drumguish (no age-statement) and
Speyside 8-, 10-, and 12-year-olds.

◄ **SPEYSIDE 12-YEAR-OLD**
SINGLE MALT: SPEYSIDE
40% ABV
The flavour of this well-balanced
12-year-old recalls nougat, with a faint
smoky edge. It is slightly richer and
more full-bodied than you would
expect from its restrained nose.

SPRINGBANK

Scotland
Campbeltown, Argyll
www.springbankdistillers.com

Springbank was officially founded
in 1823, at a time when there were
no fewer than 13 licensed distillers
in Campbeltown. Although this
end of the Mull of Kintyre stills
feels pretty cut off by car, it was
always a short hop across the
Firth of Clyde to Glasgow by ship.
And, as the second city of the
British empire boomed, distilleries
like Springbank were on hand to
quench its ever-growing thirst.
In the other direction there was
the US but, when that went dry
during Prohibition, and the big 👉

SPRINGBANK 15-YEAR-OLD ▶
SINGLE MALT: CAMPBELTOWN
46% ABV
Sweet toffee and candied peel on the
nose give way to more exotic sweet-
and-sour flavours in the mouth.

SPRINGBANK 10-YEAR-OLD
SINGLE MALT: CAMPBELTOWN
46% ABV
A complex cocktail of flavours, from
ripe citrus fruit to peat smoke, vanilla,
spice, and a faint underlying salty tang.

SPRINGBANK

 blenders turned ever more to Speyside, Campbeltown's demise was swift.

Yet Springbank survived. Much of this must have been down to its continuity: the distillery was originally owned by the Reid family, who sold out to their in-laws, the Mitchells, in the mid-19th century. The Mitchells are still in charge, and have built up a real cult following for their innovative range of single malts.

◀ SPRINGBANK VINTAGE 1997
SINGLE MALT: CAMPBELTOWN
54.9% ABV
A complex nose of toffee mixed with smoky, leathery aromas. Drier on the palate, with a meaty, mouth-filling flavour wreathed in smoke.

SPRINGBANK 100 PROOF
SINGLE MALT: CAMPBELTOWN
57% ABV
A big, full-bodied malt with a dried-fruit and butterscotch flavours, along with traces of spice, nuts, and smoke.

ST. GEORGE

USA

*St. George Spirits, 2601 Monarch
Street, Almeda, California
www.stgeorgespirits.com*

St. George Spirits was established
by Jörg Rupf in 1982, and the
distillery operates two Holstein
copper pot stills. A percentage
of heavily roasted barley is used,
some of which is smoked over
alder and beech wood. Most of
the single malt whiskey is put
into former bourbon barrels and
matured for between three and
five years, with a proportion
matured in French oak and
former port casks.

ST. GEORGE ▶
SINGLE MALT 43% ABV
The nose offers fresh, floral notes, with
fruit, nuts, coffee, and vanilla. Quite
delicate on the palate: sweet, nutty,
and fruity, with a hint of menthol and
cocoa. Vanilla and chocolate notes in
the finish, along with gentle smoke.

STEWARTS CREAM OF THE BARLEY

Scotland
Owner: Chivas Brothers

First produced around 1831, this old-established brand is today a topseller in Ireland. For many years it enjoyed great popularity in Scotland, too, not least because of its widespread distribution in public house chain of Allied, the owner at the time. Single malt from Glencadam used to be at the heart of the blend. With changes in ownership, Glencadam is now in other hands, but the blend reputedly still contains a healthy proportion of up to 50 different single malts.

◄ STEWARTS CREAM OF THE BARLEY
BLEND 40% ABV

A malty, sweet, soft, and slightly spirity nose. The fruitiness of a young spirit on the palate – spicy, raw, and a little smoky. Peppery, drying, charred-wood finish.

STRANAHAN'S

USA

Stranahan's Colorado Whiskey,
2405 Blake Street, Denver, Colorado
www.stranahans.com

Jess Graber and George Stranahan
established the Denver distillery
in March 2004, the first licensed
distillery in Colorado. Whiskey
is produced using a four-barley
fermented wash produced by the
neighbouring Flying Dog Brewery.
The distillation takes place in a
Vendome still and the spirit is put
into new, charred American-oak
barrels. It is aged for a minimum
of two years, and each batch
bottled comprises the contents
of between two and six barrels.

**STRANAHAN'S COLORADO
WHISKEY ▶**
COLORADO WHISKEY 47% ABV
The nose is quite bourbon-like, with
notes of caramel, liquorice, spice, and
oak. The palate is slightly oily, big, and
sweet, with honey and spices. The
fairly short finish is quite oaky.

STRATHISLA

Scotland
Keith, Banffshire
www.maltwhiskydistilleries.com

In 1786, Alexander Milne
and George Taylor founded the
Milltown Distillery in Keith. The
whisky it produced was known
as Strathisla and, in 1951, this
was adopted as the name for
the distillery. Over the years,
Strathisla has survived fires,
explosions, and bankruptcy, to
become the oldest and possibly
most handsome distillery in the
Highlands, with a high-gabled
roof and two pagodas. Bought
by Chivas Brothers in 1950,
it has been the spiritual home
of Chivas Regal ever since.

◀ **STRATHISLA 12-YEAR-OLD**
SINGLE MALT: SPEYSIDE
43% ABV
This has a rich, sumptuous nose
and a spicy, fruitcake character,
thanks to the influence of sherry.
It is medium-bodied, with a slight
smoky note on the finish.

STRATHMILL

Scotland
Keith, Banffshire
www.malts.com

With its twin pagoda roof, this handsome late-Victorian distillery was built in 1891 as the Glenisla-Glenlivet Distillery. Four years later it was bought by Gilbey, the London-based gin distiller, and re-christened Strathmill – a reference to the fact that it stood on the site of an old corn mill. A single malt expression was released as early as 1909, but Strathmill's long-term role in life was – and is – to supply malt for blended Scotch, particularly J&B.

STRATHMILL FLORA & FAUNA 12-YEAR-OLD ▶
SINGLE MALT: SPEYSIDE
43% ABV

On the lighter, more delicate side of Speyside, Strathmill has a nutty, malty character with notes of vanilla from the wood. It is quite soft and medium-sweet on the tongue.

SULLIVANS COVE

Australia
*Tasmania Distillery, Lamb Place,
Cambridge, Tasmania
www.tasmaniadistillery.com.au*

Part-owner and Master Distiller
of the small Tasmania Distillery
Patrick Maguire admits that some
of the early batches of spirit were
not as good as they should have
been, but the whisky is now
winning national awards. Locally
grown, unpeated Franklin barley-
malt is used. The spirit is brewed
at Cascade Brewery, distilled in
a Charentais-style pot still, and
bottled from single casks by hand.

◄ SULLIVANS COVE
PORT MATURATION
SINGLE MALT 60% ABV
This 7-year-old was matured in a
French oak ex-port cask. It has a floral
nose, developing into rich malty stout;
the taste is tannic and warming.

SULLIVANS COVE
BOURBON MATURATION
SINGLE MALT 60% ABV
Another 7-year-old, this time from
an American oak ex-bourbon cask.
It is sweet and malty, with oaky
and chocolate notes.

SUNTORY HAKUSHU

Japan
Torihara 2913–1, Hakushucho,
Komagun, Yamanashi
www.suntory.co.jp

Located in a forest high in the
Japanese Alps, Hakushu was once
the largest malt distillery in the
world, producing a vast array of
different makes for the Suntory
blenders; nowhere else offers such
an array of shapes and sizes of pot
stills. Hakushu single malt seems
to echo the location, being light,
gentle, and fresh.

SUNTORY HAKUSHU 12-YEAR-OLD ▶
SINGLE MALT 43.5% ABV
A very cool nose, with cut grass,
a growing mintiness, and a hint of
linseed oil. The palate is sweet but
quite slow; the minty, grassy character
is given depth by apricot fruitiness and
extra fragrance by a camomile note.

SUNTORY HAKUSHU 18-YEAR-OLD
SINGLE MALT 43% ABV
Once again a vegetal note, this time
more like a tropical rainforest. There's
also plum, mango, hay, and fresh ginger.
Good acidity and a toasty, oaky finish.

Whisky Tour: Japan

Tokyo is a good starting point for the whisky lover. The city has myriad whisky bars and excellent train connections to the distilleries at Chichibu, Karuizawa, Hakushu, and Gotemba. Further afield, Suntory's flagship distillery, Yamazaki, is also accessible by train, and can be combined with a visit to Kyoto or Osaka.

JAPAN

DAY 1: CHICHIBU DISTILLERY

❶ Chichibu, Japan's newest distillery, started by Ichiro Akuto, has no visitor facilities yet, but whisky enthusiasts can arrange a personal tour by contacting the distillery in advance *(+81 (0)494 62 4601)*. Chichibu city is 90 minutes by train from Tokyo's Ikebukuro station. A taxi can be taken from the station to the distillery, which is outside the city.

DAYS 2–3: KIRIN'S KARUIZAWA DISTILLERY

❷ The Kirin Distillery at **Karuizawa** is a small whisky-making plant. It is open to visitors and incorporates an art gallery. Karuizawa is a spa town that is 65–80 minutes by the Nagano Shinkansen from Tokyo Station, or by local train connections from Chichibu (3–5 hours). There are numerous spa resort hotels near to the distillery for those wishing to make an extended break.

○ MATSUE — Chugoku Expy — KYOTO

YAMAZAKI ❺

KOBE ○ — OSAKA

FINISH

OKAYAMA ○

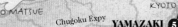

Sanyo Expy

HIROSHIMA ○

TOUR STATISTICS

DAYS: 8
LENGTH: 300 miles (480km)
TRAVEL: Shinkansen (bullet trains), local trains
DISTILLERIES: 5

Shinjiro Torii is revered in Japan as the founder of Suntory, which operates the Yamazaki and Hakushu distilleries on this tour.

DAY 4: SUNTORY'S HAKUSHU DISTILLERY

③ Hakushu is surrounded by a lovely nature reserve in the southern Japanese Alps. The nearest station is Kobuchizawa, which is accessible by slow trains from Karuizawa, or by express train (JR Chuo Line) from Tokyo's Shinjuku Station.

HAKUSHU DISTILLERY

DAYS 5–6: KIRIN'S GOTEMBA DISTILLERY

④ It is best to access Gotemba by fast train from Tokyo's Shinjuku station. The town is the start of one of the main routes up Mount Fuji, and home to Kirin's **Gotemba** Distillery. Many visitors come to visit both. They start climbing Fuji in the afternoon to reach the 8th or 9th stage by nightfall, where there are huts for pilgrims. The summit is reached at dawn. After descending, it is possible to get a bus back to Gotemba to visit the distillery. Although not the prettiest of distilleries, it has good facilities and a spectacular view of Fuji from its rooftop terrace.

MOUNT FUJI AND TRAIN

DAYS 7–8: SUNTORY'S YAMAZAKI DISTILLERY

⑤ It is best to take the bullet train to either Kyoto or Osaka to make a base for visiting the Suntory Distillery at **Yamazaki**, the company's original whisky-making plant. Local trains from either city stop at JR Yamazaki station. There are extensive visitor facilities, including an impressive tasting bar with exclusive bottlings. The distillery offers well-heeled clients a chance to buy a cask through its Owner's Cask scheme. There is also a traditional Shinto shrine to visit.

YAMAZAKI DISTILLERY

SENDAI

NIIGATA

FUKUSHIMA

Banetsu Expy

Joban Expy

Tohoku Expy

Kanetsu Expy

NAGANO

START

Nagano Shinkansen Line

② KARUIZAWA ① CHICHIBU

③ HAKUSHU TOKYO

JR Chuo Line

HONSHU JR Asagiri Line

GOTEMBA ④

NAGOYA

Tokaido Shinkansen Line

miles
0   30

0   30
kilometres

SUNTORY HIBIKI

Japan

Torihara 2913–1, Hakushucho,
Komagun, Yamanashi
www.suntory.co.jp

The fortunes of Suntory were built on blended whiskies based on malts from its two distilleries: Yamazaki and Hakushu. Although there is a move towards single malts globally, the Hibiki range is still regarded as very important.

◄ SUNTORY HIBIKI 17-YEAR-OLD
BLENDED MALT 43% ABV
This, the original Hibiki, has a soft, generous nose featuring super-ripe fruits, light peatiness, a hint of heavy florals (jasmine), and citrus. On the palate: caramel toffee, black cherry, vanilla, rosehip, and light oak structure.

SUNTORY HIBIKI 30-YEAR-OLD
BLENDED MALT 43% ABV
This multi-award winner is huge in flavour, a compote of different fruits: Seville orange, quince paste, quite assertive wood, and walnuts, followed by aniseed and fennel, and a deep spiciness. The palate is sweet and velvety, with Old English Marmalade to the fore, with sweet, dusty spices.

SUNTORY YAMAZAKI

Japan
Yamazaki 5–2–2, Honcho,
Mishimagun, Osaka
www.suntory.co.jp

Established in 1923, Yamazaki
was the first malt distillery built
in Japan, and was home to the
fathers of the nation's whisky
industry, Shinjiro Torii and
Masataka Taketsuru. Like ☞

THE YAMAZAKI 12-YEAR-OLD ▶
SINGLE MALT 43% ABV
The mainstay of the range, the
12-year-old is crisp, with a fresh nose
of pineapple, citrus, flowers, dried
herbs, and a little oak. The palate is
sweet and filled with ripe soft fruits
and a hint of smoke.

THE YAMAZAKI 18-YEAR-OLD
SINGLE MALT 43% ABV
With age, Yamazaki acquires more
influence from oak. The estery notes
of younger variants are replaced by
ripe apple, violet, and a deep, sweet
oakiness. This impression continues
on the palate with a mossy, pine-like
character and the classic Yamazaki
richness in the middle of the mouth.
This is an extremely classy whisky.

SUNTORY YAMAZAKI

 Hakushu, it produces a huge range of styles. The official single-malt bottlings concentrate on the sweet fruity expression. Single-cask bottlings have also been released. Most of the older expressions have been aged in ex-sherry casks, but there is the occasional Japanese-oak release for Japanese malt converts.

◀ SUNTORY VINTAGE 1984
SINGLE MALT 56% ABV

An award-winning, heavily sherried expression. Very dark with a balsamic nose, wood bark, yew, Christmas pudding, and espresso coffee. The palate has black cherry, treacle toffee, and prune. Interesting mix of bitter and sweet, with strong tannins.

THE CASK OF YAMAZAKI 1990 SHERRY BUTT
SINGLE MALT 61% ABV

One of a regular series of single cask releases, this has an almost opaque mahogany colour and a nose filled with date, prune, and figgy sherried notes. Some peatiness adds complexity. The palate is grippy and autumnal with light woodsmoke, walnut, espresso (with sugar), and a long, firm finish that ends with a touch of treacle.

TALISKER

Scotland
Carbost, Isle of Skye
www.taliskerwhisky.com

Talisker, founded in 1830 by Hugh
and Kenneth MacAskill, is the only
surviving distillery on Skye. Given
Skye's size and proximity to the
mainland, it seems odd that there
is only one distillery there, when
Islay has so many.

Talisker struggled through the
19th century until, in 1898, it
teamed up with Dailuaine, then the
largest distillery in the Highlands.
In 1916, the joint venture was
taken over by a consortium
involving Dewar's, the Distillers
Company, and John Walker ☞

TALISKER 10-YEAR-OLD ▶
SINGLE MALT: ISLANDS
45.8% ABV

An iconic West Coast malt with a
pungent, slightly peaty character that
has a peppery catch on the finish.

TALISKER 18-YEAR-OLD
SINGLE MALT: ISLANDS
45.8% ABV

Age has softened the youthful vigour
of the 10-year-old, and given it a scent
of leather and aromatic smoke and a
creamy, mouth-filling texture.

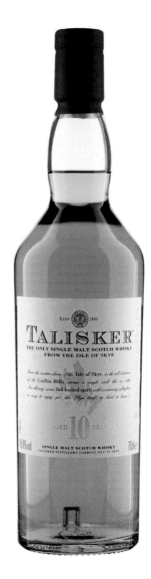

TALISKER

 & Sons. Ever since, Talisker has been a key component in Johnnie Walker Red Label.

Until 1928, Talisker was triple-distilled, like an Irish whiskey, which explains why two wash stills are paired to three spirit stills. The lyne arms have a unique U shape to increase reflux and produce a cleaner spirit, although the fact that this is then condensed in worm tubs seems contradictory, as worm tubs tend to produce a heavier, more sulphurous spirit. Whatever the rationale, it seems to work, and Talisker has won countless awards and fans.

◀ TALISKER DISTILLERS EDITION 1996
**SINGLE MALT: ISLANDS
45.8% ABV**
With a maturation that ends in Amoroso sherry casks, the Distillers Edition has a peppery, spicy character, softened by a luscious, dried-fruit richness in the mouth.

TALISKER 57° NORTH
**SINGLE MALT: ISLANDS
57% ABV**
Named in reference to the latitude of the distillery, this is rich, fruity, smoky, peppery, and spicy, with a long finish.

TAMDHU

Scotland
*Knockando, Aberlour,
Morayshire
www.edringtongroup.com*

While it may keep a low profile,
offering just one young distillery
bottling, Tamdhu is a large set-up,
with nine pine washbacks, three
pairs of stills, and a mix of dunnage
and racked warehousing on site.
There's a maltings plant, too,
and part of Tamdhu's role in the
Edrington Group is to provide
some of the malt for the company's
other distilleries, as well as all the
malt for its own whisky.

As you might expect of a
distillery with only one official
expression, there are several
independent bottlings of Tamdhu
– from Duncan Taylor, Douglas
Laing, Gordon & MacPhail, and
a 29-year-old from the Douglas
Laing Old Malt Cask series.

TAMDHU ▶
**SINGLE MALT: SPEYSIDE
40% ABV**
Bottled by the distiller to replace
the old 8-year-old, this is a
youthful introduction to Speyside, with no age
statement and a slight peppery edge.

TAMNAVULIN

Scotland
Ballindalloch, Banffshire

In 1966, Invergordon Distillers, now part of Whyte & Mackay, decided to build a big new distillery in a picturesque corner of Upper Speyside by the River Livet. Its six stills could pump out as much as 4 million litres (880,000 gallons) of pure alcohol a year. Yet, in 1995, Tamnavulin closed down – the owners, it seemed, had decided to focus their attention on their other distilleries, Dalmore and Jura in particular. The UB Group bought Whyte & Mackay in 2007, and now Tamnavulin is back up and running.

◀ **TAMNAVULIN 12-YEAR-OLD**
SINGLE MALT: SPEYSIDE
40% ABV
A light, aperitif-style malt, with a dry, cereal character and minty nose. This standard release of the so-called "Stillman's Dram" is joined by occasional older expressions.

TANGLE RIDGE

Canada
Alberta Distillery, 1521 34th Avenue Southeast, Calgary, Alberta

This whisky from the Alberta Distillery *(see p12)* is sweeter than its stablemates, although, like the other Alberta whiskies, it is made exclusively from rye. Introduced in 1996, it is one of the new school of premium Canadian whiskies: aged 10 years in oak, it is then "dumped" and small amounts of vanilla and sherry are added. The spirit is then re-casked for a time to allow the flavours to marry.

Its name comes from a limestone wall in the Canadian Rockies that was discovered by distinguished explorer, artist, and writer Mary Schaffer (1861–1939).

TANGLE RIDGE DOUBLE CASK ▶
CANADIAN RYE 40% ABV
Butterscotch and burnt caramel on the nose, velvet-smooth mouthfeel, and a very sweet taste, with a hint of sherry. Lacks complexity, however.

T

TÉ BHEAG

Scotland
Owner: The Gaelic Whisky Co.
www.gaelicwhisky.com

Although it is blended and bottled elsewhere in Scotland, this is another brand from the Pràban na Linne company on Skye (The Gaelic Whisky Company), who produce Poit Dhubh. Té Bheag (pronounced *Chey Vek*) means "the little lady" and is the name of the boat in the logo. It is also colloquial Gaelic for a "wee dram". The blend is popular in France and has won medals in international competition. Té Bheag is non chill-filtered, and Islay, Island, Highland, and Speyside malts aged from 8 to 11 years are used in the blend.

◄ **TÉ BHEAG**
BLEND 40% ABV
The nose is fresh, with a citrus note, good richness, a delicate peatiness, and a touch of cereal. Weighty on the palate, with a good touch of liquorice, a toffee-like richness, and some peat.

TEACHER'S

Scotland
Owner: Beam Global

This venerable brand can be dated to 1830, when William Teacher opened a grocery shop in Glasgow. Like other whisky entrepreneurs, he soon branched out into the spirits trade. His sons took over, and blending became increasingly important. In 1884 the trademark Teacher's Highland Cream was registered, and this single brand eventually came to dominate the business. The whisky was always forceful in character, built around single malts from Glendronach and Ardmore. Today it continues to prove popular in South America.

**TEACHER'S
HIGHLAND CREAM ▶**
BLEND 40% ABV
Full-flavoured, oily, with fudge and caramel notes on the nose, and toffee and liquorice on the palate. A well-rounded, smooth texture and quite a quick finish that leaves the palate refreshed.

TEANINICH

Scotland
Alness, Ross-shire
www.malts.com

Distillery visitors to the Highland
village of Alness rarely notice
Teaninich as they make their way
to its more famous neighbour
Dalmore. And yet Teaninich has
been quietly distilling away with
barely a break since 1817, when
it was set up by Captain Hugh
Munro. Teaninich's role was to
supply spirit for blending – no one
was interested in marketing it as
a single malt to whisky-drinkers
until 1992, when its owners, UDV,
released a 10-year-old expression.

◀ TEANINICH FLORA & FAUNA 10-YEAR-OLD
SINGLE MALT: HIGHLANDS
43% ABV
The only official distillery bottling
is polished and grassy, with a
predominantly malty flavour.

TEANINICH GORDON & MACPHAIL 1991
SINGLE MALT: HIGHLANDS
46% ABV
A deep amber, fruitcake-flavoured
malt, with notes of mint, tobacco,
cloves, and wood smoke.

TEERENPELI

Finland

Teerenpeli, Hämeenkatu 19, Lahti
www.teerenpeli.com

Teerenpeli distillery began life
in 1998 within a small brewery in
the city of Lahti, an hour north of
Helsinki. In 2002, its owner, Anssi
Pyysing, bought a restaurant
nearby, and moved the distillery
to the former car park beneath it.
The distillery used wash from the
brewery until 2010, when a new
mash tun was installed, as well
as a visitor centre. Until now, only
8,000 litres (1,760 gallons) of spirit
have been produced each year, but
the distillery's capacity is now up
to 30,000 litres (6,600 gallons).

TEERENPELI
3-YEAR-OLD NO. 001 ▶
MALT 43% ABV

A lot of grain (barley), vanilla, and
oak wood with a slightly thick body.

TEERENPELI 6-YEAR-OLD
MALT 43% ABV

In Finnish, Teerenpeli means
"flirtation". True to its name, this
malt is soft and seductive, with vanilla
sponge and baked apple flavours, an
intriguing mix of herbal and spicy
notes, and a spritzy mouthfeel.

TEMPLETON RYE

USA
East 3rd Street, Templeton, Iowa
www.templetonrye.com

Scott Bush's Templeton Rye whiskey came onto the market in 2006. It is distilled in a 300-US-gallon (1,150-litre) copper pot still before being aged in new, charred-oak barrels.

Bush boasts that his rye is made to a Prohibition-era recipe. During the years of the Great Depression a group of farmers in the Templeton area started to distil a rye whiskey illicitly in order to boost their faltering agricultural incomes. Soon, "Templeton Rye" achieved a widespread reputation as a high quality spirit.

◄ **TEMPLETON RYE SMALL BATCH**
RYE WHISKEY 40% ABV
Bright, crisp, and mildly sweet on the palate. The finish is smooth, long, and warming.

344

THOMAS H. HANDY

USA
Buffalo Trace Distillery,
1001 Wilkinson Boulevard,
Frankfort, Kentucky
www.buffalotrace.com

Thomas H. Handy Sazerac is the newest addition to the Buffalo Trace Antique Collection. It is an uncut and unfiltered straight rye whiskey, named after the New Orleans bartender who first used rye whiskey to make the Sazerac Cocktail. According to the distillers, the barrels are aged six years and five months on the fifth floor of Warehouse M – "it's very flavourful and will remind drinkers of Christmas cake".

THOMAS H. HANDY SAZERAC 2008 EDITION ▶

RYE WHISKEY 63.8% ABV
Summer fruits and pepper notes on the nose. The palate is a lovely blend of soft vanilla and peppery rye, while the finish is long and comforting, with oily, spicy oak.

345

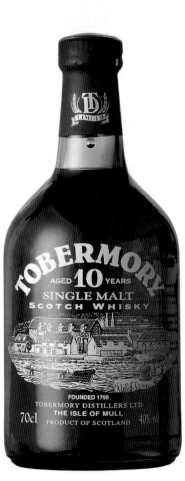

TOBERMORY

Scotland
Tobermory, Isle of Mull
www.tobermory.co.uk

Tobermory's survival has been something of a miracle, given that it has spent much of its life lying idle.

It was founded in the 1790s by local businessman John Sinclair, but closed on his death in 1837. It was revived briefly in the 1880s, but operation was sporadic and it closed again between 1930 and 1972. Again, production was sporadic until it was sold to its present owners, Burn Stewart Distillers in 1993.

◄ **TOBERMORY 10-YEAR-OLD**
SINGLE MALT: ISLANDS
40% ABV
This fresh, unpeated, maritime malt claims to have a slight smoky character, owing to the water from Mull's peat lochans. If true, the effect is subtle.

TOBERMORY 15-YEAR-OLD
SINGLE MALT: ISLANDS
46.3% ABV
The nose has rich fruitcake notes and a trace of marmalade, thanks to ageing in sherry casks. The spicy character comes through on the tongue. It is non chill-filtered and cask strength.

TOMATIN

Scotland
Tomatin, Inverness-shire
www.tomatin.com

With 23 stills and a capacity
of 12 million litres (2.6 million
gallons) of pure alcohol, Tomatin
was once the colossus of the malt
whisky industry. In 1974, at the
time of its expansion, it eclipsed
even Glenfiddich, whose capacity
remains at 10 million litres (2.2
million gallons).

Tomatin was founded in 1897,
and took a while to reach its
super-size status. Its two stills
were increased to four as recently
as 1956; thereafter expansion
was rapid until it peaked in the
1970s, just in time for the ☞

TOMATIN 12-YEAR-OLD ▶
SINGLE MALT: HIGHLANDS
40% ABV
A mellow, soft-centred Speyside-style
malt, which replaced the old core
10-year-old expression back in 2003.

TOMATIN 18-YEAR-OLD
SINGLE MALT: HIGHLANDS
43% ABV
The deep amber hue betrays a strong
sherry influence that brings out fruity
and cinnamon flavours in the malt.

TOMATIN

🐦 first big post-war slump. Tomatin struggled on as an independent distillery until 1985, when the liquidators arrived. A year later it was sold to two of its long-standing customers – Takara Shuzo and Okara & Co – thus becoming the first Scottish distillery in Japanese hands.

With 11 fewer stills, production has been cut back to 5 million litres (1.1 million gallons), which still allows plenty of capacity for bottling as a single malt. Tomatin's biggest seller is the standard 12-year-old; the 18- and 25-year-olds form part of the core range, while older expressions and specific vintages are released on a more ad hoc basis.

◀ TOMATIN 25-YEAR-OLD
SINGLE MALT: HIGHLANDS 43% ABV
With its simple packaging, this ripe, zesty malt, full of nuts, and spice is a triumph of substance over style.

TOMATIN 30-YEAR-OLD
SINGLE MALT: HIGHLANDS 49.3% ABV
A voluptuous after-dinner dram with a big, sherried nose and impressive legs.

TOMINTOUL

Scotland
Kirkmichael, Ballindalloch, Grampian
www.tomintouldistillery.co.uk

Tomintoul opened in 1964 –
a time of great confidence in the
industry, with booming sales of
blended Scotch. Its role in life
was simply to supply malt for
these blends. This role continues
under Angus Dundee, who bought
the distillery in 2000, when it was
in need of malt for its own blends
(see p17). While single malts
account for a small fraction of
the 3.3 million litres (600,000
gallons) produced each year,
the number of expressions has
increased greatly.

TOMINTOUL 10-YEAR-OLD ▶
SINGLE MALT: SPEYSIDE
40% ABV
This delicate, aperitif-style malt has
some vanilla from the wood and a light
cereal character.

TOMINTOUL 16-YEAR-OLD
SINGLE MALT: SPEYSIDE
40% ABV
Extra years give this expression a
nuttier, spicier character with orange
peel aromas, as well as more depth and
a more rounded texture.

349

TORMORE

Scotland
Advie, Grantown-on-Spey, Morayshire

Built on a grand scale in 1958, Tormore symbolizes the whisky industry's self-confidence at a time when global demand for blended Scotch was growing strongly. With its copper-clad roof and giant chimney stack, the distillery towers up beside the A95 in Speyside. It seems no expense was spared by the architect, Sir Albert Richardson, a past president of the Royal Academy. Tormore is now owned by Chivas Brothers (Pernod Ricard), who released an official 12-year-old bottling in 2004.

◀ TORMORE 12-YEAR-OLD
SINGLE MALT: SPEYSIDE 40% ABV
There is a soft malty character to the nose, with notes of melon and grass. In the mouth it has a slightly oily texture and a medium-light body that dries on the finish.

TULLAMORE DEW

Ireland
www.tullamoredew.com

In 1901, the worldwide sales
of Irish whiskey peaked at 10
million cases, around the period
that the Williams family gained
control of Tullamore Distillery.
D. E. Williams's name is still
associated with the whiskey;
as in Tullamore DEW-illiams.
But by 1954, the distillery closed
and the brand was sold repeatedly.
Nowadays, the whiskey is all
produced to order in Midleton
and it sells very well across
continental Europe.

TULLAMORE DEW ▶
BLEND 40% ABV
This whiskey is fairly one-dimensional.
It has a characteristic bourbon burn,
with not much else to recommend it.

TULLAMORE DEW
12-YEAR-OLD
BLEND 40% ABV
A considerable step up from the other
Tullamore blends, the 12-year-old is
reminiscent of a premium Jameson.
The precious trinity of pot still, sherry,
and oak is very much in evidence.

TULLIBARDINE

Scotland
Blackford, Perthshire
www.tullibardine.com

Tullibardine was a mothballed distillery until it was bought by an independent consortium in 2003. It soon launched its first official bottling – a 10-year-old – but it will be 2014 before the whisky actually distilled by the new owners sees the light of day. In the meantime there has been a raft of releases based on the inventory inherited in 2003, which included some 3,000 casks dating back to 1952.

◀ TULLIBARDINE 1993 SHERRY WOOD FINISH
SINGLE MALT: HIGHLANDS 46% ABV
Eighteen months in Oloroso sherry butts give this malt a deep amber colour and a spicy butterscotch flavour that finishes dry.

TULLIBARDINE 1993
SINGLE MALT: HIGHLANDS 40% ABV
This is more akin to a delicate Speyside than a robust Highland malt. Light citrus nose with a vanilla sweetness from maturation in bourbon casks.

TYRCONNELL

Ireland

Cooley Distillery, Riverstown,
Cooley, County Louth
www.cooleywhiskey.com

It would be hard to find anyone
who remembers the original Old
Tyrconnell whiskey. The distillery
that produced it, Andrew A. Watt
and Company of Derry City, closed
in 1925. In its day, this whiskey
(named after a race horse) was
very popular in the US, and early
film of baseball matches at the
Yankee Stadium show hoardings
advertising "Old Tyrconnel".

But the combined effects of civil
unrest in Ireland and Prohibition
in the US pushed Watt and ☛

TYRCONNELL SINGLE MALT ▶
SINGLE MALT 40% ABV
Cooley's bestselling malt and it's easy
to see why. This has the loveliest nose
of any Irish whiskey, releasing jasmine,
honeysuckle, and malted milk biscuits.

TYRCONNELL PORT CASK
SINGLE MALT 46% ABV
Port changes the nose slightly, spicing
things up. The body has aromas of fig
rolls and plum pudding.

TYRCONNELL

🥄 many other Irish distilleries into the hands of the Scottish United Distillers Company. To protect their core Scotch brands, UDC ruthlessly closed every Irish distillery they bought, bringing the industry across the island to its knees. However, The Tyrconnell was the first brand Cooley's John Teeling chose to bring back to life when he bottled his first single malt in 1992. Since then, various wood finishes have been tried on the 10-year-old.

◀ TYRCONNELL SHERRY CASK
SINGLE MALT 46% ABV
The best of the wood finishes – malt and fruity sherry fuse beautifully.

TYRCONNELL MADEIRA CASK
SINGLE MALT 46% ABV
Madeira and Ireland do each other proud here. Warm hints of cinnamon and mixed spice dance on the palate.

UBERACH

France

Bertrand Distillery,
3 rue du Maréchal Leclerc, BP 21,
67350 Uberach, Alsace
www.distillerie-bertrand.com

The Bertrand brandy and liqueur distillery in Alsace dates from 1874 and has been run by the same family ever since. The Alsace region is blessed with particularly fertile, alluvial soil and the area around the distillery produces a range of fruits that are used in some of Bertrand's spirits. The company has recently branched out to produce beer and two non-filtered whiskies, Uberach Single Malt and Uberach Single Cask.

UBERACH SINGLE MALT ▶
SINGLE MALT 42.2% ABV
Floral, fruity, and spicy, with black tea and hints of plums, as well as wax, and tobacco notes. Aromatic, with good balance and an oaky, fruity finish.

USHER'S GREEN STRIPE

Scotland
Owner: Diageo

One of the foremost names in Scotch whisky, the Edinburgh firm of Usher was a pioneer in the art of blending. In fact, it is recognized for introducing the first modern blend – Old Vatted Glenlivet in 1853. After the firm joined the DCL in 1919, the brand slowly faded away. Today Usher's Green Stripe is among the lowest- priced Scotch available to drinkers in the US, few of whom will either know or care about its distinguished history. But, Usher's whisky remains highly desirable among historians and collectors, owing chiefly to the very high standard of its promotional give-away materials.

◀ **USHER'S GREEN STRIPE**
BLEND 40% ABV
A low-priced blend with a high grain content; well-suited to mixing.

VAN WINKLE

USA

2843 Brownsboro Road
Louisville, Kentucky
www.oldripvanwinkle.com

The legendary Julian P. "Pappy"
Van Winkle Snr. was a salesman
for W.L. Weller & Sons who went
on to become famous for his Old
Fitzgerald bourbon.

Van Winkle specializes in
small-batch, aged whiskeys. The
bourbons are made with wheat,
rather than cheaper rye. This
is said to give the whiskeys a
smoother, sweeter flavour during
the long maturation period ☞

PAPPY VAN WINKLE'S FAMILY RESERVE 15-YEAR-OLD ▶
BOURBON 53.5% ABV
A sweet caramel and vanilla nose,
with charcoal and oak. Full-bodied,
round and smooth in the mouth, with
a long and complex finish of spicy
orange, toffee, vanilla, and oak.

OLD RIP VAN WINKLE 10-YEAR-OLD
BOURBON 45% ABV
Caramel and molasses on the big nose,
then honey and rich, spicy fruit on the
profound, mellow palate. The finish is
long, with coffee and liquorice notes.

VAN WINKLE

🐷 favoured by Van Winkle. All the whiskeys are matured for at least 10 years in lightly charred mountain oak barrels.

Buffalo Trace *(see p66)* has been in partnership with Julian Van Winkle, "Pappy" Van Winkle's grandson, since 2002, making and distributing his whiskeys. The current expressions were produced at a number of distilleries, and matured at the Van Winkle's now silent Old Hoffman Distillery.

◄ VAN WINKLE FAMILY RESERVE RYE 13-YEAR-OLD
RYE WHISKEY 47.8% ABV

An almost uniquely aged rye. Powerful nose of fruit and spice. Vanilla, spice, pepper, and cocoa in the mouth. A long finish pairs caramel with black coffee.

PAPPY VAN WINKLE'S FAMILY RESERVE 20-YEAR-OLD
BOURBON 45.2% ABV

Old for a bourbon, this has stood the test of time. Sweet vanilla and caramel nose, plus raisins, apples, and oak. Rich and buttery in the mouth, with molasses and a hint of char. The finish is long and complex, with a touch of oak charring.

VAT 69

Scotland
Owner: Diageo

At its peak, VAT 69 was the 10th-bestselling whisky in the world, and references to it crop up in films and books from the 1950s and 60s. It was launched in 1882 and was once the flagship brand of the independent South Queensferry blenders William Sanderson & Co, its name coming from the fact that vat 69 was the finest of 100 possible blends tested. Today its current owner, Diageo, gives precedence to Johnnie Walker and J&B, and it might not be unreasonable to suggest that – despite sales of more than 1 million cases a year in Venezuela, Spain, and Australia – VAT 69's glory days are behind it.

VAT 69 ▶
BLEND 40% ABV
A light and well-balanced standard blend with an initial, noticeably sweet impact of vanilla ice cream and a pleasantly malty background.

W.L. WELLER

USA

Buffalo Trace Distillery,
1001 Wilkinson Boulevard,
Frankfort, Kentucky
www.buffalotrace.com

Distilled by Buffalo Trace,
W.L. Weller is made with wheat
as the secondary grain, for an
extra smooth taste.

William Larue Weller was
a prominent 19th-century
Kentucky distiller, whose
company ultimately merged
in 1935 with that of the Stitzel
brothers. A new Stitzel-Weller
Distillery was subsequently
constructed in Louisville.

◄ W.L. WELLER SPECIAL RESERVE
BOURBON 45% ABV

Fresh fruit, honey, vanilla, and toffee
characterize the nose, while the palate
has lots of flavour, featuring ripe corn
and spicy oak. The medium-length
finish displays sweet, cereal notes
and pleasing oak.

WALDVIERTLER

Austria
*Whiskydestillerie J. Haider OG,
3664 Roggenreith 3
www.roggenhof.at*

The Waldviertler Roggenhof
Distillery produces two single malts
– J.H. Single Malt and J.H. Special
Single Malt "Karamell" – and three
rye whiskies – J.H. Original Rye,
J.H. Pure Rye Malt, and J.H. Special
Pure Rye Malt "Nougat".

Waldviertler uses casks made
from the local Manharstberger oak
trees. The whiskies are matured
for between three and twelve years
and offered as single-cask bottlings.
Other spirits made here include
vodka, gin, and brandy, but –
unusually for a European distillery
– whisky is the main focus.

WALDVIERTLER J. H. SPECIAL PURE RYE MALT "NOUGAT" ▶
RYE WHISKY 41% ABV
A gentle, sweet taste of honey,
harmonizing perfectly with the
light vanilla taste.

WALDVIERTLER J. H. SPECIAL SINGLE MALT "KARAMELL"
SINGLE MALT 41% ABV
Smoky and dry, with an intense
caramel flavour.

WAMBRECHIES

France

*1 Rue de la Distillerie,
59118 Wambrechies,
Nord-Pas-de-Calais
www.wambrechies.com*

Wambrechies was founded in 1817 as a *jenever* (gin) distillery and is one of only three stills left in the region. It continues to produce an impressive range of *jenevers*, as well as one malt whisky and a *jenever* beer. Wambrechie whiskies are bottled at three and eight years old, with the younger whisky consisting of a lighter, floral blend and the older having a deeper, spicy character.

◀ **WAMBRECHIES 8-YEAR-OLD**
SINGLE MALT 40% ABV
Delicate nose, with aniseed, fresh paint, vanilla, and cereal notes. Smooth on the palate, with a fine malty profile. Spicy finish, with powdered ginger and milk chocolate.

WHISKY CASTLE

Switzerland
Schlossstrasse 17, 5077 Elfingen
www.whisky-castle.com

Käsers Schloss (the Swiss name
of the distillery) is owned by Ruedi
and Franziska Käser. The couple
started producing whisky in 2000
and expanded the business in
2006 to include themed events
such as whisky dinners and whisky
conferences at their premises.
The brand name of their whisky
in English is Whisky Castle, and
there are a number of expressions,
including Doublewood, which has
a whiff of chestnut, and Edition
Käser, which is matured in new
Bordeaux casks and bottled at
cask strength.

**WHISKY CASTLE
FULL MOON** ▶
SINGLE MALT 43% ABV
This is made from smoked, malted
barley during full moon, hence the
name. It is a young whisky with
a sweetish aroma and taste.

WHITE HORSE

Scotland
Owner: Diageo

In its heyday, White Horse was one of the world's top ten whiskies, selling more than 2 million cases a year. Its guiding genius was "Restless" Peter Mackie, described in his day as "one-third genius, one-third megalomaniac, and one-third eccentric". He took over the family firm in 1890 and built an enviable reputation as a gifted blender and entrepreneur.

White Horse is still marketed in more than 100 countries. A deluxe 12-year-old version, White Horse Extra Fine, is occasionally seen.

◀ **WHITE HORSE**
BLEND 40% ABV

Complex and satisfying, White Horse retains the robust flavour of Lagavulin, assisted by renowned Speysiders such as Aultmore. With its long finish, this is a stylish, intriguing blend of crisp grain, clean malt, and earthy peat.

WHYTE & MACKAY

Scotland
www.whyteandmackay.co.uk

The Glasgow-based firm of Whyte
& Mackay started blending in
the late 19th century. Its flagship
Special brand quickly established
itself as a Scottish favourite, and
remains so to this day. Having been
through a bewildering number of
owners and a management buy-out
in recent years, the company was
acquired in May 2007 by the
Indian conglomerate UB Group.

One constant through all
these changes has been the
highly regarded master blender ☞

WHYTE & MACKAY SPECIAL ▶
BLEND 40% ABV
The nose is full, round, and well-
balanced. On the palate, honeyed soft
fruits in profusion; smooth and rich,
with a long finish.

WHYTE & MACKAY
THE THIRTEEN
BLEND 40% ABV
Full, firm, and rich nose, with a slight
hint of sherry wood. "Marrying" for a
full year before bottling gives great
backbone. A well-integrated blend.

WHYTE & MACKAY

Richard Paterson, who joined the firm in 1970 and has received a great number of awards. As well as creating the "new" 40-year-old, Paterson has overseen several aged innovations.

The backbone of the blends emanates from Speyside and the Highlands. Dalmore and, to a lesser extent, Isle of Jura are the company's flagship single malts, and Dalmore's influence can be clearly felt in the premium blends. All the blends are noticeably smooth and well-balanced.

◀ WHYTE & MACKAY 30-YEAR-OLD
BLEND 40% ABV

The flagship of the Whyte & Mackay range is a big, rich, oaky whisky with a deep mahogany hue. The sherry influence is strong, with a pepperiness mellowed by the sweeter flavours.

WHYTE & MACKAY OLD LUXURY
BLEND 40% ABV

A rich bouquet, with malty notes and a subtle sherry influence. It all blends smoothly on the palate. Mellow and silky textured. Warming finish.

THE WILD GEESE

Ireland
www.thewildgeese-irishwhiskey.com

The term "Wild Geese" refers to those Irish nobles and soldiers who left to serve in continental European armies from the late 17th century to the dawn of the 20th century. The name has come down through history to embrace all the men and women who left Ireland in the last 400 years – not just the nobles. The idea of diaspora and emigration has, of course, been a poignant theme in Irish culture and remains so today. Wild Geese raises a glass to this part of Irish history, and they've certainly produced a good whiskey for the job.

THE WILD GEESE CLASSIC BLEND ▶
BLEND 40% ABV

A boiled-sweet nose. The malt doesn't have much impact here, leaving the grain to carry things to the finish.

THE WILD GEESE RARE IRISH
BLEND 43% ABV

A rich and malty blend, with some spiciness and lemon notes in the body. You'll find a little dry oak in the finish.

WILD TURKEY

USA
*Boulevard Distillery, US Highway
62 East, Lawrenceburg, Kentucky
www.wildturkeybourbon.com*

The Boulevard Distillery is
situated on Wild Turkey Hill,
above the Kentucky River, near
Lawrenceburg. The distillery was
first established in 1905 by the
three Ripy brothers, whose family
had been making whiskey since
the year 1869.

◀ WILD TURKEY 80 PROOF
BOURBON 40% ABV
The soft, sweet nose hints at corn,
while on the palate this is a very
traditional whiskey, nicely balancing
caramel and vanilla flavours. Ideal
served on the rocks or with a mixer.

WILD TURKEY 101 PROOF
BOURBON 50.5% ABV
Jimmy Russell maintains that 50.5%
ABV (101 proof) is the optimum
bottling strength for Wild Turkey.
This has a remarkably soft, yet rich,
aroma for such a high proof whiskey.
Full-bodied, rich, and robust palate,
with vanilla, fresh fruit, spice, brown
sugar, and honey. Oak notes develop
in the powerful, yet smooth, finish.

The Wild Turkey brand itself was conceived in 1940, when Austin Nichols' president, Thomas McCarthy, chose a quantity of 101 proof straight bourbon from his company stocks to take along on a wild turkey shoot. Today, Wild Turkey is distilled under the watchful eyes of legendary Master Distiller Jimmy Russell and his son Eddie. The Russells have also created some other highly regarded brands, including Russell's Reserve and American Spirit.

WILD TURKEY RARE BREED ▶
BOURBON (VARIABLE ABV)
A complex, initially assertive nose, with nuts, oranges, spices, and floral notes. Honey, oranges, vanilla, tobacco, mint, and molasses make for an equally complex palate. A long, nutty finish, with spicy, peppery rye.

WILD TURKEY KENTUCKY SPIRIT
BOURBON 50.5% ABV
A single barrel whiskey with a fresh, attractive nose of oranges and notes of rye. Complex on the palate, with almonds, honey, toffee, more oranges, and a hint of leather. The finish is long and sweet, gradually darkening and becoming more treacly.

Whisky Tour: Kentucky

The state of Kentucky is the bourbon-producing heartland of the USA and home to many of the best-known names in American whiskey. Most of the distilleries offer visitor facilities, allowing guests to study this historic spirit. Touring them is a great way to experience the beauty of Kentucky.

▐ DAY 1: BUFFALO TRACE, WOODFORD RESERVE

BARRELS AT WOODFORD
RESERVE

❶ Frankfort, the state capital, has a range of hotels and restaurants, and is the home of **Buffalo Trace**. The distillery's large visitor centre offers tours throughout the year.

❷ Woodford Reserve lies near the attractive town of Versailles, in Kentucky's famous "blue grass" horse-breeding country. Its copper pot stills are the highlight of the distillery tour.

▐ DAY 2: WILD TURKEY, FOUR ROSES

❸ Spectacularly situated on a hill above the Kentucky River, **Wild Turkey's** Boulevard Distillery allows visitors into its production areas at most times of the year.

❹ Four Roses Distillery is a striking structure, built in the style of a Spanish Mission. Tours are available from autumn to spring (the distillery is closed throughout the summer). You can also pre-arrange to visit Four Roses' warehouse at Cox's Creek.

WILD TURKEY EMBLEM

LOUISVILLE

Route 71

Route 64

150 KENTUCKY

FINISH

❾ JIM BEAM

OSCAR GETZ

❼

❻

❺

BARTON
BARDSTOWN

HEAVEN HILL

Route 65

Loretto Rd

❽

MAKER'S MARK

TOUR STATISTICS

DAYS: 5
LENGTH: 85 miles (137km)
TRAVEL: Car
DISTILLERIES: 8

DAY 3: HEAVEN HILL, BARTON, OSCAR GETZ

5 Bardstown is renowned as the "World Capital of Bourbon", and makes an excellent base for visiting the distilleries in the area. Book a room at the Old Talbott Tavern, which offers a well-stocked bourbon bar. Then head out to the **Heaven Hill** Bourbon Heritage Center, which includes a tour of a bourbon-ageing rackhouse and the chance to taste two Heaven Hill whiskeys.

HEAVEN HILL, BARDSTOWN

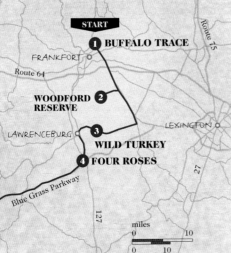

6 The Tom Moore Distillery in Bardstown, which produces the former **Barton** brands, has traditionally maintained a low profile compared to its neighbours. Nowadays, it boasts a state-of-the-art visitor centre and in-depth tours of the production areas.

7 A few blocks from Tom Moore, the **Oscar Getz** Whiskey Museum houses a collection of whiskey artefacts, including rare antique bottles, a moonshine still, and Abraham Lincoln's original liquor licence.

DAY 4: MAKER'S MARK

8 The historic **Maker's Mark** Distillery stands on the banks of Hardin's Creek, near Loretto, in Marion County. The distillery grounds are notable, being home to some 275 species of trees and shrubs. Guided distillery tours are available daily.

DAY 5: JIM BEAM

9 **Jim Beam**'s Clermont Distillery offers tours of the site grounds, a working rackhouse, and the Hartmann Cooperage Museum. The American Outpost is an on-site visitor centre, with a film about the bourbon-making process at Jim Beam and displays of whiskey memorabilia that take in more than two centuries of bourbon history.

JIM BEAM'S CLERMONT DISTILLERY

WILLIAM LAWSON'S

Scotland
Owner: John Dewar & Sons (Bacardi)

Although the Lawson's brand dates back to 1849, the "home" distillery today is MacDuff, built in 1960. Lawson's is managed alongside its big brother, Dewar's, and sells well over 1 million cases a year in France, Belgium, Spain, and parts of South America.

Glen Deveron single malt from MacDuff features heavily in the blend. MacDuff uses the highest percentage of sherry wood of any whisky in the Dewar's group, making the Lawson house style full in flavour and rich golden in colour.

◀ WILLIAM LAWSON'S FINEST
BLEND 40% ABV

Slightly dry nose, with delicate oak notes. Well-balanced palate, with hints of crisp toffee-apple. With a medium to full body, this punches above its weight.

WILLIAM LAWSON'S SCOTTISH GOLD 12-YEAR-OLD
BLEND 40% ABV

Fuller-flavoured than the standard Lawson's expression, suggesting a higher malt content.

WINDSOR

Scotland
Owner: Diageo

The name Windsor is an overt link to the British royal family, and the brand's packaging underlines its luxury position, especially in the highly competitive South Korean market. Windsor was originally developed in a partnership between Seagram and local Korean producer Doosan; later, Diageo acquired the Seagram interest and launched Windsor 17 as the first super-premium whisky in 2000. Windsor 17's sweeping popularity in Korea posed a threat to its competitors, many of whom have since emulated the older style.

WINDSOR 12-YEAR-OLD ▶
BLEND 40% ABV
Vanilla, wood, and light fresh fruit on the nose. Green apples on the palate, with honey, more vanilla, and spiciness that mellows into a smooth finish.

WINDSOR 17-YEAR-OLD
BLEND 40% ABV
A rich vanilla crème brûlée nose, with fruit and a background layer of malt. Fresh fruit and honey on the palate, with creamy vanilla oak notes.

WINDSOR CANADIAN

Canada

Alberta Distillery, 1521 34th Avenue Southeast, Calgary, Alberta

One might think that this comes from the Hiram Walker Distillery at Windsor, Ontario; actually, it is made at the Alberta Distillery *(see p12)*. The name is no doubt meant to recall the British Royal Family, but it should not be confused with the Scotch Windsor *(see p373)*. Like other whiskies made at Alberta, Windsor Canadian is exclusively rye-based.

◄ **WINDSOR CANADIAN**
BLENDED CANADIAN RYE
40% ABV
Honey, peaches, pine nuts, and cloves on the nose. A medium body and a sweet taste, with cereal and wood notes. An unassuming whisky; great value for money.

WISER'S

Canada

*Hiram Walker Distillery, Riverside
Drive East, Walkerville, Ontario
www.wisers.ca*

John Philip Wiser may well have
been the first distiller to use the
term "Canadian Whisky" on his
label, at the Chicago World's Fair
in 1893. By the early 1900s, his
was the third largest distillery in
Canada, and its whiskies were
being exported to Asia and the US.

A few years after the death of
J.P. Wiser in 1917, the company
was acquired by Hiram Walker.
Eventually, production moved
to the Hiram Walker Distillery
at Walkerville. Today, Wiser's are
the fifth best-selling Canadian
whiskies in Canada.

WISER'S DELUXE ▶
BLEND 40% ABV
A fruity and spicy nose, with cereal
and linseed oil, vanilla, and toffee.

WISER'S SMALL BATCH
BLEND 43.4% ABV
This is full-flavoured, with vanilla, oak,
and butterscotch on the nose and in
the taste. The slightly higher strength
makes for more flavour and texture.

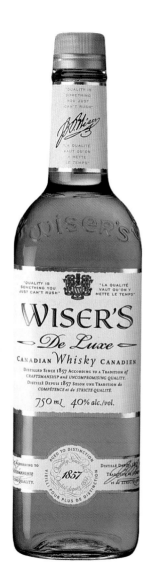

WOODFORD RESERVE

USA
7855 McCracken Pike,
Versailles, Kentucky
www.woodfordreserve.com

Woodford Reserve is the smallest distillery operating in Kentucky, and it is unique among bourbon distilleries in that it uses a triple distillation method and three copper pot stills.

◄ WOODFORD RESERVE DISTILLER'S SELECT
BOURBON 45.2% ABV
An elegant yet robust nose, perfumed, with milk chocolate raisins, dried fruit, burnt sugar, ginger, and saddle soap. Equally complex on the palate: fragrant and fruity, with raspberries, camomile, and ginger. Lingering vanilla and peppery oak in the finish.

MASTER'S COLLECTION FOUR GRAIN
BOURBON 46.2% ABV
Spicy apple pie, vanilla, caramel, and mint on the nose. The palate features more vanilla, caramel, orange, nuts, and oak. The lengthy finish exhibits pine and spicy oak. The four grains used are corn, malted barley, rye, and wheat.

In 2005, the first bottling in the Master's Collection range was released under the Four Grain Bourbon name, and two years later a Sonoma-Cutrer Finish was added to the line-up. The Master's Collection 1838 Sweet Mash was released in 2008 to commemorate the year in which the present Woodford Reserve Distillery was constructed, and also to celebrate the historic "sweet mash" method of bourbon production.

MASTER'S COLLECTION
SONOMA-CUTRER FINISH ▶
BOURBON 43.2% ABV

The first and only bourbon in the world to be finished in California Chardonnay barrels. The influence of the wine casks is very apparent in this fruity, sweet bourbon. Butterscotch and almonds on the nose; baked apples, peaches, and toffee in the mouth. Medium to long finish.

MASTER'S COLLECTION
1838 SWEET MASH
BOURBON 43.2% ABV

Maple syrup, spicy fruit, cinnamon and nutmeg aromas. Rich palate, with more maple syrup, rich fruit, rye, and mint. Lengthy finish, with soft apple notes.

A–Z OF WHISKIES BY TYPE

Page numbers in *italics* indicate whisky tour references.

A–Z OF WHISKIES BY COUNTRY

Page numbers in *italics* indicate whisky tour references.

SIMPLY

JESUS

LifeChange Books

JOE
STOWELL

This special edition is published by the
Billy Graham Evangelistic Association
with permission from Multnomah Publishers.

Multnomah® Publishers *Sisters, Oregon*

SIMPLY JESUS
published by Multnomah Publishers, Inc.

© 2002 by Dr. Joseph M. Stowell
Cover design by David Carlson

Multnomah is a trademark of Multnomah Publishers, Inc.,
and is registered in the U.S. Patent and Trademark Office.
The colophon is a trademark of Multnomah Publishers, Inc.

Printed in the United States of America

Library of Congress Cataloging-in-Publication Data

Stowell, Joseph M.
   Simply Jesus / by Joseph M. Stowell.
      p. cm.
   Previously ISBN 1-57673-856-6
   ISBN 0-913367-51-6
   1. Christian life.   2. Jesus Christ—Person and offices.   I. Title.
BV4509.5 .S85 2002
248.4—dc21

Table of Contents

Chapter 1

EXPERIENCING JESUS

*Paul said that it was the throbbing ambition
of his life to experience Jesus.... Is it yours?*

When my secretary told me I'd been invited to the White
House, my heart picked up a little speed.

I wonder if I'll get to meet the president.

Like everyone else, I'd read a lot about him and seen him
countless times in pictures and on TV. I'd followed his political career with more than a little interest. In fact, I had
voted for him. If someone had asked if I knew much about
him, I could have launched into a rather extensive description
of his background, his political philosophy, and his policies.

But this was different.

I was on the verge of actually experiencing him.
Personally.

Wearing my best navy pin-striped suit, a starched

white shirt, and a "presidential" tie, I stopped long enough at the airport to get my shoes professionally shined. I could hardly keep myself from telling the man bent over my feet, *Do a good job—these shoes are headed for the White House.*

I felt sobered as I walked into the grand foyer of our president's home. *These truly are the halls of power,* I said to myself. *Behind closed doors in this very house wars have been declared—history made.*

I found myself seated on the front row of the East Room. The small gathering hushed as a commanding voice announced, "Ladies and gentlemen, the president of the United States." We stood as he walked in briskly and took his place on the low platform. I couldn't take my eyes off of him. I was in his presence and found myself intrigued by his every move. Later, in a very brief conversation, I was surprised at how engaged he seemed. If only for a moment, he looked into my eyes and gave me his attention.

Frankly, having experienced the reality of his presence, I will never view our president in the same way again. I went away wishing I could know him better.

It's like that in your relationship with Jesus: You can be satisfied to just know about Him, or you can enter into an experience with Jesus. Only you can make the choice. And this choice determines the difference between religion as usual or the satisfaction of connecting with Jesus, the One we were created to enjoy.

More than Mere Knowledge

We all know who Jesus is. Right?

In the last two thousand years, no other individual has commanded such respect, such honor. Our entire Western civilization—from its laws to its ethics—has been marked and molded by His teaching. For over two millennia, history's greatest works of art have centered on His life, death, and resurrection. Enduring musical masterpieces have celebrated His worth and glory. But for those who have personally embraced the liberating reality of His forgiveness of sin and hope of eternity, He is so much more.

Or...at least, He should be.

We preach and teach about His will and His ways; tell His stories by heart; celebrate Him in worship; and serve Him with enthusiasm. Yet underneath it all (if we are truly candid), there is a gnawing sense that there should be something...well, more to this relationship.

Why is it that He often feels so far away? So historical? So church related? So other? The distance between knowing Him and knowing about Him is vast. And the space between these two experiences separates the spectators from intimate participants.

Think carefully. It's a pretty safe bet that if you are reading this book you know at least something about Him. You know something about Him biographically and historically.

In your more lucid moments, you might even be able to talk a little theology. But as impressive as your knowledge about Jesus may be, the unfortunate reality is that most of us stop there. Seemingly satisfied that knowing about Him is enough, we have no clue that there is more.

And there is more.

The thought of a deep richness waiting for those who get beyond knowing about Him to actually experiencing Him has either escaped us or—worse yet—has been exiled to the vague regions of religious wishful thinking.

If that's your story, get ready.

The best is yet to come.

Jesus intends for you to experience the pleasure and reassuring peace of His presence at the core of your life. He wants to be more than just another volume in your encyclopedia of biblical facts. He didn't die for you to simply strike a deal guaranteeing heaven. He died for you to make you His own and to grant you the unspeakable privilege of experiencing Him personally.

As Paul wrote to early followers of Jesus…

He [God] is the one who invited you into this wonderful friendship with his Son, Jesus Christ.

1 CORINTHIANS 1:9, NLT

And think of this invitation that Jesus extends to all of us who will respond…

"Look! Here I stand at the door and knock. If you hear me calling and open the door, I will come in, and we will share a meal as friends."

REVELATION 3:20, NLT

This is incomparably better than an invitation to the White House. The eternal God of the universe has called us into fellowship—friendship, companionship, close contact—with His Son. Jesus never intended to connect only with your head; He lives to connect with the entire you. In fact, He sent us the Holy Spirit to make the total connection possible, and gave us His Word to show the way. And, regardless of who you are or how you have chosen to live your life, you can know the pleasure of His presence.

Up close and personal.

Forgive a trip down memory lane, but I long again to experience Jesus in my grandmother's quavery voice as she sang the words of her favorite hymn:

I come to the garden alone
While the dew is still on the roses,
And the voice I hear falling on my ear
The Son of God discloses.
And He walks with me and He talks with me
and He tells me I am His own.
And the joy we share as we tarry there,
None other has ever known.

Knowing my grandmother, I have little doubt that she had moved well beyond simply "knowing about Him" into the joy of experiencing Him.

And just in case you think that a closer relationship with Jesus is about some kind of rigid morning routine, some tedious-but-essential religious exercise, think again. While regular Bible study and cultivating a life of prayer are indispensable, there is far more to a personal experience with Jesus.

—*It's about a deep and abiding sense of His nearness on the journey.*

—*It's about an unshakable confidence that only His abiding presence can give.*

—*It's about courage in the face of previously intimidating encounters.*

—*It's about a closeness that enables your spirit to commune with Him, anywhere, anytime, regardless.*

—*It's about meeting Him in places you may have never dreamed of...in the most heated of seductions, in the midst of suffering, and in acts of unflinching surrender.*

There is a marvelously mystical aspect to all this. You can't wrap words around it. You can't put it in a box and tie it up with a red ribbon. When you try to fully define it, you degrade it.

Jesus is never predictable. Just totally available. He

doesn't play hide-and-seek. In fact, He consistently rewards anyone who diligently seeks Him (Hebrews 11:6). But to many of us, tasting of that reward seems so illusive. Could it be we simply don't know how to seek Him or where to find Him?

I'll never forget the frustrating experience early one Sunday morning when I was supposed to pick up an elderly relative who had come into Chicago on the train from Milwaukee. The whole purpose of the exercise was to find her and get her safely to our house. I showed up on time, but where was she? Certainly not where I thought she would be. I checked the monitor and the train was already in. With a sinking feeling in the pit of my stomach, I scoured the early morning loneliness of Union Station…to no avail.

I was about ready to leave when I happened to glance down a hallway toward the baggage area. There she was, luggage at her feet, patiently waiting for me to arrive. She'd been there all the time. And to my chagrin, she was right where she should have been! I had been looking in all the wrong places.

The great news is that Jesus is there, patiently waiting for you. In fact, He not only waits, but is also at this very moment busily pursuing you. The fact that you are reading this book is no accident, no coincidence. It's just another one of the countless ways He hopes to get your attention.

It's time to connect.

YOU CAN'T GET ENOUGH OF HIM

The following lines of Scripture have captured my heart in recent days. Don't skip over them. Don't let your mind wander. If you really want to experience Jesus, you must read these words slowly and thoughtfully...until they have gripped your heart.

> I once thought all these things were so very important, but now I consider them worthless because of what Christ has done. Yes, everything else is worthless when compared with the priceless gain of knowing Christ Jesus my Lord. I have discarded everything else, counting it all as garbage, so that I may have Christ and become one with him. I no longer count on my own goodness or my ability to obey God's law, but I trust Christ to save me. For God's way of making us right with himself depends on faith. *As a result, I can really know Christ and experience the mighty power that raised him from the dead.* I can learn what it means to suffer with him, sharing in this death, so that, somehow, I can experience the resurrection from the dead!
>
> PHILIPPIANS 3:7–11, NLT, EMPHASIS ADDED

More than any other writer, Paul spoke most passionately about knowing Jesus. It was his singular quest in life.

Everything else became peripheral—rubbish—compared to knowing God's Son. And in this text, when he speaks of giving everything up to know Jesus, he uses the Greek word that means *to know by experience.*

But here's the thought that sets me back on my heels. Paul had already experienced Jesus in far more dramatic ways than anyone before or since. On the Damascus highway, Jesus appeared to Paul in a bolt of white fire and spoke to him in person. Sometime later, Paul found himself swept up into the "third heaven," where he had an extended season of personal experience with Jesus.

Yet what did Paul want with all his heart?

He wanted more.

He was still so taken with Jesus that the entire focus of his life was to experience more of Him. Which only proves that once you get a taste, you can never get enough of Him. Having experienced Jesus makes even the brightest treasures of life look dull by comparison.

Do you wonder if this is for you? Wonder no longer! He is at the door of your heart, wanting to come in for some serious fellowship.

Chapter 2

I'D RATHER
HAVE JESUS

If you had to choose between Jesus and something precious to you
...some alluring dream or tantalizing desire...
I wonder, would you choose Him?

The meal was just about finished when I leaned over and asked Billy Graham the question I had hoped to ask him all evening.

Martie and I had been seated next to Dr. Graham at a dinner for the staff and board of his organization. Billy, eighty at the time, was lucid and interesting. Wondering what he would say about his highest joys in life, I asked, "Of all your experiences in ministry, what have you enjoyed most?"

Then (thinking I might help him out a little), I quickly added, "Was it your time spent with presidents and heads of state? Or was it—"

Before I could finish my next sentence, Billy swept his hand across the tablecloth, as if to push my suggestions onto the floor.

"None of that," he said. "By far the greatest joy of my life has been my fellowship with Jesus. Hearing Him speak to me, having Him guide me, sensing His presence with me and His power through me. This has been the highest pleasure of my life!"

It was spontaneous, unscripted, and clearly unrehearsed.

There wasn't even a pause.

With a life full of stellar experiences and worldwide fame behind him, it was simply Jesus who was on his mind and on his heart. His lifelong experience with Jesus had made its mark, and Billy was satisfied.

I found Billy Graham's statement that evening more than convicting. I found it motivating—right to the core of my being. With everything in me, I want what he's experienced. I find my heart saying, *If I make it to eighty, I want to say the same thing.*

Even more so when you consider the story of Chuck Templeton.

"I MISS HIM!"

Templeton's name was practically a household word in evangelical homes in the fifties and sixties. He pastored one of Toronto's leading churches and—along with his close friend Billy Graham—helped found Youth for Christ in Canada. His extraordinary ability to communicate God's Word put him in demand on platforms all over North America.

But I don't remember him for his stellar gifts.

I remember him for his renunciation of the faith.

Evangelicals everywhere were rocked by the news that Chuck Templeton had left his church and renounced all he had previously embraced and proclaimed.

The former preacher went on to fame and fortune. He managed two of Canada's leading newspapers, worked his way into an influential position with the Canadian Broadcasting Company—and even took a run at the prime minister's office.

It had been decades since I'd thought of Chuck Templeton. So imagine my surprise when I noticed he had been interviewed by Lee Strobel in his book, *A Case for Faith.*

After reading Templeton's most recent book, *Farewell to God: My Reasons for Rejecting the Christian Faith,* Strobel caught a plane to Toronto to meet with him. Though eighty-three and in declining health, the former preacher vigorously defended his agnostic rejection of a God who claimed to be love, yet allowed suffering across the world to go unchecked.

Then, toward the end of their time together, Strobel asked Templeton point-blank how he felt about Jesus.

Instantly, the old man softened.

He spoke in adoring terms about Jesus, concluding, "In my view He is the most important human being who has ever existed." Then as his voice began to crack, he haltingly said, *"I…miss…Him!"* With that, Strobel writes, tears flooded Templeton's eyes, and his shoulders bobbed as he wept.

Think of it. Billy Graham and Chuck Templeton, two friends who chose radically different paths through life. And near the end of their journeys, one has found Jesus to be his most prized possession, while the other weeps for having left Him long ago.

TAPPING THE SECRET

Cynics might say that you'd expect someone like Graham to have a close walk with Jesus—and that common, ordinary folk like the rest of us can't expect to get there. But my grandmother had it as well. And she was no Billy Graham.

Born of pioneer stock in Michigan, she married a

frontier farmer and gave birth to her children in a drafty, second-floor corner bedroom at home. She simply kept house for her family, far away from the hustle and bustle of high society. No one but friends and family even knew her name. Yet she had tapped the secret as well.

And so can you.

Stepping into a deepening experience with Jesus is something more than keeping short accounts with sin in our lives. It's beyond that. It is about getting far enough beyond *self* that we can see Him more clearly and desire Him more completely.

Let me explain.

First, so there is no confusion, keeping clear ledgers in our lives is basic to experiencing Christ. As long as there is residual sin in our hearts, there will always be a distance. In His Sermon on the Mount, Jesus said, "Blessed are the pure in heart, for they shall see God" (Matthew 5:8). And the tenses in that pronouncement are not futuristic but present. In other words, if you are not pure in heart today, don't count on experiencing Christ in a compelling way.

It's really not complicated. If there is bitterness, unresolved anger, sensual thoughts and actions, pride, untruthfulness, or slander and gossip in your vocabulary, you're going to feel the distance. Jesus doesn't meet us on those playing fields. He'll meet us there to pull us out of the ditch of our own ways, but He won't stay there with us.

I hope you are in a quiet place where you can put this book down for a moment and think carefully about those things in your life that stand between you and Jesus. Go to your knees and open your life to His divine inspection. Pray as the psalmist prayed,

Search me, O God, and know my heart;
    Try me and know my anxious thoughts;
And see if there be any hurtful way in me,
    And lead me in the everlasting way.

PSALM 139:23-24

Don't shy away from this. He already knows about your secret thoughts and struggles. He has been grieving the distance between your heart and His. At this very instant, He is waiting for you, His cleansing mercy readily available.

Dealing with our sin is step one. But I have a hunch most of us understand that already. In fact, some of us may feel that we've been making fairly good progress in that regard.

So…why does Jesus still seem so distant?

If anyone's heart had a clean slate, we'd all probably agree that the apostle Paul qualifies for the honor. Yet Paul insists that his pursuit of a deeper experience with Jesus focuses on a distraction far more subtle than obvious sin. As he writes to the Philippians, he makes the case that we can never fully experience Jesus until we stop being absorbed with ourselves.

Chapter 3

ME OR THEE?

*At some point in life, we have to come to grips
with whether "He" or "me" is the main feature
of our existence.*

"Daddy, are we famous?"

Libby, my seven-year-old, looked up into my eyes.

Famous? I was pastoring a church in a small Midwestern town at the time, and it didn't take me long to respond.

"No, honey," I assured her. "We're not famous at all."

She paused thoughtfully, and then with confidence and a touch of consternation, replied, "Well, we *would* be if more people knew about us."

Poor Libby, only seven, and already concerned with what people thought about us. With whether or not we registered on the Richter scale of public opinion.

It is something that Libby will likely wrestle with the

rest of her life. She, like all of us, will spend her days struggling through the sticky web of self-absorbed perspectives. Since earliest childhood we have been very much aware of and concerned about ourselves. We mastered words like *my* and *mine* long before we knew the word for *friend* or *share*.

Now, as grown-ups, we find ourselves haunted regularly by questions like these: *Who am I? What do people think of me? Have I been sufficiently recognized for my accomplishments? How am I being treated? Does anyone care about me?*

Americans spend millions of dollars trying to get to know themselves. Books about knowing and understanding "who you really are" consistently make the bestseller lists. Obscene amounts of money go to therapists who offer to guide you on a journey through your inner self.

Frankly, can you think of a scarier thought than taking an inner journey through yourself? It's not only a scary thought, it may be an unbiblical one. If you are in the process of becoming a fully devoted follower of Christ, then life is an adventure in getting to know Jesus. And, when we live to know Him, we find that knowing Him is the key to understanding and making peace with ourselves.

Trying to discover self-worth? *You have it in Him....
He died for you!*

Plagued by failure and guilt? *He does what no one else will
or can do for you.... He forgives and forgets, kills the fatted calf*

as heaven rejoices, and clothes you with the best robes of His righteousness.

Searching for significance? *Search no more…you are His child. There is no greater significance than that.*

Wondering if there is any reason or purpose for you to take up space on this care-worn planet? *The mystery is unraveled in Him as He scripts your life to be lived for His glory and to reflect the radiance of His character.*

Let's face it, absorption with self is inadequate to satisfy the soul—and completely inept to solve the restless searching of our hearts. Life *must* be about more than getting to know ourselves. Ultimately, self-preoccupation is an empty, boring pursuit. No matter how charming, witty, or profound we may be, we were not created to enthrall ourselves with ourselves for long periods of time.

Simply put, we need Him!

TIRED OF ME

I'm only fifty-seven, and I already find myself weary of the hollow thoughts of what few accomplishments I may have mustered in my life. My failures continue to embarrass me. The inadequacies I have carried with me since my youth still frustrate me. My insecurities still trouble my soul. And the praise of others has an increasingly hollow ring. I am tired of worrying about whether or not the sermon I preached was good enough or whether or not someone will pat me on the back for a job well done. I'm tired of worrying about what people think about me. I'm weary of the carnal feeling that sometimes haunts me when someone talks about his favorite preacher and it's not me.

Bottom line, I just flat out get tired of me. But I never get tired of Jesus.

After all these years, I still find Him more compelling, more engaging, more awesome, more surprising, more fulfilling, and more attractive than ever before.

I never get tired of singing His praises or of watching Him perform. I find Him to be gripping. Absorbing. Beyond comprehension. And that's why—along with Paul, my grandmother, Billy Graham, and countless others through the years—I find myself longing to know Him better.

I am becoming increasingly aware that life doesn't go on forever. When we're young, we think we're bulletproof. We live like we'll never die. But when your knees protest certain movements and your eyesight and memory begin to grow fuzzy, reality sets in. I can see the day coming when there'll be another president of Moody—and a better one at that. There'll be other preachers who bless hungry hearts.

And me? I'll be sitting in the corner of some nursing home waiting for them to ring the lunch bell. And if life up to that point has been all about me, that is going to be a sad and empty day—no matter what they're serving for lunch. Why? Because all I will have will be me! Which at that point won't be much.

But...if my life has been about knowing Jesus and experiencing a deepening relationship with Him, as I sit in that corner of the nursing home waiting for the lunch bell to ring, He'll be there with me.

The mighty Son of God.

The Bright and Morning Star.

The Desire of all Nations.

The Great Shepherd of the sheep.

The wondrous Creator of all.

The King of kings and Lord of lords.

And He'll be more wonderful on that day than ever before. He'll walk with me as I toddle along the linoleum in my walker. He'll talk with me, and I won't have any trouble hearing Him when He tells me that I am His own. He'll say, "Well, Joe, you're almost home." And I'll say, "Lord, the sooner the better. I've heard Your voice through all these years, but I can't wait to see Your face." He and I will be having such a grand time of fellowship, I just might miss that lunch bell.

It's time that we all got real about where Jesus fits in the overall picture of our lives. At some point, the sooner in life the better, we have to come to grips with whether "He" or "me" will be the main feature of our existence. Careful, it's easy to fudge—to think that you can be fully absorbed with yourself and in hot pursuit of Him at the same time. But that isn't reality. You can't have it both ways.

Paul was well aware of the radical choice he would have to make to fully experience the presence and power of Jesus in his life. For him the decision was clear. He chose Jesus.

All right, you say, but he had an edge. After all, he had literally been in the presence of Jesus Christ. Probably twice. I doubt that any of us would be interested in a self-absorbed life if we had actually met the Lord of the universe face-to-face! Fast-food hamburgers lose some of their glow after you've tied into a killer steak!

But in spite of that, he still faced the tension of getting lost in himself. Paul's résumé offered a tempting list of accomplishments that would have seduced the best of us to become fully self-absorbed. Listen to him rattle off his credentials. In the crowd he ran with, this would have been good for some multiple "wows." He writes...

> Yet I could have confidence in myself if anyone could. If others have reason for confidence in their own efforts, I have even more! For I was circumcised when I was eight days old, having been born into a pure-blooded Jewish family that is a branch of the tribe of Benjamin. So I am a real Jew if there ever was one! What's more, I was a member of the

Pharisees, who demand the strictest obedience to the Jewish law. And zealous? Yes, in fact, I harshly persecuted the church. And I obeyed the Jewish law so carefully that I was never accused of any fault.

PHILIPPIANS 3:4–6, NLT

And yet…. And yet his choice is clear….

I once thought all these things were so very important, but now I consider them worthless because of what Christ has done. Yes, everything else is worthless when compared with the priceless gain of knowing Christ Jesus my Lord. I have discarded everything else, counting it all as garbage, so that I may have Christ and become one with him.

VV. 7–9, NLT

Hear his passion…. *You can take all the newspaper clippings, book reviews, and academic honors. Take the prized business card, retirement watch, and bowling trophies and stuff 'em in a Dumpster. They mean less than NOTHING to me compared to Jesus, compared to knowing Him better every day.*

Taking this step doesn't mean that we stop having what we have, doing what we do, or being who we are. It simply means we are no longer consumed by it all. We are consumed instead with Jesus.

As Jesus welcomes us to lose ourselves in Him, He reminds us, "Whoever finds his life will lose it, and whoever loses his life for my sake will find it" (Matthew 10:39, NIV).

What an intriguing thought.

Chapter 4

BLUE RIBBONS

*Beware the danger of losing Jesus
in the glitter of your own goodness.*

What happens—what are the consequences—when followers of Christ forget that Jesus comes first, and get absorbed in themselves and their own accomplishments?

It's never a pretty picture.

My mind jumps back to an incident from junior high days. I remember standing with my buddies in the hall outside our Sunday school room. We were way too cool to get into our chairs early for class. The name of the game was hanging out in the hall to "see and be seen" as all the Sunday foot traffic went by. On this particular Sunday we spotted a visitor—a boy about our age coming down the hall toward our classroom with his mother. Since he was new, we immediately sized him up.

As he came closer, we caught a glimpse of something that clearly marked him. It was bad enough that he was coming with his *mom,* but what was that hanging on the lapel of his suit? Closer examination revealed it to be a long string of Sunday school attendance pins.

In case you didn't grow up in this kind of a church, let me bring you up to speed. If you had perfect attendance in Sunday school for one year, you received a small round metal pin that you could wear, signifying your faithfulness. If you had another perfect year, you won a wreath that went around the pin, with two small loops at the bottom. The loops were for the bars that could be attached year after year to each other if you maintained a spotless attendance record.

This boy must not have missed a Sunday since the day he was born. He looked like a little Russian general, decked out with a chestful of battle ribbons. The bars under his award pin seemed to swing as he walked. In fact, we thought that he tilted a little to the left under the weight of it all.

And what do you think? That we guys in the hallway were blown away by this kid's stellar spiritual accomplishments? That we stood in awe and stunned admiration of his impeccable Sunday school credentials?

No chance.

It was more like, *"Who does this guy think he is?"*

Obviously, it wasn't the most gracious or praiseworthy response, but it came naturally.

This was the essence of the destructive dynamic under way among first-century followers of Jesus in the city of Philippi. And if we're not careful, it easily becomes the ruling pattern in our own lives as well.

THE HOLIER-THAN-THOU CROWD

Any way you look at it, the Judaizers were trouble.

The strident teachings of this group within the early church were more than controversial. They were explosive. Simply put, the Judaizers taught that the death of Christ wasn't enough for salvation. The Lord's sacrifice on the cross did not cancel the requirements of the law and the countless demands of the Levitical system. Therefore, in their view, authentic Christians were to continue to observe sacrifices, circumcision, the Sabbath, and other aspects of the multiplicity of rules handed down by Moses. If you had the Real Deal, you would keep all the requirements of the law.

And guess who thought they were the authentic Christians?

The Judaizers.

As you might imagine, they were rather taken with themselves. They were the "true believers" with the inside scoop on what pleased God.

Never mind that their doctrine flew in the face of the apostles' teaching that Jesus fulfilled all the law and its requirements. According to countless passages in the Epistles, the new covenant in Christ made His work supreme and final—and our good works are simply a reflection of our love and allegiance to Him.

The way the Judaizers saw it, however, they were simply better than the average "loose-living" so-called Christian.

On the other side, the "faith alone" crowd looked at the Judaizers as prime examples of legalism gone amok. As the two camps began to debate, argue, and polarize, they focused on their own distinctives and rejoiced in their own doctrinal correctness.

"We've got it right, and you've got it all wrong."

"No, WE'VE got it right, and YOU'VE got it all wrong."

"No, we don't!"

"Yes, you do!"

And guess who got lost in the scuffle?

Jesus.

That suited Satan's plans perfectly. The church at Philippi was ready to self-destruct—to implode under the weight of its own intramural "Who's the Best?" tournament. The Judaizers were convinced they had won. They kept all the Law. Their work, instead of being a reflection of their love for Jesus, was a reflection of their love for themselves.

It is a strange and subtly destructive dynamic that the better we become, the more we seem to get stuck on ourselves. The demons of pride and self-adulation lurk just around the corner of every good deed. If we're not careful, the better we are, the worse we might become.

Living to flaunt your goodness or to measure yourself by everyone else may very well be the major barrier to a deepening experience of Jesus in our lives. As we have said, life cannot be about you and Him at the same time. Either you are the feature or He is. Take your pick.

In our Christian culture there are lots of fields on which to play this "look-at-me" game....

- Keeping the longest list of rules and living as though strictness is next to godliness
- Serving in high-profile positions in churches and worthy organizations
- Serving in low-profile positions in those same places
- Finding success in the marketplace
- Raising godly kids
- Home-schooling
- Not home-schooling
- Worshiping with contemporary music
- Worshiping in the traditional way
- Using newer Bible translations

- Rejecting newer Bible translations and sticking with the older ones
- Giving large amounts of money
- Getting invitations to the "right" events

The list goes on. And while we don't actually pass out blue ribbons or medals for spiritual accomplishments, we do tend to wear them in our attitudes and self-serving chatter. And when we do, we betray the secret that we've been trying to hide: that life, even when we serve Jesus, is really about "me" after all.

So what is a Jesus seeker to do? Stop being good? Stop being blessed? Stop serving? Stop obeying? Stop sacrificing and surrendering?

Obviously not. Then what are we to do?

Having learned that experiencing Jesus requires transitioning from being self-absorbed, we are now ready to begin the journey toward Him.

Read carefully.

Experiencing Jesus begins with two attitude shifts.

Chapter 5

ON A FENCE POST

Attitude Shift #1...
REJOICE IN THE LORD.

Have you ever been around Christians who smile about everything?

Does it trouble you...just a little?

I must admit, it bothers me. From where I sit, this sort of attitude robs our Christian life of the honest emotions of grief and appropriate anger. It robs us of the healthy emotional swings we experience day by day, hour by hour. It denies the therapy of an uncontrolled belly laugh and the cleansing of a good cry. I'm trying to figure out what these smile machines know that I don't. Maybe they've gotten their signal to be happy all the time from Paul's exhortation to "rejoice in the Lord"—which was buttressed by his follow-up statement to "rejoice in the Lord always;

again I will say, rejoice!" (Philippians 3:1; 4:4).

Thankfully, when Paul opened the third chapter of Philippians with the command to "rejoice in the Lord," he wasn't asking us to go around 24/7 with a praise smile on our face. To expect anybody—much less Christians in the early church who faced excruciating persecution—to be constantly "happy" is something of a stretch.

Besides, biblical joy is never defined as an unending emotional high. Jesus wept over Lazarus, spent a season alone grieving over the brutal murder of His cousin John, and was thoroughly tested in every point even as we are.

So what did Paul mean? Given the problem of the self-inflated Judaizers and the apostle's following statements about the supremacy of knowing Christ, his conclusion is pretty clear.

It's time to stop rejoicing in ourselves and start rejoicing in Jesus. As we have learned, deciding not to be self-absorbed is important. But we will quickly slide back into its grip if we don't replace it with an active and aggressive pattern of rejoicing in Him.

Rejoicing in Jesus is the liberating response that frees us from the endless task of trying to satisfy and fill our souls with ourselves and our accomplishments. It frees us from the endless torment of worrying about being recognized, affirmed, and adequately appreciated. It soothes otherwise fragile egos that are quickly frustrated and irritated when others don't live up to our expectations or when we don't get what we think we "deserve."

Living to brag on Jesus instead of ourselves must have been what Jeremiah had in mind when he declared:

> This is what the LORD says: "Let not the wise man gloat in his wisdom, or the mighty man in his might, or the rich man in his riches. Let them boast in this alone: that they truly know me and understand that I am the LORD who is just and righteous, whose love is unfailing, and that I delight in these things. I, the LORD, have spoken!"
>
> JEREMIAH 9:23–24, NLT

When you think about it, there is far more to brag about in Him than the best of what any of us could ever hope to be or accomplish. When Paul celebrated Christ's awesome list of credentials, he could hardly stop writing for the sheer joy of it all.

He was shamelessly boasting.

He went on and on.

And it felt so right!

Who is Jesus? He's the One:

> ...in whom we have redemption, the forgiveness of sins. And He is the image of the invisible God, the first-born of all creation. For by Him all things

were created, both in the heavens and on earth, visible and invisible, whether thrones or dominions or rulers or authorities—all things have been created by Him and for Him. And He is before all things, and in Him all things hold together. He is also head of the body, the church; and He is the beginning, the first-born from the dead; so that He Himself might come to have first place in everything.

COLOSSIANS 1:14–18

Boasting is a healthy activity when it centers on Jesus. You can introduce Him to others with as long a string of superlatives as you want. You can list His accomplishments, cite His wonderful qualities, talk constantly about His kindness and mercy and love, and sing His praises for the rest of your life.

And that would be a good thing to do, because He deserves it all.

And more.

So why do we keep drawing attention to ourselves? Why do we want to get the credit and seek applause for our good deeds? Why do we boast in our accomplishments? Why do we keep kidding ourselves? Everything good we've ever managed to do is because of Him, accomplished in and through His grace and strength. If it weren't for Him—His grace to save me and supply my life with all I've needed to accomplish and succeed—I would be and do nothing of significance at all.

That isn't modesty or false humility. It's not "Aw, shucks." It's stark reality.

You simply cannot exaggerate when you are speaking of His worth. He belongs in the place of preeminence.

And if in your heart you have become preeminent, then He is not. It bears repeating: Either He is preeminent, or you are. To think that even the best of us can compete with Him is an embarrassing arrogance.

I'm not saying we have nothing to rejoice about in ourselves. Anyone who is anxious to please Christ and who has been gifted and blessed has a lot to feel good about. God doesn't want to deny you the sweet feel of a straight and long golf shot, a tender kiss from one you love, a contract won, an investment that succeeds, or the pleasure of a task superbly performed. Seeking Jesus by living to rejoice in Him does not require you to lapse into self-defacing, non-productive "woe-is-me-ness."

Nevertheless, if you and I are ever going to experience Jesus in the way we long to experience Him, we need to learn how to get beyond ourselves and our achievements *to get all the way to Him.* We need to cultivate a reflex response that immediately triggers gratefulness and praise to Him for enabling us to accomplish what we do…when something good happens in life…when we've performed well and received a few strokes…when we've been acknowledged and affirmed…when our fondest dreams have come true.

When we are blessed, we need to master the response that takes that spark of joy we feel about ourselves and lets it *explode* into the joy of celebrating His preeminent provision and grace in our lives.

The moment you do this, you connect with Him and lose yourself in His abundant goodness.

UP ON A FENCE POST

A number of years ago, a friend of mine wrote a book he entitled *Turtle on a Fence Post;* it was the story of his highly successful life. What a great title. Stop and think about it: How does a turtle ever make it to the top of a fence post?

He certainly didn't climb there.

If a turtle is on a fence post you can rest assured that someone put him there. It took a power beyond his own to place him on that lofty perch. And when you answer the question of how you got to the top of *your* fence post, then you'll be ready to turn from celebrating yourself and begin to celebrate Him.

Resisting the ever-present tendency to rejoice in our

own preeminence demands that we learn to recognize when we are tangled in its web. Do you know what those tacky strands of webbing feel like?

- Is it your knee-jerk reaction to take credit for your accomplishments, or do you instinctively recognize and rejoice in His grace in all that you have and do?
- Are you bothered or—worse yet—bitter about the times you have been slighted, and your rights and privileges have not been respected?
- Have you ever performed for the praise of others?
- Are you prone to complain that you don't have all that you deserve, and compare yourself in self-pity to others who have more?
- Is church (really) about *you* and *your* preferences?

If this is your profile, then it should be clear why Jesus and a deepening experience with Him is at best a vague notion on your spiritual wish list. But when we live to praise Him for all that He is and master the liberating art of celebrating His worthiness rather than our own, we have positioned ourselves to meet Him in a way beyond what we have ever experienced before. And it is important to note that this principle needs to be operative in bad times as well as good.

I'm reminded of Paul's arresting comment that he had

learned how to be content in both "want" as well as "prosperity" (Philippians 4:12). In "want" we rarely think about "rejoicing in the Lord." We usually spend great amounts of time fretting and feeling sorry for ourselves. We torment ourselves with a sense of being cheated out of the comfort, health, wealth, and happiness we think we deserve.

With that attitude, life is still totally about me. Big-time. And while a little dose of that feels good for a brief moment, we can't stay there. We've got to turn the corner. Rejoicing in the Lord in bad times means learning to give thanks in everything (1 Thessalonians 5:18). It means that we rejoice in the fact that a wise God gives and takes away, and we bless the name of the Lord (Job 1:21). That we are truly rich in Him even if we are poor in this world's goods (Revelation 2:9). That He never leaves us or forsakes us (Hebrews 13:5–6). That He works all things together for good (Romans 8:28). That in our weakness He is made strong and that His grace is abundantly sufficient (2 Corinthians 12:7–10). That it is by His wise and over-seeing permission that we have been placed on the fence post of trouble, and that through the darkest of trials He can bring glory and good.

We have not learned how to live in pain or prosperity until we have learned how to use them as a springboard to a life of grateful praise and adoration to our Lord.

Do you really believe that whatever benefits you receive from the hand of God flow only from His grace and are completely undeserved?

Are you convinced that even in the darkest of times He is with you, that He has a purpose, and that He will not waste your sorrows?

If you answer yes to these questions, you're on your way to a closer walk with the Son of God. The psalmist tells us that He inhabits the praises of His people (Psalm 22:3, KJV). Strangely enough, it doesn't say that He inhabits our complaints or our self-serving compliments. If your heart is full of complaining or self-pity—or of self-congratulating applause—you won't experience His nearness. Positioning our lives to experience Jesus requires seeing beyond the blessings and burdens of life…to fill our hearts with Him alone. In the process, we learn the sweet skill of boasting on Him, regardless.

He inhabits the praises of His people.
Meet Him there.

Chapter 6

THE GREATEST VALUE

Attitude Shift #2…
VALUE JESUS ABOVE EVERYTHING.

Think for a minute about the things you've treasured in your life.

At age one or two, it might have been a raggy, bedraggled baby blanket that you clung to like life itself. Woe unto the person who attempted to remove it from your grasp!

At age three or four, maybe it was a stuffed animal or doll that somehow became as real and as important to you as anything else in your world.

By six or seven, it might have been that first bike. You wouldn't have traded it for anything. Maybe you had a little collection of some kind tucked away in one of your dresser drawers, or in a shoe box under your bed…pretty rocks or dolls or comic books or baseball cards or stickers or those tiny green plastic army men.

As the years rolled along, it might have been some wonderful experience you wanted to hold onto…a winning hit at a Little League game…an A on one of your papers…a lead in the school play…an invitation to join an honor society…a date with one of those cute cheerleaders or the big man on campus.

At one point in time, those things were very precious to you. You protected them and pondered them and held them tightly in your memory. They gave you delight and pleasure. They made you feel warm all over again.

But where are they now? Life goes on, doesn't it? And we move on to encounter new and more intriguing possessions and experiences. Our picture albums, basements, attics, and garages are a living testimony to the changing values in our lives.

A CHAOS OF PRICE TAGS

You may have heard the story about the pranksters who broke into a hardware store. Strangely enough, they didn't steal a thing. Yet what they did created chaos of epic proportions.

They switched all the price tags.

The proprietor was unaware of anything amiss until the first customer stepped to the cash register with a claw hammer. And it rang up at $199.95. Naturally, the customer's jaw dropped. "What's that thing made out of?" he demanded. "Platinum?"

On further inspection, employees noticed that a big screen TV in the appliance section was selling for $14.95. The goods were all the same, resting on the same shelves as the night before, but the assigned values were hopelessly jumbled.

We are so prone to do that with our lives. More often than not we assign the wrong value to who we are and what we have.

The apostle Paul had the price tags right....

The very credentials these people are waving around as something special, I'm tearing up and throwing out with the trash—along with everything else I used to take credit for. And why? Because of Christ. Yes, all the things I once thought were so important are gone from my life. Compared to the high privilege of knowing Christ Jesus as my Master, firsthand, everything I once thought I had going for me is insignificant—dog dung. I've dumped it all in the trash so that I could embrace Christ and be embraced by him.... I gave up all that inferior stuff so I could know Christ personally.

PHILIPPIANS 3:7–8, 10, *THE MESSAGE*

There's Paul at the cash register, looking at all the price tags attached to his experiences, accomplishments, and treasures. He's got a red pen in his hand, and all those things that used to be so valuable, so precious, so terribly important to Paul, have been slashed down to zero. In fact, he's loading them up in boxes, headed for the Dumpster out back.

And what about knowing Jesus—the name Paul used to hate and assigned no value to at all? He can't even put a price on the privilege of experiencing Him. He writes Beyond Price on the tag because there's no way he can even describe how precious it is to him.

I'm reminded of a friend of ours who was an avid decorator. She had all the knack and instinct to make a room come alive. Then, in the midst of one of her decorating sprees, the doctor told her she had cancer. To that point her decorating project had her in its grip. She woke up with it every morning and fell asleep rearranging the details. Her day was consumed with fabric swatches and catalogs strewn around the house.

But on that day that she drove home from her doctor's office, the joy and fixation with that decorating project evaporated like water on a Phoenix sidewalk. Just that quickly, *life itself* had become precious. So precious that everything else that used to bring her joy was insignificant.

How often have you heard it?

—A widower lamenting over the misplaced values that robbed him of precious time with his wife.

—A dad who had valued life at the office more than time at home with his young son.

—A working mom who treasured a promotion at work more than watching her baby girl grow up.

—A retiree who spent money carelessly through his working years and had nothing left for retirement.

Getting our values straight is a critically important issue in life. And it is particularly strategic for the one seeking to experience Jesus.

In my limited experience, I've noticed two kinds of shoppers: those who check the contents listed on the side of the box for value, and those who like how the box looks. My wife, Martie, is a value shopper. She reads every label, right down to the tiny print. She compares weight to price per ounce, and when she finally throws it in the cart you can count on the fact that she has nabbed the best value.

If you value what looks good and gives you a buzz, then your heart will embrace all that is temporal and seductive. But if you look hard and long at Jesus, if you read all that the label says about His matchless worth, then Christ will have your heart. Every time. All the time.

Perhaps you've never thought of contrasting what you

value most with how you value Christ. But to experience Him in the fullness He intends, you've got to go through the exercise. And this exercise is far more than just giving mental assent to the fact that Jesus is most important. Most of us have been doing that all of our lives—and then go on to live like He was eighth or ninth on the list. *It's only when we understand why there is no one like Him and nothing else besides Him that we are able to embrace His unsurpassable value—even in the face of the fiercest of competitors.*

READ THE LABEL

Our attitude change regarding what is most important to us has to be more than "church-speak." There needs to be irrefutable substance to the claim. What is the proof of His supreme value? What is it about Him that would convince our hearts that compared to Him everything else in our life is like rubbish?

There are three all-surpassing realities that Jesus brings to our life that no one else—indeed, nothing else—even hopes to offer. These qualities ascribe unprecedented value to Christ. It is these three that gripped the apostle heart like a vise, that by comparison left the apostle counting everything else in his life as loss.

It all started at the Cross.

1. It is at the Cross that we "gain" Christ (Philippians 3:8).

If "gaining" Jesus is of substantive value, then what is it that we gain? Simply put, if you gain Him, you have all you need. Most importantly, gaining Him means gaining total and eternal forgiveness for all your sins and shortcomings—past, present, and future. There is nothing on earth that can compete with the gift of His saving grace. And the astounding reality is that *anyone* who repentantly comes to Jesus receives the irrevocable privilege of gaining Him.

One of my all-time favorite stories from the Gospels is in Luke 12. It's the account of the man who was indignant and troubled by the fact that his brother had cheated him out of his inheritance. One day, he happened to find himself in the presence of Jesus, the Nazarene. He caught the Lord's attention and complained, "Master, tell my brother to divide the inheritance with me!"

As with so many who spoke with Jesus, he got more than he bargained for in the answer. The Lord replied, "Watch out! Be on your guard against all kinds of greed; a man's life does not consist in the abundance of his possessions" (Luke 12:15, NIV). Jesus went on to tell the story of a rich and successful farmer. This man had been blessed with such a great harvest that he had to tear down all his little barns and build big ones just to store his bumper crop of grain. Inviting his friends to celebrate his good fortune, the wealthy man apparently left someone off the invitation list.

It was God.

But He showed up anyway.

On that very night God required the wealthy farmer's soul, and all of those carefully hoarded goods went to someone else. Jesus didn't mince words about the barn-building man. He called him a fool. Not because he had been so successful, not because he had so much stuff, but because he valued it as his ultimate security and placed no value on God in his life. As Jesus said on another occasion, "What will it profit a man if he gains the whole world and forfeits his soul?" (Matthew 16:26).

Bottom line? Without Jesus, all the goods and gear and gadgets this consumer culture can throw at us are just so many cheap toys; all the success in the world is of no ultimate value at all. Gaining Jesus not only settles the problem of guilt and judgment before a just and holy God, but it also showers us with an abundance of other graces with which nothing in this world can compete.

—An incomparably rich inheritance reserved for you, that no government can tax, no thief can plunder, no terrorist can explode, and no temperamental rich uncle can revoke.

—Our Lord's 24/7/365 presence, so that you have nothing to fear from man, woman, angel, or demon.

—An Advocate in heaven who sticks up for you and

pleads your case when the devil hurls accusations against you.

—A limitless supply of grace to help you in the time of need...and countless other unparalleled advantages.

2. At the Cross we are placed "in Him" (Philippians 3:9).

When we came to the Cross we not only gained Him, we entered into the privilege of being found "in Him." This is a concept so big that it's hard to bend our minds around it. As Paul notes, being found in Him means that you and I have been wrapped in the very righteousness of Jesus Christ. Try to imagine the blinding, searing, white fire at the core of a new star blazing in the heavens. Now...what if you could take that searing radiance and just slip it over your shoulders like a robe?

That just begins to describe what it means to have the righteousness of Jesus—the perfect, sinless, spotless Lamb of God—covering all of your life.

Apart from "being found in Him," we could not approach the throne of God in prayer. We could not draw near to the majestic presence of our God without being instantly vaporized. But covered in our Lord's own righteousness, we can approach a holy God with confidence and worship Him without fear. We can share our deepest thoughts and longings, knowing that He hears and cares. And we can find grace and mercy to help us in our time of need.

In the midst of a hostile and often intimidating world, He clothes us with His own robe and guarantees our safety all the way home. To put it plainly, Jesus has you covered. As my street friends say, He's got your back! And in a relationship with a holy God, that's a very big deal!

3. Having Jesus and being found in Him guarantees our resurrection from the dead (Philippians 3:11).

By far the most popular notion today regarding life after death is reincarnation. For the life of me, I can't understand why anyone would want to come back and go through the disaster of another lifetime. But if you don't have God's Word, then all you have is the hope of some vague human recycling project.

The next stop after death is not a recycled life in a different body; it is accountability for what I have done in life, and for what I have done with Jesus and His offer of eternal life. As God's Word says, "It is appointed for men to die once and after this comes judgment" (Hebrews 9:27). But in Jesus we no longer fear that judgment day. Jesus has clearly said, "I am the resurrection and the life; he who believes in Me will live even if he dies, and everyone who lives and believes in Me will never die" (John 11:25–26).

Think of it. A pass in Him at the judgment, all that is "far better" throughout eternity, and in the darkest of days here on earth, the bright hope of an eternity of sorrowless joy. In Jesus we boisterously and with great confidence sing, "O DEATH, WHERE IS YOUR VICTORY? O DEATH, WHERE IS YOUR STING?... Thanks be to God, who gives us the victory through our Lord Jesus Christ" (1 Corinthians 15:55, 57).

UNSURPASSED VALUE

So tell me.

Is there anything you have

anything you might hope to have

anything you are or hope to become

that can compare with Jesus?

Is there anyone else to whom you are more gratefully indebted? Is there a reason—any reason at all—why He would not be more highly prized in your life than anything else or anyone else?

Think back to the day when you invited Jesus into your life as Savior and Lord. In order to receive this triple-grace-bestowed benefit we just spoke of, you had to leave all that you were and had at the foot of the cross and come with no merit of your own. Remember?

You had to tear up your list of accomplishments.

Burn your journal of good deeds.

Shred your file of newspaper clippings.

Why? Because the cross is all about Christ and Christ alone.

This is exactly the point that Paul is making. In order to gain Christ, in order to be found in Him, in order to experience resurrection from the dead, Paul had to count all things loss for the exceeding value of knowing Jesus. And so did you. It was there, at the foot of His cross, that you laid all your trophies down so that you could gain Jesus.

God has never looked at a portfolio of greatness, turned to Peter (who for some reason is always at heaven's gate), and said, "Check this out! Can you believe we get someone of this caliber as a resident in heaven? Unlock the gate! This one's a keeper!" Quite the contrary. As Scripture says, we are saved by grace through faith, and it is not of ourselves. It is a gift of God. It is not of works, because if that were so, we would spend eternity boasting about ourselves (see Ephesians 2:8–9).

It is at the cross, then, that we put all our blue ribbons and trophies in a pile. We stand as it were naked before Him, pleading His mercy and grace. And instead of judging us, He touches us with His love, makes us His own, clothes us with His own perfect righteousness, and guarantees our resurrection on that final day.

Before the cross, all the value is affixed to us—all we are and have. At the cross, He alone is of supreme value.

So why, after receiving all that we have in Christ, do we dig those old trophies out of the trash heap? When did we stop clinging to the cross and start valuing our own merit again? How ludicrous, how deeply offensive it must be to Jesus when we reach back and reclaim what we gladly forfeited to gain Him—as though it were now of greater value to us again. Was He of supreme value only for the moment of salvation? Of course not. We need Him every hour of the day, with every breath we draw into our lungs.

Keep your eyes on Jesus.

Stay at the cross every day.

Remember the mercy and grace that freely flowed to cover you.

Cling to its blood-stained timbers.

Lose yourself in the glory of His amazing grace.

If you do, it won't be long until you've put "self" in its proper place—and Jesus in His.

When our attitudes have shifted to move self out of the way, and to value Jesus more highly than anything we are or have, we are ready to experience Jesus in three "meeting places." He meets us in the seductions of life, in the midst of our suffering, and in the process of full surrender. These may not be places where you thought He would be.

But He is there just the same.

And He is waiting for you.

Chapter 7

DELIVER US
FROM EVIL

Experiencing Jesus in seasons of seduction.

Temptations. All of us have them. It shouldn't be hard to think of the last time you were caught in the tension of a choice between good and evil—or even something good and not so good.

How easy to utter a quick lie, just a little one, to get off the hook.

To let an offense take us all the way to a shouting match or brawl.

To let our minds become an incubator for irritations that turn into angry words and hurtful schemes of revenge. Or a playground where fantasies burrow in and begin expressing themselves in attitudes and actions.

Temptations are everywhere. They show up in moments of victory, and they leer at us in the midst of despair. They dress like money, wear fine perfume and rich cologne, go high tech on the Internet, make anger seem sweet, and offer bitterness as a five-star luxury. Temptations lure us to give in to our doubts and to live for what seems right at the moment. They love what feels good. In short, they offer the sizzle of sin…for a season.

But for all we know about temptation, few of us have imagined that we can experience Jesus in its midst. After all, He's the sinless one. He's the one who taught us to pray, "Lead us not into temptation…." Temptation? That's Satan's territory!

Nevertheless, it's true. Temptation is one of the places where we can experience a fresh closeness with our Lord. And given the frequency of temptations in our lives, it becomes an opportunity to meet Him on a regular basis!

In a moment we will explain—or should I say, let's have Paul explain what he means when he writes "…that I may know Him and the power of His resurrection" (Philippians 3:10). But first, it's important to put meeting Jesus in times of temptation into the bigger picture of what Paul is saying.

To this point in the text, Paul has reveled in what theologians would call the *positional* blessings that we have in Jesus. If we have been to the cross, we are in the privileged *position* of having gained Christ, of being found in Him, and of being guaranteed a part in the resurrection from the dead (vv. 8–9, 11). Positional blessings are prized realities secured for us *no matter what* through the grace of His work at Calvary. Unfortunately many followers of Jesus are content to bask in what we have in Jesus without actually experiencing Jesus.

Paul, however, isn't satisfied to simply bask in these "positional" gifts. He makes it clear that gaining Jesus and being found in Him are actually intended to enable us to enjoy a real-life, day-by-day experience with Jesus.

When Paul begins verse 10 with "that I may know Him," he uses a "purpose clause." Simply put, we gain Christ and are found in Him *for the purpose* of having an experiential relationship with Him. To revel in those positional privileges without going on to experience Jesus is to abort the very purpose of the gifts!

I have a friend here in Chicago who owns a company that has skyboxes for the Cubs, the White Sox, and the Bulls. In fact, he has front row, center court, feet-on-the-playing-floor tickets for all of the Bulls games. In the Michael Jordan era, Bulls tickets were the most coveted commodities in town (my how the mighty have fallen!). Every year, believe it or not, I get a shot at these tickets. And what can I say? It's wonderful. Experiencing the Cubs at Wrigley Field from the luxurious confines of a skybox or feeling the breeze generated when giant NBA players run past you at the United Center is a super-charged experience for an unrepentant sports fan.

My friend does all he can to ensure that experience for me. He checks with my schedule and sends me the tickets (sometimes with parking passes); then he'll call me and ask how I enjoyed the game. Good buddy that he is, my friend wants to know that I not only have the tickets in my hand, but that I actually show up at the game, sit in those prime seats, and revel in the experience.

How much sense would it make if I held those tickets—flashing them around and impressing everyone with my opportunity—but decided to skip the game? Not only would I be cheating myself out of a choice experience, I would be embarrassed to see my friend, lest he should ask how I liked the game. Wasting his gracious provision would be unthinkable.

It's a similar situation—only infinitely more serious—if we waste the phenomenal price that Jesus paid that we might enjoy a close and personal relationship with Him. So what's the secret? How do we activate this kind of relationship? Paul tells us we must meet Jesus in three places:

—in the power of His resurrection

—in the fellowship of His sufferings

—and in conformity to the image of His death.

Let's figure out how we encounter Jesus in that first meeting place—resurrection power.

THE FIRST MEETING PLACE...
Experiencing Jesus in His Resurrection Power

You might say that Paul was power hungry. But in this case it was a good thing. God wants you and me to be power hungry, too. He wants to infect us with a deep longing, insatiable hunger, and overpowering desire for power.

But not just any power. If we are hungering and thirsting for the resurrection power of Jesus Christ, we're on the road to experiencing Him in a deeper way. And believe it or not, the resurrection power of Jesus Christ is most frequently experienced in times of temptation.

It may be a little hard to get a grip on this thought because we tend to think of the Resurrection as a glorious future event. And it is certainly that. The power of the Resurrection will kick-start an eternity of unhindered joy in our fellowship with Jesus.

And that, my friend, is a power worth having.

I recall D. James Kennedy preaching about the miracle of the Resurrection. In his sermon he referenced the unfortunate turn of events for Roger Williams, the founder of Rhode Island. He was buried in a rather common setting, which led his admirers several years later to get permission to exhume his body for a burial more appropriate to their hero's image. Imagine their consternation to discover that the roots of a nearby apple tree had worked their way into the casket.

I remember Dr. Kennedy's question at that point. "What now of Roger Williams?" Or of the apples that grew. Or of the people that ate the apple pies made of apples from the tree. Or of those who had eaten the pie and were lost at sea and eaten by sharks? Just think of the miraculous power required to reassemble Roger Williams!

But the real power of the Resurrection lies in its spiritual significance—for what it accomplished in realms far more strategic than the reassembly of scattered remains.

The Resurrection is at its very essence the ultimate victory over sin, death, and hell. All the forces of evil spent their best efforts to permanently ground their Archenemy behind a massive, immovable stone—guarded by imperial guards from the most powerful empire on earth. And then, with a word from God—the merest breath—death was defeated, and sin and the forces of hell no longer held sway. Jesus lives and in Him the power of sin is rendered weak and ineffective.

This is the real power of the Resurrection. And it was hunger for this power that became a mighty longing within the heart of Paul. In it and through it, the apostle tells us, we get to experience Jesus Christ in a deeper way than we've known before.

While it is true that Jesus taught us to pray that He would not lead us into temptation, it is also true that He taught us to pray that God would deliver us from evil.

He waits in every temptation to meet you there. To take you by the hand and deliver you from the hammer blows of the hooded tormentor who lurks just behind the lure of it all.

When was the last time you looked for Jesus in the midst of a pressing temptation? Our problem is that we haven't known He is there! Most of the time we try to break the spell of sin on our own power by learning to fear the consequences, by trying to "buck up" and be good, by finding an accountability partner, or by a dozen other good but inadequate mechanisms.

But only He can deliver you.

Temptation is not foreign to Him. In the wilderness, exhausted and hungry from an extended fast, the King of creation went one-on-one with the great seducer. Jesus is no stranger to our struggles. Which is precisely why Scripture reminds us that He was tempted in every way like we are. He understands and promises to give us grace and mercy to help in our time of need (Hebrews 4:14–16).

Every temptation is a choice. A choice to satisfy our own fallen desires or to satisfy Jesus. *And He is there*—right in that crisis of choice. Learn to look for Him in the very moment that temptation moves in on your desires. And weigh the choice. He always offers something of greater value than the lure being trolled through the waters of your heart.

Need to lie to avoid a problem? Give your problem to Him. *He will help you through, and the truth you tell will reward your heart with the freedom of a clear conscience.*

Feel like cheating to get some extra cash? *He will meet all your needs—miraculously, if necessary.*

Attracted by the buzz of some sensual fulfillment? *He offers the long-term pleasure of a pure heart without damaging and polluting your soul.*

Feel the need to manipulate your way through a problem? *Simply do what is right. He will guide your footsteps and clear the way.*

With every choice you make for Him, you will have met Him there and tasted His resurrection power in your life. And as He delivers you from evil, the purity in your life will open your heart's door to increasingly sweet fellowship with Him.

A listener to our radio program, *Proclaim!,* wrote of his struggle to break the spell that Internet pornography had over his heart. He knew that with every click he was denying and distancing himself from Jesus. To remind him of the choice, he finally put a picture of Jesus in the corner of his computer screen. With that reminder of the presence of Jesus, he found it impossible to pursue those alluring sights.

In the end, most sin is about enhancing or preserving your life, reputation, pleasure, prosperity, or safety. If life is about you, sin will come easily. But if you have begun to live to rejoice in the Lord instead of in yourself, you'll be glad to meet Him in temptation and let Him take you by the hand. If you value Jesus as the preeminent value of your existence, you will never dream of trading Him for the poison porridge of hell.

As you probably know, songs have a way of starting in your head in the morning and staying with you all day. Recently I woke up singing a favorite song from years past, "I'd rather have Jesus…than be held in sin's dread sway." Throughout the day, as temptations ambushed my heart, the words drove me to Him.

I sing that song in my heart a lot these days! It helps me to meet Jesus in times of temptation and to keep my heart pure and open for the One who seeks to come in and dine.

Chapter 8

THE TROUBLE
WITH INTIMACY

Experiencing Jesus in seasons of suffering.

The transatlantic connection was filled with static, but the sound of a broken heart on the other end of the line was all too clear. It was Craig's wife, Martha. As she spoke, everything inside me felt crushed.

Craig and I grew up together. We attended the same college, played soccer together, and in fact looked so much alike that we were often mistaken for brothers. He married a pretty coed in college and after graduation enlisted in the Air Force.

I hadn't seen Craig in years. Imagine my surprise when our paths crossed in the town where I began my first pastorate. Talk had it that Craig and Martha had been far from the Lord. When Martie and I heard that they had recommitted their lives to the Lord, we were overjoyed. It wasn't long before they became active in our little church. He taught our high school boys, and Martha taught the girls. Before long, God led them to work with troubled teens on the island of Haiti.

They'd been in Haiti only a week, and now Martha was telling me that Craig had suffered a serious injury while diving into a pool. He didn't make it through the night. Martha was there alone. Less than thirty years old, and already a widow. Her dreams and hopes dashed. How could this be? Only days into a fresh commitment to serve Jesus, and nothing left to show for it but unbearable loss.

THE TROUBLE WITH TROUBLE

Job's comforters may not have had a lot right, but Eliphaz certainly had a point.

"Man," he said, "is born to trouble as surely as sparks fly upward" (Job 5:7, NIV).

Let's face it: Trouble happens. In fact, as a friend of mine points out, if we really understood the depth of the Fall and the grip that sin has on this world, we would be surprised that anything good happens *at all*.

The trouble with trouble is that it seems so indiscriminate.

Good people suffer. Bad people prosper. Exploiters exploit with seeming impunity. Children are victimized by crack addict parents, and elderly folks end up being neglected and marginalized.

We have a wonderful neighbor in her eighties. Charmingly crusty, with an engaging personality, she seems to enjoy being a touch out-of-sorts about some things. It's her "gig," and we love her for it. She claims that her everyday consumption of gin and cigarettes "keeps her fresh." Her sister, on the other hand, is as proper as they come. She doesn't drink or smoke. She exercises faithfully at the local pool, and she complains about nothing. Last winter, while swimming her daily routine, she was taken ill and lay in a coma in the hospital for days, until she finally died.

Our neighbor was stunned. Her sister was her only living relative. All she could say in the days following her sister's death was, "I don't understand it. *It should have been me!* My sister was such a good person."

The truth, of course, is that none of us is exempt. Jesus stated very clearly, "In this world you will have trouble" (John 16:33, NIV). And He was talking to His closest friends!

Is there anyone left on the planet who actually feels that the world is gradually getting better and better? That we are more civilized? If you harbor such thoughts, consider the horrific events surrounding September 11, 2001—or just spend a few minutes with CNN on any given night.

The good news in all this bad news is that a special experience with Jesus is there for the taking—right in the middle of that hardship.

THE SECOND MEETING PLACE...
Experiencing Jesus in the Fellowship of His Sufferings

Our instincts tell us to resist trouble. To fight it. To resent it as an intruder. To feel cheated. To tell ourselves, *I deserve better than this.* And as those thoughts settle in, the great scramble begins. We plot, manipulate, fret, seek revenge, doubt God and His goodness, threaten, harbor anger, flirt with bitterness, withdraw, and—if all else fails—throw a major pity party. And by the way, if you throw a pity party don't bother sending out invitations. Friends may try to cheer you up—and that would wreck everything.

Thankfully, for those of us who seek the face of God in the midst of trouble, we discover that He is not surprised by the arrival of pain—and that He wants us to experience Him there.

Paul knew that in suffering he had the opportunity to gain a deeper, more experiential knowledge of Jesus. We discover the same thing—that closer, sweeter walk—when we connect with Him in our seasons of suffering. As Paul puts it, there is a special encounter with Christ when we share in the "fellowship of His sufferings" (Philippians 3:10).

If you are thinking here of the Cross, then you will struggle to meet Him in your sufferings. Most likely, none of us will be crucified—not literally. But the sufferings of Christ are far more extensive, more identifiable, than only the injustices of Golgotha.

Have you ever felt lonely, displaced, misrepresented, or misunderstood? Have you ever found yourself severely restricted? Denied of your rights and privileges? Betrayed by a close friend? Have you ever been left out of the power group and plotted against? Have you ever done right and suffered for it? Have you ever tasted the bitterness of injustice? Have you ever longed for your friends to stand with you in your moment of need, only to sense they're really too consumed with their own needs to pay much attention? Have you ever experienced unbearable pain? Have you ever felt abandoned by God?

These, and many more, are the sufferings Jesus endured on our behalf. He bore them in love, patiently and willingly for us, so that "by His stripes, we are healed."

If you found yourself nodding your head to any of those questions, you can identify with what He felt and suffered for you.

The question is not Are you willing to suffer? We have little choice about that. The real question is, Are you willing to meet Jesus there—right in the midst of your pain?

Are you willing to make that choice?

To experience Him in the midst of our pain requires that we stop whining about our trials. How often do we find our hearts complaining, *Why is He doing this to me? Does He really care? Does He truly feel the ache in my heart and the anguish in my spirit? Does He have any idea what He's putting me through?* Residual anger, revenge, bitterness, self-imposed depression, and despair are the rewards we reap from these attitudes.

Jesus has something better in mind.

If we really desire to experience Him, we need to stop blaming God, reverse our self-centered demand for release, and realize for the first time in our lives that we are getting a firsthand experience of what He felt and experienced as He suffered for us. Stop and identify the type of trouble you feel. Think through Christ's suffering and identify where His pain meets yours. Ask Him to forgive you for feeling that you should be exempt. And as you feel His pain in yours, thank Him that He loved you enough to suffer like this for you.

Stay there with Him. Refuse to let Satan draw you back into bitterness and self-pity, and you will find Jesus a meaningful companion in the midst of trouble.

We need to be deeply taken with the thought that in suffering we understand a little of what He went through for us. And maybe, just maybe, we will begin to grasp—

sand particle by sand particle—the depth of His love for us. What words cannot express in trying to explain the marvelous love of Jesus, suffering servants feel in the deepest parts of their souls.

This is the fellowship of His sufferings.

This is the intimacy of a shared experience with Jesus.

This is where He waits to meet us. It's time to stop turning our backs on Him in pain and flee to His embrace.

But we are only free to do this when we have ceased to live to rejoice in ourselves. If we are intent to celebrate "me" in life, we will resist trials and quickly become embittered when they settle in for the long haul—to say nothing of the difficulty in meeting Jesus in pain when we have valued comfort and peace more than nearness to Him. If He is the supreme value in our lives then we will be willing to meet Him in times of trouble.

SHARED EXPERIENCES

Moody has a policy that I do not travel alone. When our children were at home, I often traveled with a colleague from the Institute. After I returned home, I would reenter Martie's world of runny noses, school lunches, taxi runs, and bedtime stories.

I'd try my best to brief her on the trip and tell her about all the things I had seen and the people I had met, but there really wasn't much connection. How could there be? For one thing, I'm a man. And most men like to cut to the bottom line, rather than share details. For another thing, she simply hadn't been there. After I would give my little spiel, she in turn would try to explain to me all that happened while I was gone—all the little trials and joys of caring for growing children. I did my best to enter into her experiences.

But I really couldn't. I hadn't been there.

Now, however, our children are married and have homes of their own. Happily, Martie and I often travel together. We share the experiences of new places and new faces, of sometimes stressful meetings; we watch the Lord work through the ministry of His Word and experience the joy of His work together. We experience missed connections and delightful conversation with new friends around a dinner table in some cozy restaurant.

We come home and talk about where we've been and what we've done. We relive our experiences, smile together over the funny moments, and sigh over the stories of pain and heartache we encounter along the way. It's amazing how much closer we are today in our intimacy with one another. All because of shared experiences. Our lives are no longer two worlds that periodically merge. Our worlds are the same, and we know each other better today than ever before. And we love it this way!

It's like that in our relationship with Jesus. You've got to capitalize on where your world merges with His. And suffering is one of the places where your world and His intersect. If you choose to see your season of suffering as a moment to capture a shared experience with God's Son, your intimacy with Him will become a deepening reality. It is a firsthand experience with the reality of His love for you and the heavy price He paid for your redemption.

Yes, your pain will still be pain—sometimes extremely difficult to endure. But instead of focusing on the loss, the hardship, the obstacle, you will step through the door of a fellowship beyond words to describe.

After Craig's tragic death, questions plagued us all. Why, God? Why now? Why them? But God's grace was strengthening Martha's heart. In the midst of her hurt she chose to see the suffering as a shared experience with Jesus. She wrote to me that she had decided to view her pain through His loss at the Cross. She marked the loneliness and despair in her heart, recalling the loneliness and despair Jesus had experienced for her. His words, "My God, why have You forsaken me?" echoed in her soul. She found solace in Jesus' confidence that His loss was not in vain but that His suffering was a part of His Father's wise and bigger plan. She chose to endure the pain for the joy that was set before her, just as Jesus did (Hebrews 12).

Martha found unusual supporting grace in meeting

Jesus in her loss, and it opened the door of her heart to His strong and abiding presence. Recently she wrote in reflection: "During that time of emotional recovery, God revealed Himself in ways I could not imagine. Physical, financial, emotional, and spiritual needs were met in dramatic and supernatural ways."

Today, Martha teaches a large women's Bible class, has a ministry to women in prison, and has a son who serves as a missionary. Had she not met Jesus in her sorrow, I wonder where lesser instincts might have taken her?

Chapter 9

SWEET
SURRENDER

Going all the way to Gethsemane.

Bob always said he wanted a closer walk with the Lord, but seemed continually frustrated. No matter what he did, his longing for Jesus never seemed satisfied.

His pastor had told him he couldn't really expect such a relationship this side of heaven. But Bob knew in his heart there had to be more, more than he was experiencing. What really frustrated him was that others seemed to find that closer, more intimate walk he wanted so much. So he knew it was possible. In fact, he tried so hard that at times he felt frustrated with God. He often thought that if God was truly "a rewarder of those who diligently seek Him," then He must have run out of rewards when Bob stepped up.

He tithed and then some.

He served as an elder in his church.

He regularly met with God in devotions and prayer.

He was good to his wife and spent time with his kids.

He even fasted on occasion.

What else was there to do? What, pray tell, did God expect? What did He require anyway?

Listening to Bob's complaint reminds me of the time that Israel felt the same way. In the days of the prophet Micah they filed a grievance with heaven; in fact, their whole tone seems to indicate that they were miffed about the distance God seemed to keep between Himself and them.

> With what shall I come to the LORD
>> And bow myself before the God on high?
> Shall I come to Him with burnt offerings,
>> With yearling calves?
> Does the LORD take delight in thousands of rams,
>> In ten thousand rivers of oil?
> Shall I present my firstborn for my rebellious acts,
>> The fruit of my body for the sin of my soul?
>
> MICAH 6:6–7

You can almost feel their frustration in the text. *What's it all about, Lord? What does it really take to sense Your nearness? Have we missed something?*

The Lord graciously responded with a reminder of what it is that He requires. He named three keys to closing the distance. (I've always been thankful that our God is a God of short lists. Imagine if He had dropped a tome of detailed requirements for us to live up to. Given His holiness, He could have done just that. But He didn't.) What is it that pleases Him? To do justice. To love mercy. To walk humbly with your God.

It was the "walk humbly with your God" that Bob had unknowingly missed. One of the basic expressions of humility is complete obedience at any cost. When I say no to God, keep an area of my life to myself, or withhold what He requires, He sees it for what it is—an act of willful pride. And as Peter reminds us, He resists the proud! (1 Peter 5:5). That sounds like a clear clue as to why some of us feel kept at arm's length from Jesus.

Letting God's people go was a tough task for Pharaoh. The Israelites comprised the heart of Egypt's labor force. They were the backbone of the economy. God had asked the Egyptian king to do something of great difficulty and phenomenal risk. When he refused, Moses said to him, "Why do you refuse to humble yourself before God?"

Jesus humbled Himself and became obedient unto death, even the death of the cross (Philippians 2:8). Which is exactly Paul's point about meeting Jesus by becoming conformed to His death (Philippians 3:10).

THE THIRD MEETING PLACE...
Total Surrender

Paul writes that the third way to experience Jesus in our lives is by a willing conformity to His death (3:10). Again, we cannot think of this in terms of the Crucifixion alone. This is not about dying so that we can get to heaven to experience Jesus there. It's about coming to grips with the dynamics of Jesus' death and conforming our lives to that pattern.

Actually, the death of Jesus began long before the Cross, in eternity past when Jesus willingly surrendered to the Father's decree that He should die for the sins of the world. In our history, that surrender was reenacted in the garden of Gethsemane. There, while His friends slept, He went through the excruciating pain of the heaviest decision of His life. His Father was asking Him to go to the cross, where the pain and torment of the sins of the world would press upon His sinless soul while soldiers mocked and curious bystanders gawked.

The Gospels record that the grief of this decision was so wrenching He literally sweated drops of blood in the process. Every sweat gland is surrounded by a whole network of tiny blood vessels; this is how our body cools itself. The moment of extreme crisis was so intense for Jesus that these vessels burst under the pressure. This decision wracked every aspect of His being. The cost was beyond measure, beyond comprehension.

It is not surprising, then, that Jesus in His humanity shrank from the horror—asking His Father if there might not be another way. But in the end, through lips parched with anxiety, in a voice heavy with the weight of the cross to come, He uttered those unforgettable words of unparalleled resolve, "Not My will, but Yours be done!"

Being conformed to His death means *full surrender* to our Father's will—regardless. No excuses. No escape clauses. No negotiation. And not only is it surrender for the moment, it is about *persevering* in the resolve until we have fully obeyed. As an exhausted Jesus rose from His prayer, He could see the torches of the approaching lynch mob. Judas stepped forward and betrayed the Lord of life with a kiss of death. Jesus could have lashed out at Judas, blamed the whole mess on him, told the authorities that they were in league with a man whose motives were highly suspect.

But Jesus would not be deterred. When Peter unsheathed his sword and slashed one of the servants across the face, severing the man's ear, Jesus had every right to escalate the conflict. He could have called twelve legions of angels, exercising His rights and power in the perfectly justifiable defense of innocence. Instead, He persevered in surrender. Foreshadowing what He was about to do at the cross, He loved His enemies and healed the wounded man's ear.

It's one thing to surrender. It's quite another to persevere when we're presented with opportunities to justifiably slide out of our resolve. Through all of those horrible hours to follow, when the faultlessly righteous Jesus was dragged through the halls of the kangaroo courts, He refused to return their accusations and slander.

Peter was there. He knew. Years later he would pen, "Christ also suffered for you, leaving you an example for you to follow in His steps…while being reviled, He did not revile in return; while suffering, He uttered no threats, but kept entrusting Himself to Him who judges righteously" (1 Peter 2:21, 23).

✓This is the pattern we are to follow in our lives if we are to know Jesus. An undaunted and nonnegotiable loyalty to Jesus—regardless of the cost—is the key to a deepening, intimate fellowship with Him. Regardless of what He requires, those who want to draw close to Him meet Him at that sweat-stained rock in the Garden and brokenly repeat His words after Him: "Not my will, but Yours be done."

It is a resolve that covers the whole waterfront of our existence. Nothing is exempt. Relationships, real estate, financial resources, spouses, children, grandchildren, desires, dreams, plans, attitudes, and actions are all included.

It calls for the bold and determined cessation of that fulfilling affair.

It demands no flirting around the edges of sensuality and the immediate resolve to eliminate opportunities for voyeuristic pleasure with pornography.

It requires the expulsion of jealousy, residual anger, and the bitterness that tear at our relationships. Gethsemane asks for it all. Stay at the rock until there is nothing held back. Then rise, take up your cross, and follow Him. Remember, no cross is heavier than His was. When we are committed to rejoicing in the Lord rather than ourselves and value Jesus and His perfect will more than our own rights, privileges, and possessions, the cross of surrender will be an honor, not a burden.

But there is more. Think with me for a minute. We know that the theme of the Cross is love. Love, in fact, for those who have deeply offended God in their sin and rebellion. And Jesus was giving His very lifeblood for these people.

He was dying for the Pharisees…who falsely accused.

He was dying for the soldiers…who were caustically cruel.

He was dying for the Sanhedrin…who broke their own laws to condemn Him.

He was dying for Pilate…who caved in to political pressure.

He was dying for Herod…who mocked and sneered.

He was dying for His executioners…who had no mercy.

He was dying for all those who throughout history past and ages to come would mock and spit in the face of His Father whom He loved.

And He was dying for me and you, while we were still in our sin and rebellion.

Simply put, the heart of the Cross is about loving our enemies. It is about mercy for those who deserved nothing but retribution. It is about taking the rap for someone else, about doing justice for the unjust. Being "conformed to His death" means that I am willing to forgive those who have cruelly offended me, commit acts of love toward those who deserve my scorn, and take the rap for my enemies when necessary. I do these things understanding that God Himself will ultimately deal with my offenders in a just and righteous way. But more importantly, I conform because this is where I meet Jesus.

BOB'S COSTLY DECISION

Why did Bob meet with such frustration and disappointment when he sought to draw near to Jesus? The answer goes way back to his boyhood days. Bob's dad had left his mother when he was young. But not so young that he didn't live with the awful memories of the cruel abuse. Bob's dad had multiple affairs with women all over town, and he finally ran off with and married his wife's best friend. He lives in a town not far from Bob, and Bob long ago vowed that he would never forgive his dad.

The risk was too great.

The fear of further rejection too strong.

The thought of dredging up old pain too daunting.

The prospect of restoring that broken relationship too great a mountain to climb.

So Bob didn't make contact. He refused to move one inch toward reconciliation. In his mind, this was the last person on earth to merit his love and forgiveness. In this area of Bob's life, so near to the center of his heart, he refused to be conformed to the image of Christ's death. He refused to kneel with Jesus in Gethsemane and face the excruciating prospect of encountering and forgiving his dad. The words *not my will but Yours be done* had not crossed Bob's lips, let alone his heart.

Jesus cannot draw near to a heart steeled against His will. Experiencing Him in the fullness of His presence requires that we go with Him to the Garden and kneel in surrender, conforming to what He did—for even the most undeserving in our lives. In that light, full surrender—*regardless of the cost*—is always sweet surrender. For it is within such surrender that we come to know and experience Jesus in deeper and fuller ways.

And so He waits for us. Waits for us to love and value Him more than ourselves…waits to meet us. And when we meet Him, the experience of His presence delights our soul and makes us long for more.

THE PRAYER OF
THE SEEKER

Those who experience the pleasure of His presence have made their lives *simply about Jesus.*

They live to meet Him wherever He is found: in the wilderness of Satan's attack…in the suffering that He bore because He loved us…and at that rock in Gethsemane where surrender claimed its finest hour.

> *Dear Lord, from the depths of my heart I ask for complete cleansing. Grant me the grace to keep self in its proper place, and to make my life simply about You. In the midst of all my routines, successes, and disappointments, help me to always rejoice in You and*

value You above any earthly prize. Meet me in temptation, and deliver me from evil. And if I should suffer, help me to pause to feel Your pain and love You more for the way You suffered for me. Jesus, I will live this day on bended knee by Your side in Gethsemane. What You ask I will do.

Thank You for the promise that You will reward those who diligently seek You. I do seek You—with all my heart. I humbly ask that in Your good time and in Your way, You would satisfy my heart with the experience of Your presence.

In Your worthy name I pray. Amen.

Behold, I stand at the door and knock;
if anyone hears My voice
and opens the door,
I will come in to him
and will dine with him,
and he with Me.
—Jesus Christ, Lord of the universe

REVELATION 3:20

Steps to Peace with God

 ### Step 1 God's Purpose:
Peace and Life

God loves you and wants you to experience peace and life—abundant and eternal.

The Bible Says . . .

". . . we have peace with God through our Lord Jesus Christ." Romans 5:1

"For God so loved the world that He gave His only begotten Son, that whoever believes in Him should not perish but have everlasting life." John 3:16

". . . I have come that they may have life, and that they may have it more abundantly." John 10:10b

Since God planned for us to have peace and the abundant life right now, why are most people not having this experience?

 ### Step 2 Our Problem:
Separation

God created us in His own image to have an abundant life. He did not make us as robots to automatically love and obey Him, but gave us a will and a freedom of choice.

We chose to disobey God and go our own willful way. We still make this choice today. This results in separation from God.

The Bible Says . . .

"For all have sinned and fall short of the glory of God." Romans 3:23

"For the wages of sin is death, but the gift of God is eternal life in Christ Jesus our Lord." Romans 6:23

Our choice results in separation from God.

People (Sinful)   God (Holy)

Our Attempts

Through the ages, individuals have tried in many ways to bridge this gap . . . without success . . .

The Bible Says . . .

"There is a way that seems right to man, but in the end it leads to death." Proverbs 14:12

"But your iniquities have separated you from God; and your sins have hidden His face from you, so that He will not hear." Isaiah 59:2

There is only one remedy for this problem of separation.

Step 3 God's Remedy: The Cross

Jesus Christ is the only answer to this problem. He died on the Cross and rose from the grave, paying the penalty for our sin and bridging the gap between God and people.

The Bible Says . . .

". . . God is on one side and all the people on the other side, and Christ Jesus, Himself man, is between them to bring them together . . ."
1 Timothy 2:5

"For Christ also has suffered once for sins, the just for the unjust, that He might bring us to God . . ." 1 Peter 3:18a

"But God demonstrates His own love for us in this: While we were still sinners, Christ died for us." Romans 5:8

God has provided the only way . . . we must make the choice . . .

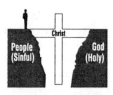

 **Step 4** Our Response:
Receive Christ

We must trust Jesus Christ and receive Him by personal invitation.

The Bible Says . . .

"Behold, I stand at the door and knock. If anyone hears My voice and opens the door, I will come in to him and dine with him, and he with Me." Revelation 3:20

"But as many as received Him, to them He gave the right to become children of God, even to those who believe in His name." John 1:12

". . . if you confess with your mouth the Lord Jesus and believe in your heart that God has raised Him from the dead, you will be saved." Romans 10:9

Are you here . . . or here?

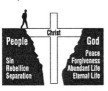

Is there any good reason why you cannot receive Jesus Christ right now?

How to receive Christ:

1. Admit your need (I am a sinner).
2. Be willing to turn from your sins (repent).
3. Believe that Jesus Christ died for you on the Cross and rose from the grave.
4. Through prayer, invite Jesus Christ to come in and control your life through the Holy Spirit. (Receive Him as Lord and Savior.)

What to Pray:

Dear Lord Jesus,

I know that I am a sinner and need Your forgiveness. I believe that You died for my sins. I want to turn from my sins. I now invite You to come into my heart and life. I want to trust and follow You as Lord and Savior.

In Jesus' name. Amen.

_____   _____
Date   Signature

God's Assurance:
His Word

If you prayed this prayer,

The Bible Says...

"For 'whoever calls upon the name of the Lord will be saved.'"
Romans 10:13

Did you sincerely ask Jesus Christ to come into your life? Where is He right now? What has He given you?

"For it is by grace you have been saved, through faith—and this is not from yourselves, it is the gift of God—not by works, so that no one can boast." **Ephesians 2:8,9**

The
Bible Says...

"He who has the Son has life; he who does not have the Son of God does not have life. These things I have written to you who believe in the name of the Son of God, that you may know that you have eternal life, and that you may continue to believe in the name of the Son of God." **1 John 5:12–13, NKJV**

Receiving Christ, we are born into God's family through the supernatural work of the Holy Spirit who indwells every believer...this is called regeneration or the "new birth."

This is just the beginning of a wonderful new life in Christ. To deepen this relationship you should:

1. Read your Bible every day to know Christ better.
2. Talk to God in prayer every day.
3. Tell others about Christ.
4. Worship, fellowship, and serve with other Christians in a church where Christ is preached.
5. As Christ's representative in a needy world, demonstrate your new life by your love and concern for others.

God bless you as you do.

Billy Graham

If you want further help in the decision you have made, write to:
Billy Graham Evangelistic Association P.O. Box 779, Minneapolis, Minnesota 55440-0779

If you are committing your life to Christ, please let us know! We would like to send you Bible study materials and a complimentary six-month subscription to *Decision* magazine to help you grow in your faith.

The Billy Graham Evangelistic Association exists to support the evangelistic ministry and calling of Billy Graham to take the message of Christ to all we can by every prudent means available to us.

Our desire is to introduce as many as we can to the person of Jesus Christ, so that they might experience His love and forgiveness.

Your prayers are the most important way to support us in this ministry. We are grateful for the dedicated prayer support we receive. We are also grateful for those that support us with contributions.

Giving can be a rewarding experience for you and for us at the Billy Graham Evangelistic Association (BGEA). Your gift gives you the satisfaction of supporting an organization that is actively involved in evangelism. Also, it is encouraging to us because part of our ministry is devoted to helping people like you discover and enjoy the stewardship of giving wisely and effectively.

Billy Graham Evangelistic Association
P.O. Box 779
Minneapolis, Minnesota 55440-0779
www.billygraham.org

Billy Graham Evangelistic Association of Canada
P.O. Box 841, Stn Main
Winnipeg, Manitoba R3C 2R3
www.billygraham.ca

Toll free: 1-877-247-2426